CUTTING THE MUSTARD

CUTTING THE MUSTARD

AFFIRMATIVE ACTION
AND THE
NATURE OF EXCELLENCE

MARJORIE HEINS

FABER AND FABER ff BOSTON & LONDON

Library of Congress Cataloging-in-Publication Data

Heins, Marjorie.
   Cutting the mustard.

   1. Richardson, Nancy—Trials, litigation, etc.
2. Boston University—Trials, litigation, etc.   3. Sex
discrimination in employment—Law and legislation—
Massachusetts—Boston.   4. Women clergy—Legal status,
laws, etc.—Massachusetts—Boston.   5. Affirmative
action programs—Law and legislation—Massachusetts—
Boston.   I. Title.
KF228.R49H45   1987   344.73'0133'0269   87–9294
ISBN 0–571–12974–9   347.3041330269

Printed in the USA.

ACKNOWLEDGMENTS

ALL of the people who spoke with me about the struggle over affirmative action and employment discrimination at the Boston University School of Theology contributed to this book. Through such conversations I became aware that, beyond the academic infighting, positioning for power, and quibbling over legalisms, a moral drama was taking place.

Above all, Nancy Richardson informed the conception and writing of this work. Her support and friendship over the past six years has made me understand why the dean of the School of Theology received so many dozens of heartfelt letters of protest after Richardson's firing. As one former student wrote, Nancy Richardson "has gifts and graces that can only benefit each of us if we choose to learn from her wisdom and style of ministry."

Richardson's close colleagues at BUSTH, among them Paul Deats, Bob Treese, Lynn Rhodes, and Jim Fraser, were unfailing in their help and support. Others on the STH faculty or staff talked with me, either during the litigation or during the preparation of the book, among them John Ward, Horace Allen, Linda Clark, Elizabeth Bettenhausen, John Cartwright, Laurel Burton, Alex Stewart and Dolores Williams. Political Science Professor Howard Zinn, a veteran of many earlier civil liberties battles at Boston University, shared both memories and wisdom.

Friends, colleagues, students, and supporters of Nancy Richardson and the Committee for Justice that organized to protest her firing assisted in many ways, from volunteering for tiresome litigation tasks to publicizing what was at stake in the case. They include: Gerrie Casey, Marian Hachten, Marjorie Mollar, Kathryn Johnson, Eugenie-Myrna Bernadel, Willard Rose, Amelie Ratliff, Elaine Huber, Emily Hewitt, Donald Leach, Ruthlyn Palmer, Thomas Eckhardt, Traci West, Jerry Avise-Rouse,

Douglas Edwards, Andrew Glasgow, Jon Hattaway, and staff at the Boston-Cambridge Ministry in Higher Education. I apologize to anyone I have forgotten.

Conversations with Beverly Wildung Harrison, Nelle Slater, Stephen Breck Reid, Julius Scott, Odette Lockwood-Stewart, and Robert McClain helped me prepare either for trial or for the present literary effort, or both.

Heidi Urich, my co-counsel during the trial, was a source of immeasurable support as well as a great friend. Scott Lewis, an attorney at Palmer & Dodge, offered sound legal advice, and, at a later stage, Professor William Levin of Bridgewater State College was a literary mentor.

Finally, my two teenagers, Matthew and Catherine Heins, were helpful, enthusiastic, affectionate, and companionable, and only occasionally demanded access to the word processor while I was trying to figure out how to use it.

CONTENTS

PROLOGUE

SEVERAL weeks after the trial of Nancy Richardson versus Boston University, I mentioned my idea of writing a book about the case to an old law school friend. "Wait and write about one you win," was his blunt advice, reflecting the good logic of his competitive world.

The advice seemed, even then, sadly ahistorical. On such a theory, books about truly momentous American trials, from the Haymarket martyrs, Sacco and Vanzetti, or Tom Mooney, to Alger Hiss or the Rosenbergs, would never have been written. Of these famous encounters with American justice, only Mooney's ever resulted in even partial vindication by the courts.

Of course, Nancy Richardson did not lose her life as did the Rosenbergs, or even her liberty, as did Hiss; she lost only her job. And unlike those celebrated litigants, she initiated the case: she sued Boston University and the boss who fired her, Richard Nesmith, dean of the Boston University School of Theology. But even when one examines the civil side of justice in the American scheme—the civil rights or employment discrimination cases—those with the claim of moral vision, of "prophesy," to use one of Dean Nesmith's favorite words, did not necessarily win.

Indeed, for years (in the case of racial segregation, almost a full century) they lost and lost again. And on the fundamental political and moral issue from which Nancy Richardson's controversy with Boston University sprang—the rethinking of "qualifications," the nature of "excellence"—courtroom victories are equally elusive. So writing about a case *is* perhaps a way to retry it, "in the court of public opinion," as the controversial Alger Hiss titled his own book.

Often, during the three weeks in December 1982 that I and others acted out the trial of Nancy Richardson versus Boston University, I was filled with the sense that this was no ordinary lawsuit. It was a story that ought to reverberate beyond the small audience of a Suffolk County superior courtroom, with its sixteen Bostonian jurors, its iconoclastic presiding judge, Paul Garrity, and its gallery of some dozen or so interested members of the Boston University School of Theology faculty, staff, student body, and religious community. The material was simply too emblematic of moral struggles to have no larger audience than this, to be girdled and distorted by the law's elaborate webbing of evidentiary rules against hearsay and the like, and to be consigned, once the litigation ended, to the oblivion of the Suffolk courthouse vault and the untranscribed stenographic notes of court reporters.

Yet it was more than two years after the trial ended before this book was underway. In the interim a new, pressing reason for writing it emerged. The struggle about affirmative action, which had been the driving issue in the case, intensified. Its proponents, like Nancy Richardson, found themselves more thoroughly on the defensive. By the summer of 1985 the Civil Rights Division of the Reagan Justice Department was devoting itself with great energy and diligence to challenging and undermining affirmative action remedies wherever they might be in place. Our hopes of educating that Boston jury about the true nature of excellence, and of persuading them to condemn the dean and Methodist minister Nesmith, not only for his small and ultimately trivial prevarications in the Richardson case but also for his political goals and the direction he was taking the once-prophetic BU School of Theology, began in retrospect to seem even more unrealistic than they had at the time. Perhaps the case had always fit more comfortably into the structure of a morality play than into any of the legal theories I had woven to litigate it in the Massachusetts courts.

Affirmative action is in peril both institutionally and legally. Although the Supreme Court, by narrow margins, has upheld some affirmative action plans, the ideal itself has too often bogged down in numbers, in paperwork, in results (or lack of results) logged on timetables. The remedial concept has become more socially divisive, and bias-reinforcing, as it is more widely viewed as a preference for "less qualified" women and members of minority groups. Affirmative action programs rarely come to grips with the underlying issue of how "merit" and "qualifications" are defined in our society, and thus how power, money, influence, and prestige are divvied up.

If the story of Nancy Richardson's legal struggle against Boston University and its School of Theology can infuse context, narrative, character, and specificity into these issues, then the case, indeed, is not over. All of the characters in this story—the dean, the church, the university, writers, ministers, intellectuals—would agree on the primacy and permanence of written exegesis. This, then, is the exegesis of a moral as well as a legal battle, and a reflection upon its larger meaning.

Newton, Massachusetts
May 1987

CHAPTER 1

CUTTING THE MUSTARD

IN 1978, the Boston University School of Theology was seeking a full professor for a prestigious chair in social ethics. The newly endowed Walter Muelder chair was named after a much-loved former dean of STH. Feelings ran high in some quarters that female scholars should be heartily recruited, for the seminary was without a single tenured woman on its faculty. This was hardly a unique situation in academia, although the federal law banning sex discrimination in employment had been on the books for fourteen years. STH did at the time have a female associate dean, Nelle Slater, and she was appointed to head the search committee for the Muelder chair.

Professor Beverly Wildung Harrison of Union Theological Seminary in New York City was one of the relatively few acknowledged academic stars in feminist theology. That emerging school of thought, while adhering to Christianity's eschatology and ethics, challenged much of its mythology and tradition. Feminists, Harrison prominent among them, asked why the major symbols of divinity—the Father, the Son, and their messengers, priests and the pope—were male. Where were female symbols recognized and worshiped, and where were women's religious experiences cherished or expressed?

Beverly Harrison had not, like her contemporary, the Catholic feminist theologian Mary Daly, come essentially to repudiate Christianity in favor of a totally woman-centered spirituality drawing on witchcraft and pagan ritual. Harrison had published dozens of articles in theological, scholarly, and feminist journals; the most widely noted was probably her 1975 piece on "The New Consciousness of Women," in which she had described the long and painful struggle that a new moral consciousness would have to undergo in the face of comfortably established social assumptions, both secular and Christian. She was also an activist in the Religious Coalition for Abortion Rights, and, within Union and other seminaries, a resource for women students pressing for curricular and administrative change, or simply looking for ways to adjust Christian theory and practice to their needs. Harrison was much in demand as a speaker at feminist theological gatherings, and had a growing following among younger academics, ministers, and students.

Would Harrison be interested in the possibility of abandoning Union for an endowed chair and full professorship at the seminary that had played a formative role in educating Martin Luther King, Jr.? When Nelle Slater made the inquiry, Harrison was receptive but wary. It was no secret to her, or indeed to scholars generally, that John Silber, president of BU, was hostile to radical philosophical and academic trends.

Silber sometimes obscured that hostility behind paeans to "excellence" and "elitism." In a 1976 *New York Times* op-ed article entitled "Above the Rabble," the BU president wrote:

> As long as intelligence is better than stupidity, knowledge than ignorance, and virtue than vice, no university can be run except on an elitist basis. A university that strives for the commonplace and is content with mediocrity would be roughly comparable to a Supreme Court on which seats were reserved for mediocrity. Thus handicapped, these institutions could not fulfill their missions in society.

Silber's theme here, as elsewhere, was that universities should select on the basis of a natural aristocracy of talent, that "rejecting excellence in the interest of women and minorities is in effect a condescending adoption of a lower standard for them." Here, he echoed an opinion popular among many in academia, as in the professions generally, but he did not say what he meant by excellence. Indeed, proponents of affirmative action might have suspected that this was exactly where the horse was buried.

At STH in particular, with its "prophetic" social ethics tradition of ministry, affirmative action was debated as a matter not just of legal but of moral and religious imperative. A graduate school of theology, some said, could not be truly excellent, the education it offered could not address the issues of contemporary Christian ministry, if its faculty lacked diversity of intellect and experience.

Nelle Slater informed STH Dean Richard Nesmith, who had been hired by Silber the previous year, that Beverly Harrison was at least interested in the faculty position. The dean thereupon telephoned Harrison for that form of economic courtship, a luncheon date. There (at New York's Russian Tea Room), Nesmith enthused about the many wonderful things he had heard of Harrison from Slater and Lynn Rhodes, one of the two female instructors at the seminary. He sounded like a man who fully intended to hire whomever he desired.

In short order, Harrison was invited to Boston for a speech on "Feminism and Ministry," and for interviews with the theology school faculty. That group voted overwhelmingly to invite her to become the Walter Muelder Professor of Social Ethics. Nesmith informed Harrison of the offer, adding casually that it could not be official until the formality of central administration approval was complete.

Nesmith called Harrison several weeks later to tell her that all signs looked favorable, but that an informal interview was being arranged because "John Silber liked to know what he was getting." He asked her to send a few of her articles, preferably something not feminist.

"Dick, my publications began when I became a feminist," Harrison responded. "I don't have anything else." She then remembered a critique that she had written several years before on the theology of Reinhold Niebuhr, and sent that along with a packet of other essays.

Toward the end of the 1977–1978 academic year, John Silber assembled an interview committee of ten professors, headed by himself and philosophy department chair, Alasdair MacIntyre. From the School of Theology, Silber invited Dean Nesmith, Professor Howard Kee (a relatively recent appointment in New Testament), Professor Lee Rouner (who headed BU's Institute of Philosophy and Religion), and Nelle Slater.

It was not until Harrison arrived on campus that she learned that this was to be no informal chat designed simply to introduce President Silber to the new Walter Muelder Professor. It was evidently to be an academic joust of the classical type, with ten members of the graduate faculty in attendance. She had not been told to prepare for a grilling, and had not looked at those essays she had sent in over a year. Harrison took about fifteen minutes in Nesmith's office to review them, but with a growing sense of trepidation that a trap had been laid.

The attack lasted some two hours. It was an almost uninterrupted trashing by Silber and MacIntyre of Harrison's work and thought, with only one, not very effective, attempt at defensive interference by Nelle Slater. As Professor Lee Rouner later summed it up for the School of Theology faculty, Silber "went for the jugular."

The crux of the battle was Harrison's view of Reinhold Niebuhr and in particular of Niebuhr's acceptance of the Kantian principle of individual transcendence. Silber is an expert on Kant and an enthusiast of the Kantian tradition. Feminist theology, as Harrison later explained, is like some other nontraditional bodies of Christian thought: it questions the centrality of individual transcendence, the lack of a social or collective anthropology in the Kantian moral and religious universe. Harrison's essay made a brief, somewhat disparaging reference to Kant, and this inspired a whirlwind of abuse from Silber.

MacIntyre functioned as Silber's backup. Responding to Harrison's assertion that one could ground social ethics, not necessarily in a transcendent view of the self, but alternatively in a vision of groups of individuals interacting to make history, MacIntyre declared, "That sounds like pure Marx."

"I wouldn't go that far," countered Harrison. "But I agree with Marx about conflict. Conflict being the generating locus of moral norms."

MacIntyre accused her of undermining the essence of the Christian tradition. Harrison responded that yes, there was no need for hierarchy, no papacy, in her Christianity.

Defending one's work on such a battleground is a dubious proposition. The attackers are also the judges. As Harrison said later, "I knew that every time I scored a point, I was digging my own grave."

Harrison also, on principle, rejected the warlike approach to scholarship and theology. At points she stopped fighting and told her inquisitors, "It appears we simply disagree on this."

After about two hours, Silber departed. A few of the others present began to talk. One professor said, "I never saw anybody go through anything like that." The only woman there aside from Slater opined, "Maybe I should have said something. I'm sorry I didn't say more." Compliments were offered on Harrison's well-known article, "The New Consciousness of Women," in which she had observed of feminism: "We live daily with the knowledge that our hard-won sense of what is going on may yet be consumed in the fires of our thwarted indignation. Consequently, much depends on what men, particularly white professional males, make of what is going on with women."

The official word was that Harrison had not "performed well" at the interview. As Lee Rouner had said, Silber went for the jugular, presumably an appropriate technique for discerning academic excellence. In discussions that followed, Nelle Slater questioned the relevance of hand-to-hand combat as a test of competence to teach in a seminary; but she accepted the verdict that Harrison had not jousted well.

The poor performance explanation, however, did not go entirely unquestioned. When that fall the STH faculty, and students at a forum, asked Dean Nesmith why he had said nothing during the interview to present Harrison as STH's chosen candidate, to defend her against attack, or to convey to Silber the urgency with which the appointment was desired, he explained that this simply was not how the academic game was played. The purpose of the interview was to test how a person responds under fire. As Nesmith was to put it much later, Harrison simply hadn't "cut the mustard."

Nesmith also told the faculty that Beverly Harrison's "Marxism" had been a serious problem. Since Harrison believed that social change occurs when people act in groups, thus minimizing the role of the individual, her understanding of history was inadequate, she was not a competent scholar. He pointed to Florence Nightingale as an example of an individual who had made a historical difference.

Richard Nesmith was worried, with reason, about how the Harrison disappointment was to be explained to the STH community. He met with his associate director of student and community life, Nancy Richardson, whom he viewed as his main link to students. Richardson, however, an ardent feminist herself, was outraged by the entire episode, said she thought Harrison had been treated abominably, and would not defend what Boston University did. Nesmith was conciliatory, saying he didn't expect her to.

Some months later, Richardson was one of several dozen women theologians, ministers, and administrators in the Boston area, part of a consortium known as the Womens' Theological Coalition of the BTI, or Boston Theological Institute, who signed and sent an angry letter to Nesmith. Failure to appoint Beverly Harrison, they declared, hurt not only Boston University but all of the institutions involved in the BTI.

It is a further indication that our male colleagues fail to appreciate the challenges of feminist theology or to recognize that the issues raised by women theologians are, in fact, on the cutting edge of theological scholarship today. That it is difficult to fit such women into traditional models should not be surprising. It is surprising and disheartening to see that male faculty and administrators do not have the vision to recognize the value of change and challenge and to allow for new models to develop.

The Commission on Women in Ministry of the National Council of Churches wrote to BU President Silber in similar terms. "We are extremely disappointed and grieved that Dr. Harrison was not invited to join the faculty of the School of Theology, despite her excellent credentials and the support of the student body and many faculty members.

The loss will be felt not only by the women of the School. The academic and professional integrity of your entire institution has suffered by your inability to do justice where justice is long overdue."

Finally, some of the students and staff wrote to the STH dean. These had been people intimately involved in the search process and, as they wrote, "genuinely excited about what was and would be happening at Boston University" when Harrison arrived. The excitement, of course, had "evaporated . . . for at the end of the process a small group of faculty and administrators met with Dr. Harrison," and turned her down, "discounting all that had gone before."

> You have asked us to "find women." In this case, a committee "found" one of the very best—but we were told, in essence, that she was not good enough. We cannot help but wonder, then, who we could ever find to satisfy this administration.

CHAPTER 2

A GELDING IN A MULE FARM

JOHN Silber arrived at Boston University in January 1971 with ambitious plans—plans to bring glory, or in his word, "excellence," to the sprawling academy poised on the Boston side of the Charles River. In the coming decade at BU many battles—political and moral as well as intellectual—would be fought over excellence.

Even before Silber's arrival the student rumblings of the 1960s had shaken the ordinary placidity of BU, the fourth largest private university in the country. A prospering, politicized food co-op; an inventive, wide-ranging free school; and one of the premier publications of the rebel student press, the *BU News*, were founded and funded by BU students in the sixties. Protests over Vietnam and the bombing of Cambodia, culminating in a student strike, precipitated the resignation of Arland Christ-Janer, Silber's predecessor, in 1970. Seminarians at the School of Theology, the founding school in the BU conglomerate, joined in the antiwar protests by establishing sanctuary for draft resisters at Marsh Chapel, on campus.

Although the first president in Boston University history not to be a Methodist minister and a teetotaler, Christ-Janer, appointed in 1966, had fit the mold of prior BU executives. A Presbyterian layman, Christ-Janer had presided over the smaller, rural, and vastly less complicated Cornell College in Iowa before coming to BU. His departure precipitated a lengthy, frustrating search for a successor willing to brave and manage BU's urban empire.

In John Silber BU's trustees certainly found something new. A Yale Ph.D. in philosophy, a former preacher and law student, Silber had earned a reputation, while dean of the College of Arts and Sciences at the University of Texas, as a combative maverick. His brutal battle with

Frank Erwin, Jr., the Texas-style chairman of the UT Board of Regents, led to his ouster from UT in the summer of 1970. Shortly thereafter *Newsweek* quoted a clairvoyant Texas professor on the level of the academic "infighting" that had preceded Silber's departure. "I have never before seen such low, hard-knuckle Boston-style ward politics," the scholar said.

One of Silber's first public acts at Boston University was calculated both to stake out his political ground and to set the tone of his leadership. Wrapping himself in the rhetoric of the free marketplace of ideas, Silber invited Marine recruiters back to campus. (They had been driven off several years before, and had since been doing their business without apparent complaint from an office in nearby Kenmore Square.) Radical students rose to the bait and in March of 1972 attempted to block the entrance to BU's Career and Planning Office. Silber called in Boston's notorious tactical patrol, complete with dogs and clubs, to crush the rebellion. Thirty-three were arrested; one professor was bitten on the hand by a dog. The faculty voted that the situation was cause for "grave concern and dismay." But it defeated a call for Silber's resignation, a position that it would reverse in April 1976 and again in December 1979 after a bitter series of faculty and staff strikes. Silber was to invite police on campus again in 1974, to stop an unruly demonstration at a symposium sponsored by the university's Center for Latin American Development Studies.

In that ambiguous decade, the seventies, Silber's noisy clashes with student protesters, and his bitter, ultimately successful attempts to drive off campus radical or dissident student press, made frequent and juicy Boston newspaper copy. Between 1976 and the end of the decade, the president's vitriolic war with the editors of the *bu exposure*, a successor to the *News*, shocked academicians accustomed to a higher tone in campus discourse. After these former student government officers published an issue of the *exposure* that was particularly distasteful to Silber—describing him in a headline as a "mediocre philosopher" and "expert chiseler"—he blasted back: "To call me an expert chiseler may be fun and games to somebody, but it's a goddamned libel. . . . In the old days there wouldn't have been any problem there: that youngster would have been rusticated the next day." Silber was quoted on other occasions as telling a student editor that an article was "shit," calling a student leader "a goddamned son of a bitch," and, during a question-and-answer period following a speech, announcing to a student, "I'm not scared of anything, fella."

The *bu exposure*'s student activity funds were frozen after the "expert chiseler, mediocre philosopher" episode in 1976, and another allocation voted by the student board the next year was never released by the university. A trusted consultant wrote to Silber in February 1977, in the context of the dispute over the *exposure:* "John, you've got to devote your time to running the university—and stop wasting your energy on worrying about these sort of radical potshots."

Perhaps Silber's most notorious clash with the student press was the 1977 housecleaning at WBUR, the highly regarded BU public radio station. Silber had written to a journalism professor and consultant to the administration on the state of the station: "We should not lend ourselves to the advocacy of drug usage, homosexuality, quack psychotherapy, or . . . anything else that is likely to frustrate the optimum personal fulfillment of our students or of citizens." BU management's subsequent efforts to refocus the station's coverage led to resignations that were well publicized in a city that had begun to wonder just what it had gotten itself into when the trustees of the BU conglomerate had invited the feisty Texas dean north. As one of the professors who had recruited Silber told a colleague (as reported by Nora Ephron in a 1977 *Esquire* article entitled "Academic Gore"), "'I pray to God every day to forgive me for what I did, and you know how serious that is for me, because I don't believe in God.'"

But Silber was not only busy fighting students. He set out to remake BU, and at first he had many on the faculty behind him. As Paul Deats, a senior professor at the School of Theology and a vice chair of the search committee that had recommended the new president, later said, Silber was "a knight in shining armor in Texas" for having opposed capital punishment, supported racial integration, and, generally, "fought all the right people." Upon arrival Silber announced, to the delight of Deats and others, that he was going to make BU a "teaching university."

Only later, recalls Deats, did it become clear that the president's major criterion for hiring was not in fact teaching ability but his own particular notion of elitism or academic stardom; and that Silber's abrasive, street-fighting style, at first considered only a peripheral drawback, had begun to drive more good people from BU than its upgraded academic image was attracting. As Ephron wrote, "The notion that Silber's personality was somehow irrelevant to his abilities as president was quite bizarre: an academic community cannot thrive in an atmosphere of paranoia and mistrust." She offered another sample of Silber's eloquence: " 'Every time someone raised questions of decency,' said a Silber opponent, 'he talked about his warts. "I'm doing great things," he would say. "If you're afraid of warts, you've got no balls." ' "

One of the first schools within BU's rattling empire at which John Silber took a good hard look was "BUSTH," the Boston University

School of Theology. The Methodist seminary (originally the Newbury Biblical Institute) was BU's founding school when the university was chartered by the Massachusetts legislature in 1869. Those links to United Methodism still brought money and moral authority, though perhaps more of the latter, to the graduate seminary. It now drew students from a variety of Protestant denominations, and also enrolled a sprinkling of Catholics, Moslems, Hindus, and Jews.

BUSTH was not only the United Methodist Church's oldest training ground in the United States; it had a deserved reputation for socially committed religious leadership. Between 1953 and 1968 nearly three-quarters of the black Ph.D.s in religious studies nationwide were products of BU. Inspired, integrated preaching and praying in a community of personal idealism were typical of BUSTH even in the fifties. During the sixties, under the deanship of Walter Muelder, the school was world famous for leadership in social ethics.

Martin Luther King, Jr. trained there in the early fifties (choosing BU over Yale), while polishing his preaching style most Sunday evenings at the South End's Twelfth Baptist Church. His sermons were remembered years later as "spellbinding." Now, a sculpture dedicated to the martyred King sits on one of the Commonwealth Avenue plazas that compose BU's concrete campus. After his death, STH established a Martin Luther King, Jr. Program with the purpose of developing curriculum and ministerial talent that addressed the religious needs of racial minorities. A 1981 report on the progress of the King program began by noting:

> Each of United Methodism's thirteen seminaries is distin-
> guished by both elements of distinctiveness and commonly
> shared qualities. The School of Theology, Boston University,
> is distinguished by a long history of innovativeness and social
> concern. It played a significant role in the early fundamentalist
> controversies around Biblical scholarship and, at another point,
> its prophetic stance led to the charge that it had a "pink fringe."

Whatever John Silber may have felt about this supposed "prophetic stance" and "pink fringe," he now claimed that he wanted to return, or prod, the School of Theology to greatness. His definition of greatness came in part from his graduate student days at Yale, where the faculty boasted such intellectual luminaries as H. Richard Niebuhr, brother of the more flamboyant Reinhold. It included lots of published scholars, it included big names, it cared about scholarly brilliance defined in terms of the received Christian theological tradition, and, as events at STH were to demonstrate, it tended to resist attempts at intellectual or moral change. As Silber's newly presidential gaze fell on STH, it seemed to him that the place needed some pretty thorough shaking up, and that a stodgy, entrenched faculty was standing in his way.

There was no question that BUSTH had administrative problems. Enrollment had declined since the heady days when draft-anxious students in large numbers had heard the call to ministry. Now the tenured faculty was too large for the student body.

Then also, in President Silber's opinion, the School of Theology faculty was by and large mediocre, not movers and shakers on the academic scene. Big names, authors of standard texts, were not much in evidence. The school's emphasis had been field work, practical education for ministry, and social activism.

Silber was at loggerheads with BUSTH on a variety of fronts in the early and mid-seventies. He considered closing the school at first; it was not a source of financial blessings, and its students' tuition was heavily subsidized by the more lucrative of the university's educational enterprises.

Ultimately Silber decided to remake STH instead. In 1974, he proposed a thorough evaluation by an outside board of visitors. Professor Robert Nelson, the then recently appointed interim dean, protested. (A search in the 1972–73 period for a permanent dean satisfactory to both Silber and STH had failed.) Dean Nelson stepped down, largely because of the debate over the outside visitors' study.

That left two major possible candidates for interim dean: Professor Merle Jordan, the current president of the faculty, and Professor Paul Deats, the prior president. Deats wanted nothing of this mess, and Jordan reluctantly assumed the post. The visitors' committee eventually recommended severance of four tenured professors, a proposal that was never adopted, though it left a bad taste within STH. A few people elected early retirement.

Conflict with Silber persisted. In December 1975 the president wrote a memo to Acting Dean Jordan and members of the faculty's executive committee, excoriating them for what he perceived to be intransigence and parochialism in resisting institutional changes he had imposed. First, Silber told them they should stop complaining about his decision to take over an STH dormitory, where one-fourth of the student body had lived in common, and convert it into academic space. "I am appalled," Silber wrote, "at your suggestion that [this space conflict was] 'the most crucial issue at this time.' . . . . Gentlemen, if you believe that, you have overlooked all of the critical issues."

What were the "critical issues" for President Silber? Selecting a permanent dean for STH was the first; adding big names to the faculty was the second. Responding to requests that he assure them that the search process for dean would comply with proper procedures, Silber, in this December 1975 memo, took a characteristic tone. He announced that he would give no such assurance since he always complied with proper procedures.

Next, Silber informed the faculty that he was putting the search for a professor to fill an endowed chair, named in honor of Martin Luther King, Jr., on hold, pending the selection of a new dean. His reasoning was as follows: "You may believe that first-rate people will move into a situation as chaotic as our present situation in Theology, but I assure you you are wrong." As to the sex of the person who would fill the King chair, Silber had no doubts: "You will ruin our opportunities to recruit a first-rate man for the King Chair if you do not let me settle this Deanship issue first."

Silber closed the memo by lecturing the faculty on the perils of its resistance to his vision for the school:

> The easiest decision I could have made would have been to close the School of Theology. It would have been a popular decision with most of the faculty. It would have been a popular decision in many quarters of Methodism. It would have been popular with anyone who cares about the economic future of Boston University. I refused to close the School of Theology because this University and this society needs a great center of theological learning and theological teaching, but I am not going to lift a finger to perpetuate mediocrity in theological education. And if you can't stand with this administration in the pursuit of excellence and if through your vacillation, indecision and rhetorical abuse you so undercut the confidence of the students and the faculty in the School of Theology that the students fail to return, you will then reap the harvest of your own sowing—namely, the closing not by decision but by neglect of this theological center.

Silber's loaded language to the STH faculty was interesting for many reasons, not the least of which was his expert employment of the rhetorical techniques that he accused his adversaries of heaping upon him. His calls to greatness are appealing, but one must ask for his definition of greatness, or excellence, and his reasons for thinking the school mediocre. That judgments of greatness or excellence, including John Silber's, are saturated by values and ideologies should not have come as a surprise to the School of Theology faculty.

Silber's memo, bristling as it was with impatience at a recalcitrant faculty, and brimming with his visions of excellence, failed to comprehend that something as mundane as dormitory space could be a "critical" issue for people seriously concerned with becoming "a great center of theological learning." But why doubt the sincerity of those who did think the issue critical? Silber knew that the respected former dean, Walter Muelder, had opposed converting the dormitory space, and that the United Methodist Church had contributed money for the building on the understanding that its activities would encompass both teaching and living. Apparently these parties had something in mind about theological education and Christian community apart from, or at least in addition to, Silber's appreciation for academic publications, fame, verbal combativeness, or even erudition about the Western Christian intellectual tradition.

In the finale of his memo, Silber rattled the ever-ready saber of school closing, while simultaneously announcing that it would be STH's own fault, not his own, if it occurred.

While the president was thus antagonizing STH, the entire BU faculty was gearing up for its first major assault on the Silber regime. In 1975 the faculty voted to unionize and become affiliated with the American Association of University Professors. Silber and the board of trustees refused to negotiate and went to court to challenge the validity of the vote. Enough questions were being raised about both the style and substance of the administration to infuse life into what had initially been a perfunctory five-year review of the Silber presidency. By April 1976, ten of Boston University's fifteen deans, bristling at a combination of administrative indignities and fiscal autocracy, agreed to request Silber's resignation. Merle Jordan of STH was among them. On April 8 the faculty voted 377 to 117 in favor of Silber's resignation, with twelve abstentions. Despite the overwhelming numbers, Silber remained feisty. As he told STH Professor Paul Deats, one of his early supporters who now voted for resignation, "Paul, you're a good man but you're going to lose this battle."

The story of how Silber marshaled his forces at the board of trustees and saved his hide in 1976 is well told by Ephron in *Esquire*. To a proposed compromise—kicking Silber upstairs—the metaphorically minded executive responded: " 'I am too young for that position. I am not about to be a gelding in a mule farm. I am not going to go out and heat up all the mares and then let some dirty little jackass come in and have all the fun.' " The trustees loved it and voted to keep John Silber.

CHAPTER 3

NOT JUST A WOMAN'S WOMAN

IN December 1980 a Methodist minister from Virginia wrote to the Boston University School of Theology to inquire about a teaching position. A response dated January 14, 1981, went out on School of Theology stationery over the name of its dean, Richard Nesmith: "Unfortunately, faculty appointments are now so hedged about with requirements regarding distribution in accordance with race, sex, and age, that it is extremely unlikely that your interest can be honored here. I will pass your biographical information along to the Executive Committee of the Faculty, but I would not be optimistic about the outcome."

The writer's unconcealed hostility toward what he described as "requirements regarding distribution in accordance with race, sex, and age" was, by 1980, not uncommon among university administrators. However warm and genuine the urge had been in the early 1970s to remedy discrimination through "affirmative action," by 1981 a chill had begun to descend. As one advocate of affirmative action (J. Stanley Pottinger, a former HEW administrator) described the academic attitude:

Once it is assumed that quotas are required, of course, there is no end to the horrors and hysteria that can be generated. University officials, it is said, will be obliged to hire regardless of merit or capability. Standards of excellence will crumble. . . . And if there are not enough qualified women engineers to fill the Engineering Department's quota, never mind; the positions will be filled with female home-economics teachers (a favorite stereotype), and don't blame the university if the country's next suspension bridge looks like a plate of spaghetti. If there are not enough black surgeons to teach surgery, no matter;

they'll be hired anyway, and when scores of hapless patients (hopefully Office for Civil Rights personnel) are left bleeding on the table, don't come to the universities for so much as a Band-Aid. If there are not enough qualified Chicano professors of Latin and Greek to fill their quotas, Latin and Greek can be dropped from the curriculum, and don't blame the universities for the fall of Western civilization.

Pottinger's parody was telling because it recited the crucial code words—merit, capability, excellence, quotas—that came to define the debate about affirmative action. From a judge-made remedy in employment discrimination cases, affirmative action by the mid-1970s had become for most employers a game of number crunching, paper shuffling, and, depending upon the commitment of the bureaucrats involved, trying either to manufacture results or to bury the fact of their absence. In the process, the essence of the endeavor was forgotten.

The original logic of affirmative action was that dramatic statistical imbalances in a school or workforce raised an inference that discrimination, or discriminatory assumptions about qualifications, were at work. Ending discrimination meant finding new ways of doing business, including rethinking the assumptions that had led to the skewed results. Once the forms and numbers took charge, however, it was easy for defenders of the status quo, in university admissions as well as employment selection, to claim that affirmative action meant the hiring of unqualified or less qualified minorities or women over more qualified or meritorious white men.

The term affirmative action derives from Title VII of the massive 1964 Civil Rights Act. Title VII made it illegal for the first time, as a matter of federal law, for private employers to discriminate on the basis of race, sex, national origin, or religion. A section of the law empowers courts, once they have found an employer guilty of discrimination, not only to prohibit further illegality but to "order such affirmative action as may be appropriate." Such court orders did not initially include race-conscious goals and timetables, but federal judges gradually came to comprehend that the intractability of discriminatory patterns in the workplace made them necessary.

In the early days of Title VII litigation, discrimination was often direct and explicit, and legal proof, if not always easy, was at least less convoluted and circumstantial than it was, by necessity, later to become. Race discrimination in employment flourished uninhibited throughout the southern and border states. In factories, job categories and seniority lines were often strictly segregated. Dismantling this system was the first step. Then came the tougher question for litigants and courts: how to remedy the system's pernicious and disabling past and continuing effects? "The nature of the violation determines the scope of the remedy." This epigram, articulated by then Chief Justice Warren Burger in a 1971 school desegregation decision, summarizes the breadth of judges' powers to issue injunctions that are reasonably calculated to compensate victims of discrimination or other wrongs and assure that such acts do not recur. The federal courts applied this maxim in desegregation cases when they ordered reassignnment of pupils and teachers, by race, sometimes facilitated by busing, to correct and undo the effects of decades of discriminatorily motivated school assignments and gerrymanders by local officials. In Title VII job discrimination cases, courts began to order this sort of race-specific remedy.

To compensate for the many black workers who were not hired, or transferred, or promoted, and the many others who had been discouraged from even applying for jobs, transfers, or promotions because of known discrimination, courts would command guilty firms to hire, transfer, or promote, until given goals—roughly corresponding to the racial composition of the available workforce—were in sight. The theory was that absent discrimination, the employer's own workforce would have approximately reflected the racial makeup of the qualified pool of available workers in the first place.

The key to the remedy was that those minority workers who would benefit from the race-conscious preference need not have been the identical workers who suffered racism at the hands of the particular employer-defendant in the past. Those original victims might be old, retired, dead, not interested, impossible to identify or locate. But if not for the race-specific remedy, it could take decades to correct and undo the effects of past evils, effects felt by a new generation of black children and young workers in terms of inadequate schooling; insufficient income; threatening, hostile, or merely alien work or school environments; and lack of exposure to parents, friends, or other role models working in integrated employment settings and at jobs other than janitor or maid.

Racism, sexism, any type of invidious discrimination, by definition categorizes by groups and inflicts group harm. Just as remedies for school segregation required the revamping of discriminatory assignment patterns with specific attention to pupils' and teachers' race, so remedies for racial bigotry in the employment sector demanded focusing on the victimized group, as a group. And just as the Supreme Court had realized, and ruled, in the late sixties, that the many "freedom of choice" plans offered up by southern school districts as a response to the Supreme Court's order to desegregate "with all deliberate speed" were painfully, even cynically, inadequate as remedies for racism, so the advocates of affirmative action understood that simply eliminating the explicit barriers, the signs that said "no blacks need apply," would not in themselves, without more affirmative efforts, result in job equality.

At about the same time that courts began experimenting with affirmative action remedies, similar concepts were emerging on the executive side of government. President Lyndon Johnson's 1965 Executive Order 11246 required employers who had sizeable government contracts to take "affirmative action" to remedy employment discrimination. As implemented by the executive branch, this meant that contractors were supposed to compile statistics on their employees, compare these numbers with the racial composition of the locally available qualified workforce, and take action to remedy significant imbalances. Each federal agency that entered into contracts was supposed to monitor this process, although inevitably some agencies were more conscientious about it than others.

Meanwhile, HEW and other executive departments that each year bestowed federal largesse upon private institutions such as universities or hospitals, or local governments, began to impose similar affirmative action requirements. Although the progress in hiring minorities and women that resulted from these federal impositions was often not dramatic or even discernible, the amount of data gathering and paperwork engendered by the emerging affirmative action regime was impressive. A new breed of government bureaucrat was born, the affirmative action expert, whose counterpart could soon be found in the personnel offices of large corporations.

What did the volumes of new affirmative action guidelines and regulations mean? At their least controversial, they meant that employers had to post and advertise notices of job openings, and make affirmative efforts to recruit minorities and women—or, at least, put a plan on paper describing their intention to do so. At their most cumbersome, affirmative action regulations meant keeping careful records of applications, searches, hires, and promotions, and analyzing statistics on the racial and sexual makeup of the available labor force. These numbers in turn helped determine whether women and minorities were "underutilized" or whether nondiscriminatory hiring practices were leading, as one would expect they should, to representation of these previously disenfranchised groups on the job in approximate proportion to their availability. The statistical analysis was usually followed, in affirmative action reports, by a lengthy and turgid text setting out the employer's plan for improving its hiring record.

This plan had to include statistical goals for hiring (and promoting) minorities and women in numbers approximately consistent with their current or predicted availability, as well as timetables for achieving the goals. In job categories where qualified women were scarce, for example plumbers or electricians, the goals were, predictably, modest.

This apparent infirmity in the affirmative action structure as it solidified became more marked where the definition of "qualified" was subjective or problematic. It was easy enough to accept that a qualified electrician was a person who had successfully completed an apprenticeship or training program of some sort, but what about a qualified associate professor? The goals for hiring women and minorities in this category were often remarkably low because the baseline "qualification," the Ph.D. degree, was usually not questioned. Then, even with the pool of "qualified" candidates thus narrowed, subjective, value-laden notions of merit, excellence, "cutting the mustard," impeded the hiring of women, and permeated evaluation of their work.

A professor at City College of New York made the point:

> Evaluation of a candidate's experience, to determine entry-level salaries, is almost exclusively subject to male judgments. In last year's [1972's] job market, for example, a woman's dossier contained this statement: "Mrs. ———, though a woman and older, should be as well received as a younger man." But "the dossier of a forty-year-old man asserted that one should hire this man; his distinguished career record (army, public relations) 'has been a better preparation for the university than uninterrupted schooling could have been.' "

Similarly, a black professor at Harvard Law School, Randall Kennedy, recently observed:

> [M]any black beneficiaries of affirmative action view claims of meritocracy with skepticism. They recognize that in many instances the objection that affirmative action represents a deviation from meritocratic standards is little more than disappointed nostalgia for a golden age that never really existed. Overt exclusion of blacks from public and private institutions of education and employment was one massive affront to meritocratic pretensions. Moreover, a longstanding and pervasive

feature of our society is the importance of a wide range of non-objective, nonmeritocratic factors influencing the distribution of opportunity. The significance of personal associations and informal networks is what gives durability and resonance to the adage, "It's not *what* you know, it's *who* you know." As Professor Wasserstrom [another of many legal academics who has wrestled with this subject] wryly observes, "Would anyone claim that Henry Ford II [was] head of the Ford Motor Company because he [was] the most qualified person for the job?"

[M]any beneficiaries of affirmative action recognize the thoroughly political—which is to say contestable—nature of "merit"; they realize that it is a malleable concept, determined not by immanent, preexisting standards but rather by the perceived needs of society. Inasmuch as the elevation of blacks addresses pressing social needs, they rightly insist that considering a black's race as part of the bundle of traits that constitute "merit" is entirely appropriate.

A little more than a year after the Beverly Harrison incident, Boston University School of Theology Dean Richard Nesmith wrote to President John Silber proposing an interim faculty appointment in church history for Dr. Clarissa Atkinson, then a research associate at Harvard Divinity School. Apparently pressed by the university's affirmative action office to come up with some female and minority appointments, if only temporary ones, Nesmith wrote to Silber on May 4, 1979, that Atkinson was to be recommended because in Nesmith's opinion, she was "not just a woman's woman," but on the contrary, according to Nesmith, she "possesses a good sense of balance which will serve her well in the classroom and in other activities with both men and women." He quoted one of his academic sources as saying that Atkinson "doesn't have those edges we expect nowadays." Ironically, and evidently unbeknownst to the dean, Clarissa Atkinson had excellent feminist credentials. She received the temporary job at BU but left before her three-year appointment ended, and returned to a tenure-track position at Harvard.

Mary Daly, a theologian whose edges, one suspects, Dean Nesmith would not have admired, wrote in an early book of the "negative sanctions in seminaries, churches, and theological schools . . . for those who do not 'think right' . . . [and the] positive sanctions for remaining or appearing to remain orthodox. . . . The orthodox or semi-orthodox who are academics can hope to be called 'scholarly.' "

Richard Nesmith's hostility to the idea of a "woman's woman," and his apparent expectation that President Silber would share it, may help explain why, the year before, Professor Beverly Harrison was treated as she was. When concepts of excellence or merit become so hopelessly politicized as they were in Nesmith's memo about Clarissa Atkinson, one need not search far for clues to the defeat of affirmative action in academia. Whether based on aptitude test scores (as those opposing affirmative action argued in the 1978 *Bakke* case), or on a ritual of combat that prizes verbal aggression and ideological conformity above creativity, originality, or depth of thought, politically driven assumptions about "merit" constituted the immovable impediments to job gains for minorities and women in the upper echelons of economic and academic life.

CHAPTER 4

THE NATURE OF EXCELLENCE

JOHN Silber hired a new dean for the Boston University School of Theology in the spring of 1977. Richard Nesmith moved into his headquarters at 765 Commonwealth Avenue that summer. Nesmith had earned a Ph.D. at BUSTH in 1957; several of the older professors, including Social Ethics Professor Paul Deats, and Bob Treese, the director of field education, had known him as a struggling graduate student.

Nesmith's career path afterward had been peripatetic: dean of a small men's college, MacMurray, in Jacksonville, Florida; then dean of students there; professor of sociology of religion at a Methodist seminary in Kansas City; director of planning at the national division of the United Methodist Church Board of Global Ministries in New York; and finally, after difficulties in that New York bureaucracy, a move to a large parish in Lincoln, Nebraska.

In the early days of his career Nesmith had taken a group of students to Alabama to confer with local black civil rights leaders; their meeting had been raided by local authorities and a night in jail followed. Nesmith was to make much of the experience during the battles over race and affirmative action at Boston University some twenty years later.

John Silber had liked Nesmith at the deanship interview: the man fumbled but kept talking. He could not be cowed into silence. In the years ahead, Nesmith's considerable gift for words and images would be one of his assets at the School of Theology, although it would also occasionally get him into trouble.

Before Nesmith's arrival, and in the absence for some time of a permanent dean, STH had essentially been run by its faculty executive committee. Paul Deats was a commanding figure in this group: a professor at BU since 1954, chair of the faculty in the 1960s, a member of the trustees' advisory committee on investment policy since 1972, chair of BU's Division of Theological and Religious Studies from 1969 to 1981. Deats had written essays on ethics and peace, civil rights, corporate responsibility. He had been active in the Fellowship of Reconciliation, a Protestant peace group that had articulately, effectively, sometimes even by civil disobedience, and often to the consternation of more conservative Christians, opposed the Vietnam War. Chair of the School of Theology's "Area B" (Philosophy, Theology, and Ethics), Deats taught courses in ethical-religious issues such as war, capital punishment, and abortion; in church-state problems; in social theory and the social gospel; and in missionary work in Mexico and the Caribbean. In 1980 he was to travel to Cuba and consult with church groups there; in subsequent years he would take STH students with him on Cuban trips.

At the start, Deats strongly supported the new STH dean. Like the rest of the STH faculty he was delighted to have someone at last who could run interference for the seminary with the unpredictable forces at central administration. And with Nesmith's arrival in 1977 the stormy waters between STH headquarters at 765 Commonwealth Avenue and the presidential suite did temporarily calm. Nesmith milked his Methodist connections across the country to raise money, cultivate alumni, and recruit students. Enrollment began to climb. Although not a careful administrator, Nesmith put together a creditable staff: Nelle Slater, associate dean for academic affairs, ran the curricular side of the school; Earle Beane was a competent director of admissions; Bob Treese stayed on as director of field education, the important clinical component required of all students in the Master of Divinity program.

Nesmith wanted to add to Treese's responsibility the administration of "student and community life" programs, which he thought vital to a theological community. The task would include assisting seminary students, almost by definition impecunious, with financial aid and housing options in a notoriously high-rent, and largely segregated, city.

Treese said it was too much to take on, especially given his teaching load, and he suggested hiring an assistant. Nesmith accepted the advice, and in the fall of 1977 hired Nancy Richardson, a United Church of Christ minister and a BU campus chaplain, to be associate director of student and community life. This soft-spoken Southern woman, schooled at Duke University during the heyday of the civil rights movement, created and ran the BUSTH student life programs.

Boston University's refusal in 1978 to appoint Professor Beverly Harrison to an endowed chair in social ethics at the School of Theology was still a fresh wound when, without warning the following year, Dean Nesmith decided to fire his associate dean, Nelle Slater. Nesmith was never able to give a reasoned explanation of why he fired Slater, who was by most accounts a solid intellect and crack administrator. The dean's most telling explanation, stated at a student forum in his characteristic metaphorical style, and much repeated thereafter by those who had heard it, was that he and Slater did not "dance well" together.

When asked by an enterprising seminarian whether his problem might not be in working with competent women generally, Dean Nesmith demurred. In contrast to Slater, he said, he had a good working relationship with his associate director of student and community life, Nancy Richardson. Because Richardson kept in close communication with him, they were able to "stay in the saddle together."

Nancy Richardson was at best sourly amused by this comment. As to the explanation about not dancing well, Richardson was not the only person at STH to perceive sexist overtones in the remark. Or perhaps she and other critics of the decision were being overly literal. But the fact remained that Nesmith had found something in Nelle Slater's leadership discomfiting. As the dean told a Ph.D. student at about this time, apropos of a female teaching candidate, he preferred to hire women who were or had been married, because they "knew the meaning of compromise."

The protests, from students and faculty, over Nesmith's decision to terminate Nelle Slater lasted the full 1979–80 academic year. The faculty's executive committee engaged in much tormented negotiation with the dean, which ultimately resulted in his offer to extend Slater's teaching contract (stripped of administrative duties) for an additional year. Slater chose not to accept, and left for a teaching position in Indiana.

Nancy Richardson privately told Nesmith her opinion that nondiscrimination and affirmative action meant a commitment to hiring and working with people of diverse types. It included accepting women in nonstereotypical, nonpassive, leadership roles. It could not be accomplished by creating and maintaining an administrative team or faculty in one's own image. Nesmith listened, but did not change his mind.

Faculty turmoil over his firing Slater so disturbed Dean Nesmith that he drafted a letter to BU Provost Robert Mayfield, explaining that he had become "sufficiently pessimistic about the potential and future of the School of Theology" that he wished "to initiate a line of legal inquiry so as to avoid later complications. I would like to formally request that your office assign legal counsel to assist me in exploring proper steps leading to discussions on the closing of the School of Theology."

This tentative, still exploratory decision, wrote Nesmith, was "based on current circumstances in the faculty and its Executive Committee which suggest a persistent pre-occupation with self-interest and an unwillingness to genuinely be sensitive either to the mandates of the Trustees or the Church, and an unwillingness to be supportive of any Dean attempting to give leadership."

If this was somewhat vague, Nesmith became more explicit about the ways in which he felt his leadership was being undermined: "measured reluctance as in the case of our D.Min. [Doctor of Ministry] program or the assumption of an adversarial stance as in the case of my termination of an Associate Dean."

It is unlikely that this letter ever reached Provost Mayfield or BU's president, John Silber, although Nesmith probably discussed its general subject matter with them or others in central administration. Senior STH faculty members got wind of the letter and, with the help of high personages in the region's Methodist hierarchy, were able to dissuade Nesmith from sending it. Closing STH had been one of Silber's favorite threats, and handing him this sort of weapon would ultimately not be to Nesmith's advantage.

The conflict over Nelle Slater's firing was, as Nancy Richardson had told Nesmith, fundamentally a conflict over the nature of affirmative action. That debate had been brewing for some time, certainly since the Beverly Harrison debacle. Apart from central recordkeeping and reporting requirements—imposed by HEW and its successor, the Department of Education, for institutions receiving federal funds—the job of recruiting and keeping racial minority and women teachers and administrators was largely left at Boston University to the individual schools. At STH the Methodist concern with "inclusiveness," as a matter of religious community, and with civil rights as a matter of morality, heightened the passion and rhetoric of the debate.

At its core was the definition of merit or "credentialling," as the concept is denoted in some of the memoranda that circulated at STH in this period. The position taken by those, including Nancy Richardson, who saw affirmative action as the obligation of a community committed to racial and sexual equality, was that it required a rethinking of assumptions about merit and qualifications, assumptions that by definition were evolved by white male elites based on criteria they had satisfied in their own successful careers. The opposing view was that, whatever affirmative action meant, it could not compel a "lowering of standards," and acceptance of those "less qualified."

In 1980, STH had a tenure-track opening in Old Testament studies.

The search committee found a young black scholar named Stephen Breck Reid, who was teaching at the Interdenominational Theological Center in Atlanta, and had just finished the courses for his Ph.D. at Emory University. He was still at work on his doctoral thesis. Reid showed interest in the job as early as January 1980, when he had delivered a lecture at STH. He returned to the campus in October to teach again and be formally interviewed. He preached to an enthusiastic crowd at BU's Marsh Chapel.

STH's request to hire Reid for the Old Testament position went to central administration for approval in November or early December of 1980. Dean Nesmith, who was responsible for monitoring the process, assured both students and faculty that the appointment was in the bag; only formalities remained.

Afterward, Nancy Richardson, STH Professor Paul Deats, and others faulted Nesmith for not monitoring the process more aggressively, for not being, as he had not been during the Beverly Harrison episode, an advocate for the person whom the School of Theology had selected. They contrasted his passive approach to Reid's candidacy with his inspired advocacy during the same period of a faculty slot for the well-known sociologist, Peter Berger.

It is unlikely, however, that more enthusiasm from Nesmith would have diluted President Silber's negativity about Stephen Reid, or ultimately produced a different result. From Nesmith's viewpoint, that of a skilled politician negotiating the academic shoals, he would probably only have lost credibility with Silber had he taken a more activist approach. Nesmith's false assurances to the STH faculty and students that Reid's appointment was a certainty appear in retrospect to have been only momentary expedients, helpful in defending his affirmative action record when lobbying for the near-simultaneous appointment of Peter Berger.

The question of Reid's appointment remained suspended at central administration from December 1980 to early March 1981 when President Silber, Provost Mayfield, and others began exchanging memos. A note to Silber dated March 5, 1981, from an assistant who had checked some references, described Reid as "a good preacher with an 'ironic' style . . . a witty and charming teacher, but . . . not a scholar." It faulted Reid for being a black man who "does not relate well to Black people" (this apparently being the opinion of a minister who was questioned on the subject). "Having him at Boston University would not give us a Black perspective in Theology," Silber's informant concluded. "Reid's background and training is Mennonite."

The same ministerial source was reported as counting Reid "an indifferent scholar . . . an Old Testament scholar with New Testament languages." Silber's source added, however, "I don't know how factual this is. . . . Simon tells me Reid can read Hebrew" (Simon being Simon Parker, a trusted Silber lieutenant in central administration whose academic background was in Biblical studies).

The memo went on, in a confidential tone: "My assessment is that there are larger issues here than Mr. Reid. . . . STH should be able to do better in recruiting proven scholars. The question is whether we wait for them to do it or hire Reid for a year to see how he works out. At 28 he is very young as a Biblical scholar."

This memo to the boss contained a number of questionable assumptions. First, why was good teaching and preaching considered such a marginal asset, if not in fact a negative? Second, was the only purpose in hiring a black teacher to obtain "a black perspective"—as defined by whites? Presumably a white teacher would not be disqualified because it is thought that he would not convey a "white perspective." When it came to women faculty, it may be recalled from Nesmith's letter of recommendation regarding Clarissa Atkinson, that having a female perspective (being a "woman's woman") was not an asset.

On March 6, Silber sent a memo to Mayfield. "I have serious doubts about Mr. Stephen Reid," he began. "Frankly, I don't believe this man has the linguistic accomplishments claimed on his behalf." Silber picked apart Reid's letters of recommendation. One said, "Mr. Reid, I am confident, will become a publishing scholar." Silber's riposte: "That, I would remind you, is the least—not the most—we can expect of a candidate."

Another Reid advocate, thought Silber, "patronizes Boston University. He can give Reid the strongest possible recommendation for an opening at our School of Theology. Considering the present situation there, I can understand [his] point of view." Was this paranoia, or clever reading between the lines? Certainly Silber was projecting onto the author of this recommendation letter his own opinion of STH, not necessarily a universal one.

Silber shipped the file back to the provost's office for further work: up-to-date recommendations, Reid's dissertation, and evaluations of it by three STH professors. "I am at a loss to know what you were approving in approving this appointment," the president snapped.

The next week, Provost Mayfield telephoned Stephen Reid and formally requested a copy of his Ph.D. dissertation, recently completed except for one chapter. Although this in itself was hardly an unreasonable request, Reid felt that its timing, after he had waited nearly five months, was ominous. Reid read the signals correctly and accepted an outstanding job offer from the Pacific School of Religion in Berkeley.

A March 12, 1981, memo from Mayfield to Silber notified the president that Reid "has taken a position at another institution, thus resolving the problem." Scrawled at the bottom in large bold handwriting is Silber's comment: "Good."

Dean Nesmith handled the aftermath badly. His first approach, in attempting to placate the aroused STH faculty, was to accuse Reid of "selling out," reneging on his promise to come to BU because he had received a better offer with a "promise" of tenure. The implication was that Reid had rejected an offer from BU. The faculty and students learned soon afterward that this was untrue, in part because Reid had written to a black student, Willard Rose, who headed BUTSA, the Boston University Theological Students Association.

Reid told Willard Rose that he had accepted the position at Pacific School of Religion for two reasons: "First, I received a better offer from PSR, which was surprising given the size of that institution in comparison to BU. The reason I made the decision to go to PSR is that they were able to offer the job with dispatch. One week after the interview I was unanimously selected as the person for the position by the faculty. A week after that I was selected by the executive committee of the board of trustees for the position. Not long after that I received a contract. This is in marked contrast to the procedure that happened with BU.

"Another factor was that my colleagues and professors all implied that the long process I was going through was not what they would have expected. There was some feeling from people I talked to that somehow things were not going as they should. Further, part of the process was the constant request for more and more information. This request caused me to infer that my appointment was somehow not as strong as the provost or others might have liked. The specter of turning down other jobs only to be rejected by BU haunted me throughout the process . . .

"I have no reason to doubt that Dean Nesmith did everything in his power to secure the position for me after the seminary faculty made that decision. The implementation of the faculty decision was hampered by the bureaucracy of the university. It is my guess that as long as there are schools that act decisively for minority appointments those schools will be able to make minority appointments. The hesitation of the university sent all the wrong signals."

Nesmith, now questioned more closely by the faculty, offered a new explanation for BU's hesitation and delay. It was a necessary product of the extreme care that the university must take in deciding to offer a tenure-track position to a black candidate. (The tenure decision usually follows the tenure-track appointment by about seven years.) The university must, Nesmith explained, be sure that the candidate is tenurable at the outset, because it would not do to deny tenure to a black teacher. Thus, the reasoning went, the university could take a chance on the average young white scholar, but could not take the same chance with a black.

The racially discriminatory impact of this logic did not escape the notice of a number of STH faculty members. In imposing a more rigorous standard for entry-level jobs on black applicants, it not only ignored the remedial and re-evaluative principles underlying affirmative action; it turned them upside down.

Joe Williamson, a minister at the Church of the Covenant in Boston's Back Bay, and a part-time STH teacher, wrote a statement protesting the assumptions that underlay the loss of Stephen Reid:

> The refusal to appoint Stephen Reid to the Old Testament po-sition at BUSTH violates all of the criteria for determining the nature of excellence. To claim that the appointment was not made in order to protect standards of excellence of Boston University is indefensible.

> In the mid-eighteenth century Jonathan Edwards wrote, "There has nothing been more without a definition than excel-lency." Now two hundred years later the same lament is heard. In an effort to correct that lack of definition I propose the following criteria.

> First, all "ideal" categories such as "excellence" must be placed within a social matrix. . . . Excellence must pertain to the be-lief systems and the moral definitions which are espoused by the church as well as those espoused by the university.

> Second, excellence requires a relational, comparative, and dy-namic component. For Edwards the highest excellency requires diversity in order that the dynamism of the relation be set in motion. Monolithic notions of excellency are by definition not excellent.

> Third, excellence must include a moral element . . . some sense of beauty, harmony and proportion. Such are also trans-lated into the moral categories of justice, peace, love.

CHAPTER 5

BUILT-IN HEADWINDS

THE Duke Power Company's Dan River Steam Station in Draper, North Carolina, practiced explicit race discrimination until July 2, 1965, the date that the 1964 federal Civil Rights Act took effect. Of the company's five operating departments—Labor, Coal Handling, Operations, Maintenance, and Laboratory—blacks could be employed only in the Labor Department, where the highest paid workers earned less than those who were paid the least in any of the other areas.

When in 1965, responding to passage of the Civil Rights Act, the company eradicated its blatant segregation, it simultaneously instituted two new requirements for positions that had formerly been all-white. The new qualifications were a high school diploma and a passing grade on a standardized aptitude test.

The results were not surprising. Although the new requirements eliminated some white applicants, they devastated the hopes of blacks. As the Supreme Court was later to note, in North Carolina in 1960, thirty-four percent of white males but only twelve percent of Negro males had completed high school. Standardized tests of the type used by Duke Power resulted in passing rates of fifty-eight percent for whites and six percent for blacks.

When the new requirements were challenged in court as violating Title VII of the Civil Rights Act, the trial judge dismissed the claim. Despite the suggestive chronology, the court said there had been no proof of intentional discrimination.

The Supreme Court reversed. Writing for the majority, Chief Justice Burger made some profound observations about the purpose of Title VII and the nature of discrimination. His words have been quoted with ritual regularity, and for good reason, by plaintiffs' discrimination lawyers ever since:

> The objective of Congress in the enactment of Title VII . . . was to achieve equality of employment opportunities and remove barriers that have operated in the past to favor an identifiable group of white employees . . .

> Under the Act, practices, procedures, or tests neutral on their face, and even neutral in terms of intent, cannot be maintained if they operate to "freeze" the status quo of prior discriminatory employment practices. . . .

> The Act proscribes not only overt discrimination but also practices that are fair in form but discriminatory in operation. The touchstone is business necessity. If an employment practice which operates to exclude Negroes cannot be shown to be related to job performance, the practice is prohibited. . . . [G]ood intent or absence of discriminatory intent does not redeem employment procedures or testing mechanisms that operate as "built-in headwinds" for minority groups and are unrelated to measuring job capability.

Because the Duke Power Company did not show its new diploma and test requirements, with their disparate impact on blacks, to be job-related, the Court held that they violated Title VII and must be eliminated.

This Title VII "disparate impact" analysis, accepted by the Supreme Court in *Griggs v. Duke Power Company*, had startling implications. It is not surprising that the Supreme Court has been reluctant to apply the insight to areas of civil rights law other than employment discrimination, and has steadily retreated from it even in Title VII cases. For the decision contains the implicitly radical recognition that to combat age-old patterns of discrimination, the assumptions underlying apparently "neutral" standards, qualifications, and notions of merit must be re-evaluated.

In the years after *Griggs*, plaintiffs brought legal challenges to written tests that disproportionately disqualified minority applicants, to height or weight standards that eliminated disproportionate numbers of women, or Hispanic or Asian men, and even to certain types of educational or experience requirements. The challenges were often successful when it turned out that the employer could not justify its tests or standards as job-related. Employment exams, especially in civil service, were time after time shorn of their mystified coat of validity; when scrutinized, such test questions as, for example, "Who was Betsy Ross?" or "Who is the longest-standing director of the FBI?" (both of which appeared in 1985 in a Rhode Island test for state police applicants) were understood to be unrelated to the jobs for which they consistently excluded large numbers of minority aspirants.

After *Griggs*, statistical analysis of test results and "validation" of tests for job-relatedness became staples of Title VII litigation, and spawned a subprofession of statisticians and validation experts to assist in the prosecution, and defense, of employment discrimination class action cases.

But the disparate impact mode of proving a Title VII case encountered noticeably less success when applied to more prestigious and influential jobs. Judges who had little trouble enjoining reliance on test scores or educational requirements for factory jobs balked at demanding the same sort of justifications from businesses hiring or promoting managers on the basis of grades or graduate degrees, law firms selecting associates or partners on the basis of the prestige of the law school attended, or universities choosing, firing, or tenuring professors on similar criteria.

Disparate impact theory was seen as even more radical and unworkable when applied to "facially neutral" employment practices that were not so discrete and easy to isolate as short-answer tests or height-weight requirements. When more subjective criteria, such as personality, "communication skills," or judgments about the value of an academic candidate's teaching and scholarly work were challenged, somehow the disproportionate impact on women or minority applicants, no matter how dramatic, did not trigger the same judicial demands for employer justification.

A handful of courts did recognize the discriminatory potential of these subjective evaluation schemes. These decisions generally involved challenges to overly discretionary systems in factory or other nonprofessional work settings. Thus, one court, commenting on the use of highly subjective evaluations to choose foremen at a General Motors plant, observed that

> procedures which depend almost entirely upon the subjective evaluation and favorable recommendation of the immediate foreman are a ready mechanism for discrimination against Blacks. . . . We and others have expressed a skepticism that Black persons dependent directly on decisive recommendations from Whites can expect nondiscriminatory action.

As the case law developed, however, and discrimination grew more subtle—perhaps even unnoticed or unconscious—courts became increasingly reluctant to treat subjective evaluation systems as they treated other "facially neutral" criteria that had a *Griggs*like disparate impact. Such evaluations were simply too fundamental a part of the employment process. Thus in the higher echelons, institutional attitudes—those pervasive impediments to the advance of women and minorities—were left almost entirely undisturbed by the upheavals wrought by Title VII in the less rarefied job world. Only occasionally would a judicial decision be reported in which, for example, an employer's rejection of a woman as either not aggressive enough, or alternatively, as "overbearing," was recognized as sex discrimination.

The problem got even thornier where, as in the average Title VII case, the plaintiff was not suing on behalf of a class, or challenging some pervasive or systemic hiring or promotion practice (such "class action" cases are monumentally expensive and time-devouring) but instead was simply asserting an individual claim of race or sex discrimination. The standard pattern, and one explicitly invited by the Supreme Court in cases involving such individual discrimination suits, was for the employer to articulate "legitimate, nondiscriminatory reasons" for its decision, be it a firing, a failure to hire, a refusal to promote, or some otherwise adverse act.

In other words, the employer was encouraged to, and usually did, attempt to impale the employee who dared complain of discrimination with a pointed bill of particulars enumerating, elaborating upon, often no doubt embroidering, every flaw in the complainant's job performance. Instead of concentrating on the real issue—whether discrimination played a part in the treatment of this less-than-perfect individual—the case became sidetracked on the manufactured question of the employee's overall performance, and on whether the employer's witnesses were lying as they embellished their "legitimate, nondiscriminatory reasons." Moreover, the reasons themselves were often highly subjective—those ineffable factors such as personality, presence, communication skills, hard or soft edges, that so often and so naturally lead personnel decision makers to prefer, and rate highly, those employees or applicants most like themselves. As a former director of the U.S. Commission on Civil Rights observed,

> We pay lip service to merit and competence, but so many hiring decisions are made on the basis of extraneous factors. . . .
> Nor, I suspect, do we agree on who is "competent" to be a teacher. I have known all too many persons, as I am sure you have, with a string of degrees who did not have the vaguest idea of what he or she was doing in the classroom.

The same phenomenon occurs when sacrosanct judgments are made in selecting, for example, law school faculty. At "first-rate" law schools, baseline criteria for selection to most tenure-track positions include: first, the prestige of the law school from which one has graduated; second, the number and prestige of the judges for whom one has labored as a law clerk after graduation from law school; and third, membership during law school years on the editorial board of a journal usually known as "law review," the qualification for which is ordinarily high first-year law school grades. No matter what an attorney has achieved in practice, no matter what her verbal brilliance, practical experience, courtroom success, or pedagogical skills, she will very rarely be able to install her feet on the tenure track of a major law school without having attended a prestige school herself, made law review, and "clerked" for a recognized judge or two.

These threshold criteria, defended with words like *qualifications* or *merit*, in fact reflect an exceedingly narrow understanding of these concepts, if indeed they correlate at all with the qualities that make a superior law teacher or innovative legal thinker. Even as a "paper credential," performance on first-year law school exams is surely less relevant to professional merit than is achievement after graduation.

The outcome of this system is that a major law school faculty often contains many members whose legal careers reached their height in that apprentice year of clerkship for a prestigious court. Many have no experience at all, or only minimal experience, actually practicing law. It is small wonder that mastery of the narrow range of verbal and writing skills so prized in traditional law schools ill prepares a student for the exigencies of practice that lie ahead. More phenomenally, it is a measure of the "Emperor's New Clothes" syndrome that is so profound a part of human nature that "merit" and "excellence" are still invoked as the reasons for maintaining law faculties on which people who have little or no knowledge of actual legal practice often predominate. That is to say, faculties may proudly parade their paper qualifications, but few if any of those cheering on the sidelines pause to notice the bareness of their legal experience.

The myth persists that law faculties are chosen on the basis of merit. In fact it appears that by maintaining a large if not dispositive role for such irrelevant or only marginally relevant factors in the hiring process as law review membership, law faculties succeed primarily in validating and perpetuating themselves. The same mechanism of self-validation operates in the selection process for numerous other plush jobs in business, academia, and the professions.

It is of course sobering for those who succeeded in school, scored high on aptitude tests, and derived self-respect and even self-importance from these achievements, to realize that what these measurements primarily showed was their capacity to do precisely that—attain high grades and do well on examinations. They said little about broader qualities of intelligence, sensitivity, judgment, introspection, or creativity, and even less about the capacity to lead a productive and "successful" life.

Likewise, it is difficult for anyone on the inside to look at his faculty, corporate boardroom, or law firm; perceive that it is overwhelmingly white and male; and then take the next step and say, "What's wrong with our evaluation system?" instead of the more comfortable, "There just aren't enough qualified minorities and women to go around."

Because no one, or so few people, in power over personnel choices at the higher levels have been willing to face this fundamental issue, the ideal of affirmative action, the crux of it, re-evaluating subjective judgments about "credentials" and "qualifications" and "merit," was forgotten, or lost, or often not even articulated. And "affirmative action" became a mundane bureaucratic matter of compiling reports, accumulating and pushing paper, combined with a few helpful but relatively ineffective gestures like posting jobs, which eradicated the appearance but often not the reality of old-boy networking. As for those anti-meritocratic-seeming goals or quotas, they were viewed primarily as paper requirements when they were paid attention to at all. Women and minorities who were hired often found themselves in a revolving door of dead-end or short-term jobs, as the upper ranks of tenured professorship and top management continued to elude them. The proper use of numerical measurements— examining the workforce for dramatic imbalances that would suggest discriminatory headwinds are at work in the selection process—was usually buried, and the numbers became ends in themselves.

In many affirmative action plans ordered by courts or agreed upon to settle litigation, for example, job candidates were chosen from two race-segregated lists, based on test results, with the scores of minority applicants inevitably being lower. The questionable tests that produced the disparate scores with their message of racial inferiority remained. As late as fall 1985, when the themes of *Griggs v. Duke Power Company*, disparate impact, and job-relatedness, ought to have penetrated to most writers on the subject, no less a journalistic eminence than *The New York Times* headlined a page-one story about a classic "disparate impact" police exam case with the inflammatory word, quota. Only near the end of the article, continued in the second section, was it mentioned that the test had been invalidated by a court because its questions were not "sufficiently job-related."

The cultural bias of standardized aptitude tests has been documented. They rely upon the test-taker's knowledge of the test-maker's cultural milieu, which up to this point in our history has invariably been middle class and white. The persistence of schools and employers in relying upon these tests, and upon similar, if less readily quantifiable, measures of "qualifications" that perpetuate notions of racial or sexual superiority, remains the fundamental challenge of affirmative action.

These contradictions and unresolved issues festered throughout the 1970s as affirmative action expanded from a creative judicial remedy in Title VII litigation to a bureaucratic requirement for thousands of recipients of federal funds or contracts, and sometimes also to voluntary efforts by colleges or employers—albeit efforts galvanized by political pressure—to improve minority and female representation. Affirmative action enforcement varied greatly, not only with changes in administrations. Within administrations, it depended upon the leadership and commitment at the different agencies that were responsible for enforcement.

The U.S. Department of Labor's Office of Federal Contract Compliance Programs (OFCCP) had the unenviable task of enforcing its affirmative action guidelines in the notoriously resistant construction trades. Here, antagonism to women workers often proved even more intractible than racism, though the goals for women were modest. Frequently, a single woman was hired for her usefulness as a number on an affirmative action report, and promptly laid off thereafter. A more sophisticated variation on the theme occurred in academia and other places where the receipt of federal funds or federal contracts triggered "compliance reviews" by OFCCP, HEW, or later, the Department of Education; or even absent compliance reviews, where administrators responded to the perceived exigencies of affirmative action by making temporary, adjunct, or part-time appointments of minorities and women.

"Who were the gainers from affirmative-action quotas?" one vocal black critic of the system, Professor Thomas Sowell, has asked.

> Politically, the Nixon administration, which introduced the
> program, gained by splitting the ethnic coalition that had
> elected liberal Democrats for decades. Blacks and Jews, for ex-
> ample, were immediately at each other's throats, after having
> worked together for years on civil-rights legislation and other
> sociopolitical goals. Whether the architects of Watergate had
> any such Machiavellian design in mind is a question on which
> each can speculate for himself.

CHAPTER 6

PARISH AND SYSTEMIC
REALITIES

IN the 1980–81 academic year, differing political tendencies at the BU School of Theology began to look like factions, and disagreements over affirmative action stopped being polite. The past few years of frustration and rejection—the trashing of Beverly Harrison, the unceremonious departure of Academic Dean Nelle Slater—had begun to fray the patience of those activists like Professor Paul Deats or Community Life Director Nancy Richardson who cared deeply about integrating the seminary. The rejection by delay of the black scholar Stephen Reid was another serious blow, as much to Dean Richard Nesmith's credibility as to affirmative action efforts. But even more upsetting to trust and morale was Nesmith's simultaneous campaign that academic year, in apparent defiance of agreed-upon affirmative action procedures, to create an STH sinecure for the well-known white sociologist Peter Berger.

Author of numerous volumes on the sociology of religion, including a classroom standard, *Invitation to Sociology*, Berger was known to be available, teaching at Boston College and looking for a change of scene. Through Professor Howard Kee at STH, Dean Nesmith and BU President John Silber were both aware that Berger was interested in BU. Berger was said to have certain liabilities, however: difficulties, as a teacher, with female students; hostility to feminism; and indifference to administrative and collegial obligations. Although Berger had written much on the crisis in religious faith, he was not a theologian; as he had acknowledged in a preface to his 1969 book, *A Rumor of Angels*, "I'm fully aware of my lack of expertise in theology."

But the lure of Berger's fame was irresistible. And Nesmith's campaign to hire him was fueled in large measure, if not entirely, by John

Silber's well-known attraction to big names, and his intention to snag Berger if he could for some sort of position at BU.

Nesmith approached, in turn, each of the four academic "areas," or departments of BUSTH, trying to persuade them to find a need for Berger's skills and offer him a position, at least part-time. Questioning the need, and remembering affirmative action, none of the four would go along. In fact, in December, the three-man executive committee, a particularly venerable faculty group, penned a blunt note to the dean. The three were Earl Kent Brown (chair of Area A, Biblical and Historical Studies), Paul Deats (chair of Area B, Philosophy, Theology, and Ethics), and Merle Jordan (former acting dean and an associate professor of pastoral psychology in Area C). They wrote:

> We affirm the principle that the School of Theology needs to have another outstanding scholar on the faculty. However, in our assessment it appears that such a scholar is needed with primary competence and reputation in the field of theology.

> In accordance with faculty policy, it is imperative that Affirmative Action procedures be rigorously followed in any appointment at the risk of serious division in the faculty and student body if they are not so followed.

> Our judgment, drawn from our knowledge of our respective areas, is that very substantial division exists on the Berger appointment proposal. We suggest that it would be unwise and impolitic to further exacerbate that division by trying to force the issue.

Nesmith was undeterred by this advice. He next approached the APT (Appointments, Promotion and Tenure) Committee at STH, which could also have created a position for Berger. This committee consisted of Earl Kent Brown, chair of Area A; Bob Treese, the director of field education and chair of Area D (Ministry in Church and Society); senior faculty members Homer Jernigan and Orlo Strunk; and John Cartwright, a BU Ph.D. and the "first-rate man" who had finally been hired to fill the Martin Luther King, Jr. chair after three earlier appointees to that post had, in quick succession, decided to go elsewhere. Now the sole black tenured professor at STH, Cartwright had been a student there in the 1950s when Martin Luther King was working toward his Ph.D. After King was murdered, Cartwright, by then teaching at the new Santa Cruz campus of the University of California, was persuaded to return to STH to head the newly-formed King Center. After a few years, he left to teach at Northwestern, but, having criticized his alma mater for what he perceived as its waning commitment to the King program, came back again in 1978 as the Martin Luther King, Jr. Professor of Social Ethics.

Nesmith wrote these five members of the APT Committee a long memo in February, announcing his intention to "seek your support for a Presidential appointment of Dr. Berger to the Unviersity Professors Program and to the School of Theology." He added that the appointment "will be subject to the condition of an affirmative action review, a review I have asked Dr. Cartwright to assist in making."

It is not easy to make out what Nesmith meant by referring to an "affirmative action" process that would occur after an appointment had been decided upon, and concerning a position that had been created with a specific appointee in mind. Professor Cartwright neither made any such "review" nor recalls being asked to do so. Nevertheless, in a March 1981 letter to the university's affirmative action office Nesmith asserted that he himself had conducted an affirmative action search by personally making a few inquiries, but had located "no known minority or female scholar who could be viewed as a viable candidate, and certainly not as a peer to Dr. Berger."

Nesmith's memo to the APT committee marshaled his arguments for Berger: his fame would "strengthen the recognition of our faculty"; his "dialogical capability will enhance conversations across the university"; and his views "would bring a needed measure of political balance." Here the dean added a note of explanation: "Personally, I do not want to see our graduates be less prophetic, but it is clear that their experience needs to be tempered by a diversity of political judgment and styles so that they are not one-sidedly naive when they confront parish and systemic realities."

This last argument was apparently a defense of Berger's well-known conservatism. In church parlance, moral fire was "prophetic," while conservatism, at least in Nesmith's view, equated roughly with "parish and systemic realities."

Nesmith's argument now moved from politics generally to the even touchier specific question of sexism:

> The issue of sexism is not without its relevance as a counter-
> point. Even this has some positive dimensions, however; Ber-
> ger is attempting to shift our language, not unlike some of the
> other men on our faculty. At the same time, he is not "caving

in" to an ideology. He continues to raise critical notes where he thinks it appropriate. I suspect some of our women students would, in the long run, be better equipped for the Feminist cause if they faced occasional critical notes.

Nesmith made clear that his status with President Silber was on the line: "Thus far I have resisted the 'star syndrome' in the rebuilding of our faculty," he wrote. "When an assumed 'star' is set on our doorstep, with some presidential support, however, it becomes a difficult matter. Inaction on our part will not be without its long term consequence. A faculty which is now viewed as making progress will once again be labeled 'second rate.' This will not be without consequence here when I seek merit salary funding, policy adjustments . . . or unrestricted fund increases. You can be sure that I will face the question, 'Why should I give more help to a faculty that can't see far enough down the road to help itself?'

"Finally," declared the Dean, "I personally want the chance to look at this appointment. As a new Dean I have not asked you to make inordinate sacrifices. The one time I did come home with a sharp need (re Nelle Slater), I received a very mixed answer."

By this point in mid-semester, the controversy over Berger's proposed appointment had become a general campus topic. Even assuming, as everyone did, based on Nesmith's assurances, that Stephen Reid had been hired, affirmative action was not something you forgot about just because you'd managed to appoint one black scholar. Students, staff, and faculty all debated with Nesmith in this period, urging him to drop the idea and insisting that creating a position for Berger, or anybody, could not be squared with the principle of conducting affirmative action searches for known job openings.

Nesmith countered with all the arguments in his arsenal. He told one female student, Jan Burdewik, that he was tired of hearing rumors about Berger's sex life (which he attributed to an instructor named Lynn Rhodes, who chaired STH's powerless affirmative action committee). He interrupted Burdewik at prayer in the chapel to invite her and other women student leaders to a dinner with Berger so they could get to know him.

Linda Clark, a recently hired teacher of sacred music, wrote to the members of Area C: "Whereas the usual differences exist among colleagues about Berger's work, there is one point on which everyone has agreed: his deep hostility to feminism. Hiring someone holding his views about feminism seems to me to fly in the face of the commitment of the school to struggle with issues of sexism. . . . What are the reasons to bring Berger here that override the commitment to dealing with issues of sexism?"

Before the APT Committee met, Earl Kent Brown, not ordinarily a vocal critic of the administration, wrote a lengthy memo summarizing the concerns that he had heard voiced around the school, and adding his commentary. Brown touched on several issues: whether STH actually needed another sociologist of religion, the relevance of widespread perceptions that Berger was sexist, and the problem of "equal opportunity," which Professor Brown described as "far broader than Berger. It is the context indeed that makes the Berger appointment controversial." Brown pointed out that in the last three and a half years female and minority appointments had been primarily part-time and not tenure-track, while the dean continued to place white males in full-time and tenure-track positions, and had announced an intention to replace Nelle Slater with Simon Parker, a white male Silber assistant from central administration. "We hear what we say to each other about equal opportunity," wrote Brown, "and we want to believe it. Others see what we do and judge us by what we do. Query: Can the above development actually be honestly described as that of an 'equal opportunity employer'?"

Finally, responding to Nesmith's political and personal plea, Brown wrote:

> The issue of consequences
> [Nesmith] lists several matters which will be affected by presidential attitude towards a school which "won't help itself."
> Those who have worked closely with John can hear his saying just such things. But it is argued, these are not the only consequences. The appointment itself has consequences. Student moral consequences. A feeling of betrayal of stated equal opportunity commitments. There are also faculty moral consequences. Did the Dean really say the male tenured faculty fears the appointment because of Berger's brilliance? Students say he did. Even if he was half joking, the effect is that the dean is demeaning his faculty to the students they are supposed to teach. That is exactly where John Silber got into the deepest water in the 1974ff period, or at least so it seems to those who argue this way.

Dean Nesmith ultimately failed to assemble any serious backing for the Berger appointment within STH. In April, nevertheless, Berger was appointed to the elite University Professors Program with a half-time position in STH. This was managed by central administration through a special procedure designed to permit emergency hiring when time was not sufficient to employ the usual channels.

In apparent accordance with affirmative action requirements, an advertisement in a professional journal appeared—also in April. The text described the job that had been created for Berger:

> Boston University, tenured, distinguished, scholar bridging theology and sociology. Ph.D. and extensive teaching and writing required.

Nesmith also filled out the required "affirmative action report form," duly recording that one white male had been interviewed for the position. It might have been less offensive, at least to some observers, had he simply refused to go through these motions, and said plainly that he didn't think affirmative action should apply when a known star appears on your doorstep. To some, like affirmative action chair Lynn Rhodes or her friend Nancy Richardson, the dean's shallow pretense of following an affirmative action procedure only cheapened and mocked the principle on which it was based.

Peter Berger and Stephen Reid were, obviously, treated very differently by Boston University. One was courted by the people who counted; a place was made for him; the other was courted by people who, it turned out, did not count very much. The presumed justification for the difference was that Berger was a big name and Reid was unproven and unknown. Affirmative action should ask whether those presumed justifications are necessary or proper. It depends on what the institution is trying to achieve. If the qualifications for a faculty position in a Christian seminary are thought to include teaching skill, quality as a ministerial role model, and diversity of ethnic experience, as well as fame, connections, and the writing of numerous books, then Reid would have rated well ahead of Berger.

CHAPTER 7

A THEOLOGICAL VERSION OF A SMALL TOWN ROTARY CLUB

In 1971 a thirty-one-year-old engineer named Allan Bakke wrote a letter to an associate dean of the University of California Medical School at Davis, expressing his desire to become a physician and asking how his age would affect his chances. The reply was that "when an applicant is over thirty, his age is a serious factor which must be considered. One of the major reasons for this is that such an applicant can be expected on an actuarial basis to practice medicine for about ten years less than the applicant of average age." Bakke did not apply to Davis that year, but in 1972 he did seek admission to two other medical schools, Southern California and Northwestern, and was rejected by both. The Northwestern letter explained that his age was "above their stated limit." In 1973, Bakke applied to Davis.

The medical school at Davis had an affirmative action admissions program under which sixteen places out of an entering class of one hundred were held open for special consideration of "disadvantaged" minority applicants who did not meet the ordinary numerical standards of the regular admissions process. Those ordinary standards included a college grade point average of at least 2.5 out of a possible 4.0. Davis further quantified the process by computing benchmark ratings for each applicant, which were a compilation of grade points, Medical College Admissions Test scores (MCATs), and other factors such as references and interviews. Allan Bakke's benchmark rating in 1973 was 468 out of a possible 500. He also applied late in the year, after most places had been filled. He was not accepted.

On July 18, 1973, an assistant to the dean for student affairs and admissions, Peter Storandt, wrote to Bakke, encouraging him to study the *DeFunis* case, then on appeal to the U.S. Supreme Court, in which a white law school aspirant had successfully challenged the University of Washington Law School's minority preferential admissions program. (The *DeFunis* case was ultimately dismissed as moot, as the plaintiff was about to graduate from law school by the time the matter was argued in the Supreme Court.)

Bakke replied to Storandt on August 7 outlining his thoughts about legal strategies and asking, "Mr. Storandt, do you have any comments on these possible actions? Are there any different procedures you would suggest? Would Davis prefer not to be involved in any legal action I might undertake or would such involvement be welcomed as a means of clarifying the legal questions involved?" Storandt's reply of August 15 suggested that a suit against Stanford Medical School might be pointless "[w]ithout the thrust of a current application for admission," and advised Bakke to "press the suit . . . at the institution of your choice."

Bakke applied to Davis again in 1974. This time his benchmark rating was 549 out of a possible 600. Again he was rejected. In both years his MCAT scores were far above the average for either the special or the general admittees. Bakke sued, claiming that the special admissions program violated both the Equal Protection Clause of the U.S. Constitution, and Title VI of the 1964 Civil Rights Act, which prohibited race discrimination by programs that received federal funds.

The university's defense strategy was questioned early and often by civil rights groups, associations of minority students, and others with a stake in affirmative action. From the beginning the university sought a definitive ruling on the overall legality of race-conscious preferences in admissions, rather than trying to defeat the suit on any of a number of less lofty grounds, such as the argument that Allan Bakke, whether because of his age or other factors, would not have been admitted to Davis even if sixteen places had not been reserved for disadvantaged minority applicants.

There was also a perhaps technical but not unimportant question of whether the number sixteen was a rigid quota, or simply a goal. In 1974 only fifteen students were admitted through the special program; the sixteenth slot had been returned to regular admissions because the special admissions task force did not think any of the other applicants from whom it had to choose was sufficiently qualified. The university's defense team made nothing of this fact, and thus permitted the case to be litigated as one involving inflexible "quotas."

The university failed to offer evidence on another crucial point, the existence of past or continuing discrimination in medical school admissions, or in California public education generally. Remedying past discrimination, after all, was the reason for affirmative action; a string of federal court precedents supported the use of race-conscious preferences to make up for prior racial exclusion or to combat the "built-in headwinds" that are encountered by minority groups.

The Regents of the University of California and their attorneys made no effort to show, for example, the racially discriminatory impact, or limited utility, of judging aspiring physicians primarily on the basis of college grade point averages or standardized tests such as the MCAT. By 1974 there was a significant body of research debunking the relevance or reliability of these numbers. Investigators had reported that neither college grades nor MCAT results accurately predict physician performance; a number of studies actually showed *negative* correlations between MCAT scores and the clinical work of physicians.

It was not exactly news that standardized aptitude tests contained cultural biases that discriminated against minority students. In requiring a student to choose the "best" of four or five possible answers, aptitude tests inevitably embody cultural presuppositions. In one example given by an authority in the testing field, many black children chose an "incorrect" answer to a question asking what they would do if sent to the store for a loaf of bread and told by the grocer that there was no bread left. The "correct" answer was "go to another store"; the black children had chosen, "go home." The difference was that many of them lived in neighborhoods with only one store, or only one at which they could buy. Professor Stephen Jay Gould of Harvard has written a detailed and fascinating book, *The Mismeasure of Man*, about the racist origins of intelligence testing, and the cultural assumptions that still pervade supposedly neutral or bias-free "aptitude" tests.

The interest of a cultural group in the subject matter of test questions may also affect test scores. One study, sponsored by the Law School Admission Council and quoted in the *Harvard Civil Rights-Civil Liberties Law Review* found "that five LSAT [Law School Admission Test] questions related to reading a passage on social customs among certain Indian tribes were easier for minority groups. The study suggests, 'If this material proved more interesting to the minority groups than to the white groups, on the average, then the minority groups might be expected to recall the details more readily.' There is no suggestion, moreover, that the questions 'easier' for the minority groups failed to measure the skill to be tested."

The author of the Harvard article continued:

[S]tandardized tests produce gaps between the test scores of white and minority students that are disproportionately wider than the gaps in academic performance. . . . [T]he performance gap between majority and minority students at the University of California on the SAT . . . is larger than the gap in their high school grades or their college grades. . . . [B]lack medical students who had successfully completed their first two years of medical school . . . had lower average scores on the . . . MCAT than whites who had been dismissed for academic reasons. The LSAT differentiates white and black law students more than a comparison of their undergraduate grade point averages or their first year law school grades. And the performance gap between majority and minority students for the Colorado bar examination is larger on the Multistate [the standardized test] than on the essay portion of the examination.

The Regents' failure to enter into the record in the *Bakke* case evidence of their own discriminatory practices, in particular their use of standardized aptitude tests, was, if not admirable, at least understandable. Indeed, many of the institutions of higher learning that submitted "friend of the court" briefs to the Supreme Court in favor of some form of preferential admissions also failed to confront the fundamental problem of bias built into their standard notions of merit and qualifications. As Professor Derrick Bell, Jr., of Harvard Law School observed, "Rather than overhaul admissions criteria that provided easy access to offspring of the upper class and presented difficult barriers to all other applicants, officials chose to 'lower' admissions standards for minority candidates. This act of self-interested beneficence had unfortunate results." Special admissions programs like Davis's helped reinforce assumptions about racial superiority.

The point had been nicely illustrated at oral argument before the Supreme Court in the *DeFunis* case. Justice Douglas had asked the Attorney General of Washington, who was defending the preferential admissions program,

Mr. Attorney General, when I was teaching law many years ago, I discovered to my consternation that these tests, these so-called tests, had a built-in racial bias. Is there any finding in this record as to your test?

The candid but otherwise not surprising response was:

There is no finding in this record, Mr. Justice Douglas, because neither party wished even to bring that subject up. Obviously Mr. DeFunis would not make that claim, and the University of Washington did not attempt to prove that it engaged in previous racial discrimination.

The state of the court record in *Bakke* thus made it possible for the California Supreme Court, beginning its opinion in the case, to frame the issue as whether the medical school could constitutionally favor "less qualified" minority candidates over higher-scoring "better qualified" white ones. The answer seemed inexorably to follow from the question: such a preference violated the Fourteenth Amendment's Equal Protection Clause.

Justice Matthew Tobriner, dissenting from the California Supreme Court's decision, recognized that this less qualified–more qualified dichotomy begged the affirmative action question:

> [T]he majority incorrectly asserts that the minority students accepted under the special admissions program are "less qualified"—under the medical school's own standards—than nonminority applicants rejected by the medical school. . . . This is simply not the case. The record establishes that all the students accepted by the medical school are fully qualified for the study of medicine. By adopting the special admission program, the medical school has indicated that in its judgment differences in academic credentials among qualified applicants are not the sole nor best criterion for judging how qualified an applicant is in terms of his potential to make a contribution to the medical profession or to satisfy needs of both the medical school and the medical profession that are not being met by other students. In asserting that the accepted minority students are less qualified than rejected applicants, the majority in effect endow standardized test scores and grade point averages with a greater significance than the medical school attributes to them or than independent studies have shown they will bear.

When the Supreme Court accepted the *Bakke* case for review, those who cared deeply about affirmative action were understandably alarmed. As litigated in the California courts by attorneys for Mr. Bakke and the University Regents, the case was structured to raise the broad issue that the Regents had wanted decided: whether race preferences, voluntarily engaged in to integrate professional schools—or, by the same token, to

integrate undergraduate schools, faculties, or other employment settings—
were permissible under the Equal Protection Clause of the U.S. Constitution, in the absence of specific findings that a particular institution
or employer had discriminated. The socially more interesting underlying
issues, of how prizes like professional school admission or prestige jobs
are distributed, were buried by assumptions about "merit" that were
shared not only by the litigants but, as it turned out, by most of the
Supreme Court as well.

The position of associate dean for academic affairs at Boston University School of Theology had been vacant since the dean of the seminary, Richard Nesmith, had fired Nelle Slater at the end of the 1979–
80 academic year.

To replace Slater, who had been the highest-ranking woman in the
STH administration, Dean Nesmith was considering Simon Parker, a
Biblical scholar and expert in Semitic languages who held a post in BU's
central administration and was trusted by John Silber. Nesmith asked a
committee of student government leaders who had been vocal about
participating in the selection process to interview Parker in July 1980.
They did so, then wrote Nesmith a memo asking when they could see
the other applicants.

Earlier in that year Professor Paul Deats and others on the School
of Theology's faculty executive committee had interviewed Parker and
two other white male candidates. They told Nesmith that despite reservations they considered Parker the best of the three, but that they
would not recommend him because an affirmative action search should
be done. The committee urged Nesmith to interview a number of likely
minority candidates for the position.

Deats, for example, suggested that Nesmith pursue Dr. Julius Scott,
then president of Paine, a predominantly black college in Atlanta. Nesmith promised to do so. Later, he said that Dr. Scott had told him in a
telephone conversation that prior commitment to a fundraising drive at
Paine made him unable to apply for the BU job. As it turned out, the
academic deanship remained open that entire year, awaiting Simon Parker's completion of his duties in central administration. Scott's understanding, as he told Deats, was that he was still a candidate, and was
awaiting follow-up from Nesmith.

As Deats wrote to Scott in August 1980, "the position is still open.
Dick is 'around-the-world-in-thirty-days.' We are hoping you and he can
work something for 1981–82." Scott responded on August 27: "I won-
dered what had happened to Dick. He was to get back to me in antici-

pation of a trip to Atlanta." Deats answered in September: "Dick tells me he missed you in June but anticipates calling you for an appointment this month."

Why Nesmith played this game is not clear. He was later to acknowledge that he had decided before the commencement of the 1980–81 year to hire Simon Parker as associate dean. Possibly that decision had simply been dictated by President Silber. As with the near-simultaneous hiring by STH of the noted sociologist, Peter Berger, however, an affirmative action charade proceeded after Nesmith's decision to hire Parker had been made. The dean filled out forms, placed ads, sought input from students.

The faculty, already in turmoil about the hiring of Peter Berger over its protests, and about the refusal of BU central administration to extend an offer to the young black scholar, Stephen Breck Reid, denounced the apparent *fait accompli* in the case of the new academic dean as well. At an April 1981 retreat the faculty discussed and refined a set of recommendations that had originally been drafted during an anti-racism workshop conducted by staff members of the United Methodist Church Commission on Religion and Race the previous December. One of these recommendations had proposed the hiring of a minority person as associate dean to replace the departed Nelle Slater. By April, this recommendation was obviously moot, as Nesmith had just announced the appointment of Simon Parker, a white man, to the position. Nevertheless, the faculty approved the recommendation along with a number of other suggestions for improving the affirmative action process at the school.

The faculty's recommendation that a minority person be hired as associate dean particularly vexed Nesmith since he perceived it as a direct affront to both himself and Parker, and he said as much to the two people who had been assigned by the faculty to compile the final anti-racism recommendations. These two were Paul Deats, a senior, tenured professor, and Nancy Richardson, whom Nesmith had promoted from associate director to director of student and community life about two years before. Nesmith expected one of the two—presumably Richardson, his untenured subordinate—to edit out this particular recommendation before the document was presented to the full faculty for a final vote in May. If Richardson even perceived that Nesmith wanted or expected this, however, she was hardly the person to do it. A feminist and civil rights activist, Richardson was not the kind to manipulate paperwork in the service of academic politics.

Other recommendations that the STH faculty put into final form at the April retreat also pointedly reflected the events of the 1980–81 academic year. In hardly concealed references to the Stephen Reid episode, in which STH's request to hire a black scholar had been stalled for months at central administration because of Silber's opposition, the faculty voted that the dean, the Appointments, Promotion, and Tenure Committee, and search committees should develop "a careful strategy for the presentation of credentials and review by the Provost and the President. . . . Someone should be responsible in each case for monitoring the review process of a dossier forwarded to central administration to prevent delays which may be disastrous in recruiting minority candidates."

Moreover, "[a]n important part of this strategy and in the definition of excellence is that the faculty and administration of the school be committed to careful review of all tenure candidates, including minority candidates. We need to develop this consensus to counter the argument [made by Nesmith and attributed to Silber in the context of BU's failure to hire Stephen Reid] that once a minority person is in the tenure track it is impossible to make a negative decision on tenure."

The faculty's anti-racism recommendations also grappled with the concept of excellence, that loaded word on which afirmative action efforts in academia so frequently foundered. The April retreat called for a definition of excellence "which includes serious attention to the inclusiveness of the faculty. We do not see excellence as defined with a ranked list of criteria so that when these are all satisfied we ask the question of Affirmative Action. We see excellence as a characteristic not only of individuals but also of the faculty as a whole so that diversity becomes one criterion of the excellence of a faculty, especially in theological education."

In early May the anti-racism recommendations drafted at the STH faculty's April retreat went to the executive committee (Professors Paul Deats, Merle Jordan, and Earl Kent Brown). This was a necessary step for their presentation to the entire faculty later in the month. Here Dean Nesmith again sought deletion of the reference to a minority person as associate dean, since Simon Parker had already been hired. Brown, Jordan, and Deats agreed to this, but the meeting was far from congenial.

A discussion began of affirmative action in general. Reviewing the events of the year, Deats declared that he had lost confidence in the commitment of Boston University's administration to serious compliance with affirmative action procedures. He added that he was tempted to include the administration of the School of Theology in that judgment. This provoked an agitated diatribe from Nesmith, who recounted to the committee with some passion a story of his youthful involvement in the civil rights movement. As Deats later recalled, "[h]e told about his wife and child having been involved in civil rights demonstrations, about his child having been taken from them while they were both put in jail overnight; that no one had any business accusing him of being a racist.

"At that point I interjected that I was not accusing him of being a racist; I was talking about compliance with affirmative action procedures. I then said that I thought that if he had pursued the matter of the appointment of Stephen Breck Reid with the same vigor that he pursued the appointment of Peter Berger, Reid would be on the faculty."

Nesmith shot back, "Your opposition to Berger can be explained in terms of ideology and in terms of the typical faculty fear of this kind of a person of excellence coming onto the faculty."

This remark set Deats steaming. It was the same explanation of faculty resistance to Berger's appointment that Professor Earl Brown had said Dean Nesmith tried out on students earlier in the year. Deats retorted that he resented being psychoanalyzed by someone who was not trained in that profession.

Each year, the Boston University Theology Students Association compiled a report to the faculty on the "Concerns of the Student Body," and read the text aloud to a faculty meeting in May. In the discordant academic year of 1980–81, BUTSA's report, as usual, canvassed various areas of campus life, but reserved its deepest concern for what it called "the lack of any serious engagement by University and STH administration in dealing with the issues surrounding institutional racism and sexism at the School of Theology, particularly in the areas of faculty and staff hiring." The report said that the failure to appoint Stephen Breck Reid was "a grievous disappointment to all students," and opined: "The filling of the associate dean position, once occupied by a woman, with a white male is another illustration of the front office's seeming disregard for student and faculty concerns about the need for an inclusive faculty and administration."

The seminarians continued:

Despite words of support for affirmative action, the administrative complement of the School of Theology continues to look like, as one third-year student put it, "a theological version of a small town Rotary Club." With the exception of the Director of Community Life and Financial Aid [Nancy Richardson], every major administrative position in the School of Theology . . . is held by a white male. . . . The pattern of hiring ethnic minority and female faculty and staff for part-time, adjunct, and non-tenured positions has become the rule and not the exception. Women students, who make up nearly half of the student body, anxiously await the day when there will be tenured women on the faculty and in key administrative positions.

CHAPTER 8

To Get Beyond Racism

THE U.S. Supreme Court's decision in *Regents of the University of California v. Bakke*, handed down in June 1978, came as a relief to many advocates of affirmative action. Although widely read as a hypocritical invitation to institutions to do indirectly what they could not do as explicitly and clumsily as the University of California at Davis had, at least the *Bakke* decision didn't close all the doors.

The nine justices divided at least four ways, with six separate opinions comprising 156 pages of text in the United States Supreme Court Reports. Justice Powell, although no other justice joined him, provided the swing vote and wrote the opinion for the Court. This was because Powell agreed with four other justices (Brennan, Marshall, Blackmun, and White) that race could sometimes be a factor in admissions decisions; but he agreed with the other four (Stevens, Stewart, Rehnquist, and Chief Justice Burger) that the form taken by affirmative action at the Davis medical school was unconstitutional. Powell's vote thus created a slim majority of five to affirm the California Supreme Court's order striking down the Davis program, and an equally slim majority of five to reverse the California decision insofar as it prohibited the use of race as a factor at all in public university admissions.

Powell's analysis started with the proposition that racial classifications are inherently suspect, and must be subjected to "strict" judicial scrutiny, regardless of whether their asserted purposes are invidious or benign. This issue of strict scrutiny was a critical one. Over the years the Supreme Court had erected an analytical framework for Equal Protection cases that came, in legal parlance, to be known as the "two-tier" standard. Tier I, strict scrutiny, almost always meant invalidation of the program involved; it was generally reserved for discrimination based on race, national origin, and certain "fundamental rights," such as the constitutional freedom to travel interstate or vote. Under strict scrutiny, the government agency defending the discrimination had to show that it was necessary to achieve a "compelling state interest."

Tier II, "rational basis," originally was reserved for everything else, and usually meant that the Equal Protection challenge to the legislation, policy, or program would fail. The government had only to articulate some arguable rational reason for classifying or discriminating as it had.

Of late, largely in response to increasingly obvious inadequacies in the rigid two-tier approach, an intermediate level of analysis had been invented. Under "intermediate scrutiny" a challenged program had to "serve important governmental objectives and . . . be substantially related to achievement of those objectives." This was sometimes known as "rational basis with bite." It was unclear, as the *Bakke* case headed toward Supreme Court resolution, exactly what sorts of classifications would trigger intermediate scrutiny. Sex discrimination, once briefly thought to inhabit the strict-scrutiny tier, had ultimately been relegated to this middle level.

Obviously, whatever standard of review was adopted by the Supreme Court in *Bakke* would go a long way toward determining the outcome of the case. Thus, Allan Bakke's counsel argued for the standard applied by the California Supreme Court, strict scrutiny; the university and many of the organizations that submitted friend of the court briefs (there were fifty-five such briefs, including one by the Carter administration) urged an intermediate standard, on the ground that the racial discrimination involved in the case was benign, not invidious, and was designed to further racial equality, not retard it.

Justice Powell, the swing vote, insisted on strict scrutiny. He rejected the argument that it made a difference, for constitutional purposes, that the racial preference was not intended invidiously, and did not impose a stigma, as Jim Crow laws and other manifestations of racism had done. Moreover, he argued (with some force), "preferential programs may only reinforce common stereotypes holding that certain groups are unable to achieve success without special protection based on a factor having no relationship to individual worth." Unlike Justice Douglas, who four years earlier in the *DeFunis* case had expressed his aversion for race preferences but gone on to argue that race must be used to understand the bias of standardized tests, Justice Powell simply assumed that these tests showed the inferiority of the minority applicants.

Justice Powell's opinion acknowledged that race classifications had been permitted, indeed required, in school desegregation cases, in voting reapportionment, whether court-ordered or voluntary, and in judge-ordered remedies for employment discrimination. He noted also, as the U.S. government's brief had taken great care to point out, that Congress and various federal agencies required numerically specific race-conscious preferences of their contractors and of recipients of federal funds. All these exceptions to his general rule Justice Powell distinguished as having been justified by specific findings of past discrimination, whether by a court, an administrative agency, or Congress. The University of California, by contrast, he said, had made no such findings, indeed, was not even competent to do so, and had put no evidence in the record to justify a remedy that took account of race.

Here Justice Powell took advantage of the poor factual record upon which the case was being decided. He enumerated four possible justifications for Davis's race classification that might enable it to survive strict scrutiny: "reducing the historic deficit of traditionally disfavored minorities in medical schools and in the medical profession"; "countering the effects of societal discrimination"; "increasing the number of physicians who will practice in communities currently underserved"; and "obtaining the educational benefits that flow from an ethnically diverse student body." A possible fifth goal was mentioned only in a footnote:

> Racial classifications in admissions conceivably could serve a fifth purpose, one which petitioner [the University] does not articulate: fair appraisal of each individual's academic promise in the light of some cultural bias in grading or testing procedures. To the extent that race and ethnic background were considered only to the extent of curing established inaccuracies in predicting academic performance, it might be argued that there is no "preference" at all. Nothing in this record, however, suggests either that any of the quantitative factors considered by the Medical School were culturally biased or that petitioner's special admissions program was formulated to correct for any such biases.

The key words here were "in this record," for substantial outside evidence existed of precisely such cultural bias.

Thus, Mr. Justice Powell could rely upon the presumed legitimacy of the medical school's quantitative standards to reject the assertion by other justices in *Bakke* that the concept of "disparate impact" under federal employment discrimination law, the understanding that apparently neutral standards or tests could act as "built-in headwinds" for minorities, should apply under the Equal Protection Clause of the Constitution as well. As Justice Powell pointed out, quoting the Supreme Court's decision in the *Griggs v. Duke Power Company* case, where the "disparate impact" or "built-in headwinds" rule had originated, what federal employment discrimination law requires "is the removal of artificial, arbitrary, and unnecessary barriers." Since the standards for determining admission to the medical profession had not been shown to be artificial, arbitrary, and unnecessary, the insights of *Griggs* did not apply.

Thus, as law professor Derrick Bell, Jr., wrote of the *Bakke* decision:

It remained simply for the Supreme Court to accept without question the definition of qualifications, that is, grades and test scores, proffered by both Bakke and the Regents. They did so, or a majority of five Justices did so, thereby simultaneously writing off the adverse impact of past discrimination on the gap between majority and minority test scores and grades, and presuming the validity of traditional admissions standards as accurate predictors of successful professional performance. In what was potentially the most important civil rights case since *Brown v. Board of Education*, racial disadvantage, like a birth defect, was treated as an unfortunate accident of nature for which charity was appropriate, not as a massive, historic, and intentional racial crime for which virtually all institutions are responsible and for which a compensatory remedy is essential.

In dismissing the notion that test scores and grades might be culturally biased, Justice Powell concerned himself only with these data as predictors of academic performance, not as predictors of performance as physicians. That second point, which had been discussed at length by Justice Matthew Tobriner, dissenting in the California Supreme Court, was virtually lost in the Supreme Court litigation. Yet, as one commentator on the *DeFunis* case had written three years earlier, "As difficult as it may be to identify the skills needed for good lawyering, a state law school could properly decide to admit those who would make better lawyers in preference to those who would make better law students."

Justice Powell's opinion turned to the four possibly compelling justifications for race-conscious admissions that he had identified. He dismissed the first, "reducing the historic deficit of disfavored minorities," as "facially invalid. Preferring members of any one group for no reason other than race or ethnic origin is discrimination for its own sake. This the Constitution forbids."

The second justification, "countering the effects of societal discrimination," did not fare much better. The concept of "societal discrimination" was too amorphous, said Powell; it "may be ageless in its reach into the past." Race-conscious remedies relying on this justification had to be based on "judicial, legislative, or administrative findings of constitutional or statutory violations." The University of California "does not purport to have made, and is in no position to make, such findings. Its broad mission is education, not the formulation of any legislative policy or the adjudication of particular claims of illegality."

The third possible justification was "improving the delivery of health care services to communities underserved," which Powell assumed for purposes of argument could be "sufficiently compelling to support the use of a suspect classification." But, he said, "there is virtually no evidence in the record indicating that petitioner's special admissions program is either needed or geared to promote that goal." Asking applicants whether they intended to practice medicine in disadvantaged communities would be a more logical method of achieving the goal than establishing racially select admissions slots.

Justice Powell did, however, find the fourth goal, "attainment of a diverse student body," to be compelling, since it derived from the First Amendment right of academic freedom. He quoted "a wise graduate" of Princeton University as "commenting upon this aspect of the educational process, 'People do not learn very much when they are surrounded only by the likes of themselves.' "

The next step for Justice Powell, under Tier I strict scrutiny, was to decide whether the Davis program's racial classification was "necessary" to achieve the compelling interest in academic diversity. Asserting that diversity did not encompass only race and ethnicity, Justice Powell concluded that a special program meant to achieve diversity but limited to racial minorities was not necessary to accomplish the goal. Here he relied heavily upon a friend of the court brief submitted by Columbia, Harvard, Stanford, and the University of Pennsylvania, which described the Harvard College affirmative action program:

> In recent years Harvard College has expanded the concept of diversity to include students from disadvantaged economic, racial, and ethnic groups. Harvard College now recruits not only Californians or Louisianans but also blacks and Chicanos and other minority students . . .

> In practice, this new definition of diversity has meant that race has been a factor in some admission decisions. When the Committee on Admissions reviews the large middle group of applicants who are "admissible" and deemed capable of doing good

work in their courses, the race of an applicant may tip the balance in his favor just as geographic origin or a life spent on a farm may tip the balance in other candidates' cases. A farm boy from Idaho can bring something to Harvard College that a Bostonian cannot offer. Similarly, a black student can usually bring something that a white person cannot offer.

Thus, said Justice Powell, race could be taken into account, but not so blatantly as Davis had done.

The last words in *Bakke*, and some of the most memorable, were in the separate opinion of Justice Blackmun. Until the early 1970s, Blackmun began by pointing out, fewer than two percent of the nation's physicians, attorneys, and medical and law students were members of racial minorities. About three-quarters of the black physicians had been trained at just two medical schools, Howard and Meharry.

It is somewhat ironic to have us so deeply disturbed over a program where race is an element of consciousness, and yet to be aware of the fact, as we are, that institutions of higher learning . . . have given conceded preferences up to a point to those possessed of athletic skills, to the children of alumni, to the affluent who may bestow their largesse on the institutions, and to those having connections with celebrities, the famous, and the powerful. . . .

I suspect that it would be impossible to arrange an affirmative-action program in a racially neutral way and have it successful. To ask that this be so is to demand the impossible. In order to get beyond racism, we must first take account of race. There is no other way. And in order to treat some persons equally, we must treat them differently. We cannot—we dare not—let the Equal Protection Clause perpetuate racial supremacy.

Despite all the heat and rhetoric and fear, the *Bakke* decision left little actually decided, apart from the legality of the UC-Davis program itself. It hardly invited employers or universities wrestling with affirmative action to engage in the sort of deeper debate about "credentialling" that was to go on at some institutions, among them the Boston University School of Theology, in the next few years. Occasionally one would read, however (as in the May 13, 1985, *New York Times*), that a medical school (in that event, Johns Hopkins) was dropping its requirement that applicants take the MCAT, which is heavily weighted toward science. "We want people who are not monochromatic," the dean was quoted as explaining.

> We do not think we need it to make our selections. . . . We rely on a transcript of grades, letters of recommendation and interviews. . . .

> The MCAT assumes tremendous importance to the undergraduate population. . . . It tends to displace all thinking about a general education. A student may think about taking a course in astronomy or European history, but then he thinks about that test. The whole thrust of the undergraduate experience becomes a multiple choice standardized test.

The article reported that three of the nation's 127 medical schools had made the MCAT optional.

CHAPTER 9

IDEOLOGICAL DIFFERENCES

IN May 1981 Boston University School of Theology Dean Richard Nesmith was worried. His angry confrontation over affirmative action with Paul Deats, a senior professor and former president of the STH faculty, was indicative of the malaise and suspicion that pervaded the dean's relations with the faculty as a whole and particularly its three-man executive committee. The Deats-Nesmith exchange had gone *ad hominem* with the dean's hot assertion of his credentials as a former civil rights activist, and his intimation that Deats and others simply felt threatened by the presence of such a brilliant man as Peter Berger.

The executive committee, frustrated over the year's events, and its apparently limited role in influencing Nesmith's decision making with respect to hiring Peter Berger and others, disbanded. Or rather, it recommended this course of action to the faculty, which accordingly, at its May 15, 1981, meeting, voted to place a moratorium on its executive committee's existence.

Nesmith worried that by abolishing the executive committee the faculty was embarking upon a political process that could easily become factionalized, "easily charged," as he later put it. In this situation, he felt, "I not only had to have a staff that could perform their operational responsibilities, but a staff that knew how to communicate and work in concert."

Central to that effort, in the dean's mind, was his director of student and community life, Nancy Richardson. But Nesmith no longer trusted Richardson. Although he recognized her administrative abilities, and her contribution to the school, she simply had not been backing him up on political issues. The problem went back at least three years, to Richardson's joinder in criticism over the loss to STH of the feminist scholar

Beverly Harrison. The next year, with most of the STH faculty, Richardson had protested Nesmith's decision to fire Nelle Slater.

Richardson's role in the traumas of the past year over the hiring, with less than a passing glance at affirmative action, of two white males, the sociologist Peter Berger and an administrator to replace Slater, Simon Parker, had not endeared her any further to the boss. Nor had the executive committee blowout with Professor Deats, Richardson's cohort in preparing a report on a series of anti-racism recommendations that had been agreed upon at a faculty retreat in April. These recommendations were sharply critical of STH failures to attract women and minorities or to hire them as faculty when they did appear. One recommendation in particular was loaded with implied criticism of Nesmith's failure in 1980–81 to push for the appointment of Stephen Breck Reid as an assistant professor of Old Testament studies. Nesmith's complaisance and President Silber's hostility had combined to kill the appointment. As Paul Deats explained, the dean blamed Nancy Richardson for these criticisms, "as well as me. [But] I'm a tenured faculty member and not subject to reprisal."

Nancy Richardson had gotten support from Nesmith in earlier years. In 1979 he had recommended her for a faculty appointment as a lecturer, writing to the provost in praise of her "strengths: administrative, analytical, and as a person whose work elicits authoritative response. Throughout the Ecumenical church," he said, "there is recognition of her leadership. She has given, and continues to give, content and process to issues related to mission and ministry. Her feminist perspective calls forth a response which helps in realization of the full humanity of all persons regardless of race or sex."

Nesmith had also, in 1979, promoted Richardson from associate director to director of student and community life. As director she had first-line responsibilities as liaison to student government and other student groups, creator of community life programs, and administrator of STH financial aid. As director she also became a member of Nesmith's inner staff circle, the "administrative team."

Bob Treese, the field education director, had been Richardson's nominal boss before her promotion. A likable, easygoing man, Treese sometimes helped resolve misunderstandings between the dean and Richardson. In the spring of 1979, for example, Nesmith complained to Treese "about Nancy's allowing the students who were serving the luncheon [at the weekly STH lunch forum] to operate the serving process within the dining room itself, rather than out in the hallway. There was some level of irritation. So I arranged a meeting between Richard and Nancy and me too. And the first item on that discussion was this serving issue and then a couple of other issues came up, one of which was the Beverly Harrison issue and the Dean was irritated at a couple of things. At the way the students were berating him . . .

"He accused her of saying something in a meeting of BTI women, Boston Theological Institute women, that was derogatory of him. Then he went on to to say that the women students are still angry with him, and he gave an example of one woman student who berated him for sweeping the floor [and thereby, in the student's view, scabbing] once when we had a buildings and grounds strike the previous fall . . .

"I remember Nancy saying something about feeling that it must be difficult to be a dean and to be in an ambivalent position, to be a dean and an ethicist at the same time."

In January 1981 Nesmith again unloaded a pile of grievances. The triggering event was an administrative-team training session in communication and decision making, one of a series of such encounters that had been going on all year, under the supervision of a consultant. The focus of the session was student housing, a serious need given the economic realities of Boston and the mammoth size of the BU student population.

The group had been assigned several readings to discuss, including the New Testament Parable of the Talents, or, in the Lucan version, Parable of the Pounds. In the parable, a lord gives several of his servants an amount of money to use; those who increase it are given rewards in proportion to the return on their investments.

In the discussion that followed, Nancy Richardson said she disliked the parable. It reminded her of the capitalist system: those who have, get. She applied the theme to the subject of the day, student housing. Here was Boston University busily seeking housing for students, in a city where, just the other day, *The Boston Globe* had reported that some two thousand homeless women were roaming the streets in the middle of winter. Tears began to flow; Richardson kept talking.

Treese said he shared her ambivalence. Others around the table agreed. When the dean's turn came, he pointedly articulated the dangers of allowing ideology to interfere with administrative style.

"Richard," said Treese, "are you saying that Nancy is not a good administrator?" Nesmith replied that this was not what he meant.

After the meeting, Nesmith pulled Treese and Richardson aside. He began a speech of some ten minutes' duration about the necessity of capitalism. He then raised two other issues, regarding rumors he had heard. One involved a black woman who had come to STH back in September expecting that housing had been arranged for her and her child. It had not, and after Richardson undertook some efforts to help, the woman left. Nesmith angrily accused Richardson of having told the woman that BUSTH was a racist school, thus accounting not surprisingly for her departure. Richardson denied the accusation and explained that the woman had simply consulted her about housing possibilities. Richardson, offering what help she could, had warned the prospective black student against certain notoriously racist sections of the city.

Not long after this exchange, Nesmith drafted a memo to Richardson. He did not send it. He claimed to have sent her a later draft (dated March 23, 1981). She said she'd never received it.

In any event, the contents accurately reflect Nesmith's state of mind. He began by reminding Richardson of the Parable of the Pounds conversation. "The lines of that discourse have been a source of some continuing reflection on my part."

> You will recall that we had this conversation as a result of some quite basic differences which emerged once again in a staff session, this time around a housing discussion. It is obvious that we are in deep trouble in our housing program once again, but at the moment I want to discuss relationships. . . .

> There have been differences between us across these years . . . which have often been picked up by students. . . . A position such as yours does not have a wide tolerance range for variation in interpretation with a Dean. . . . Usually we have been able to talk such differences through after the fact or have simply accepted the consequent friction resulting from the difference as a part of the load we each have to carry in relation to the other. This is obviously becoming unworkable for each of us . . .

> You are a person with deep social commitments and interests. This was reflected in the staff session that triggered the last conversation, for example, the issue of the housing of indigents in our community. You responded to that item in a manner marked with feeling, compassion, and drive. In other words, you gave a warm or hot response, if I may use such a figure to describe your reaction.

> This is an appropriate response for you given your style, and your commitment to be engaged in issues in a prophetic social change type of ministry.

> By contrast, an administrative position often calls for cool re-

sponses. Whatever one's feelings, there are usually organizational and policy concerns which require a more objective, cool
response. . . . This is the side of you we see when a question
of variation in financial aid/need policy is at stake.

However problematic this analysis, it was helpful for me to
use this figure of warm or cool response as a way of catching
an element of your administrative style. The warm response
quality of your style which may be a genuine asset as you look
to a potential career in social issues and change, is probably a
liability at times when you work in areas of student personnel
administration, areas where the competence of coolness is often
requisite.

Nesmith closed with a very hot warning indeed: "We are near a breaking
point in our relationship once again, Nancy. We seem to agree on long
term goals, but we cannot work well in the short term. This analysis
helped me understand our differences. I hope it may help you understand
our situation and its difficulties."

The memo sounds like a letter of termination. If Richardson had
indeed received it, one might expect that it would have elicited an alarmed
response—meetings, negotiations, more memos. As it was, business continued much as usual that spring of 1981, until the end of May. The
discussions of affirmative action at the April faculty retreat were not
altogether pleasant, to be sure; much of the faculty was appalled to learn
from Nesmith that the young black Old Testament scholar, Stephen
Reid, would not be coming to BU after all, because President Silber felt
that one could not hire a black person to a tenure-track position without
assurance that he would be tenurable seven years down the road. A
farcical pass at affirmative action procedures in the Peter Berger hiring—
an advertisement that was published after the appointment had been
made—also unsettled the faculty. A year-end report by the BU Theology
Students Association, with its snide comparison of the racial and sexual
makeup of the faculty to "a theological version of a small town rotary
club," further strained Nesmith's fortitude. And as if all this were not
enough, a final miscalculation of Richardson's at the very end of the
semester enraged him even more.

A joint faculty-student retreat was scheduled for September. With
everyone about to depart for the summer, it was necessary to set up a
committee, preferably of people who would be around town, to start the
retreat planning process. At its final meeting the faculty, as was standard
procedure, instructed the dean to convene such a committee. Several of

those present volunteered to serve. Nesmith declared that he wanted church representatives, people from outside the school, to be part of the planning. As was also standard procedure, and as she had done several times over the past few years, Nancy Richardson assumed the responsibility of calling together the first meeting of the retreat planning committee. She sent a memo to those professors who had volunteered, and to several students who were responsible for orientation of newcomers the following fall. She also sent Nesmith a request for names of those church people he would like to include.

Nesmith had a week of travel coming up, and he either did not see Richardson's memo before he left, or if he did, forgot it. When he returned, so it seemed to him, Nancy Richardson had organized the committee. He was infuriated, more so, perhaps, than anyone without an intricate sense of academic and church politics could have foreseen. Later, he was to describe Richardson's action as "insubordination." Nesmith did not say whether he had actually intended to stack the committee in some way, or disinvite some of the faculty or student volunteers who were not to his liking.

May 29, 1981. Nesmith's yearly review of Richardson's job performance began unthreateningly enough. The dean talked about a housing report Richardson had given him a few days before, then asked about her progress toward her Ph.D.: How many courses remained for her to take? Had she chosen a topic for her dissertation? Nesmith recommended that she write a paper based on library research rather than fieldwork or interviews: it was faster, and she was good at reading, synthesizing, and analyzing materials.

The next topic was his house in Maine. They talked about the beauty of the landscape. He said he had been getting his sailboat ready for summer outings. Richardson looked at her watch; about forty minutes of the allotted hour had passed.

Nesmith said he was glad that they had had the time for this friendly chat, because he had some difficult matters he would like to discuss. He told Richardson that he wanted to "rearrange" her "relationship with the school." The last two weeks had been very difficult. He mentioned commencement, difficulties he'd had in obtaining cooperation, in planning the type of ceremony he had in mind, from the student group that was responsible with him for creating the program. Then there was the blistering address that the student speaker, B. J. Norrix, had delivered at the ceremony itself. Norrix had criticized BUSTH for advertising—falsely, he said—an open, participatory approach to theological education, where students were taken seriously.

Nesmith said that with this kind of criticism of his office from students, he simply had to have someone else in Richardson's position. "What are you telling me?" said Richardson. "Are you terminating me?"

Nesmith answered: "I intend to rearrange your relationship with the school, and you would probably experience it as termination."

Richardson asked him why. Nesmith said there were two basic reasons, pedagogical and ideological. He gave two examples of the pedagogical reason. The first was "the level of grace and decorum in the dining hall": the students tended to treat it like a cafeteria, or McDonald's, while Nesmith preferred the atmosphere of a church supper.

The second, and more politically charged issue, concerned the recent student government, or BUTSA, report excoriating the administration. Richardson was BUTSA's adviser; she should not have allowed the group to meet and write the report without her. She should have been involved in the writing and presented his office in a more positive light. Likewise, she should have brought the senior class commencement committee together earlier in the year. He disputed her defense that commencement had always been the registrar's responsibility, not hers.

Richardson reminded the dean that she had done much over the year to "cool" the students down. This class had been angry at Nesmith ever since he had given them color-coded exams in their introductory sociology of religion course. (The three different colored papers on which the tests were distributed clearly signaled Nesmith's suspicion that these aspiring ministers might cheat. The students resented being treated with such distrust.) Richardson had tried to minimize these difficulties, had in fact talked the students out of a boycott, picket line, and similar actions they had contemplated during the past year.

As examples of ideological differences, Nesmith mentioned Richardson's participation in protest over BU's refusal to hire Professor Beverly Harrison three years before; he mentioned her work with the STH Women's Collective; he pointed to her role in the debate over the failure to make an offer to Stephen Breck Reid. In that situation as in others she had not represented the administration position. He mentioned the December 1980 anti-racism workshop, and accused her of organizing the reports that emerged from the workshop to reflect negatively on his office. He referred to his hiring of the two white men, Simon Parker and Peter Berger, which the faculty protested so bitterly. He brought up the team meeting at which she had wept when describing the plight of homeless women, freezing on the streets. That reflected an emotional and ideological involvement that was administratively inappropriate.

They talked some about her future, and the options for termination. Nesmith said she could resign, she could be terminated with protest, or she could be terminated without protest. He suggested the advantages of the first course, or as he called it, a negotiated settlement. It all depended on what she wanted the record to show when it was sent back to the United Church of Christ, where she was ordained.

Richardson read these last comments as not-too-subtly veiled threats of some bad outcome in whatever personnel record might be maintained by her church if she did not voluntarily resign. She saw also in Nesmith's "options" a desire to coerce her resignation and thereby avoid yet another brouhaha within STH over his personnel decisions.

Richardson wanted some time to think about the options. Nesmith assured her that she could work through August, and take her time moving out of her office. She would be entitled to four months' severance pay after that. They scheduled a second meeting for June 8 to work out the details.

Richardson immediately telephoned Bob Treese to tell him the news. "How did it go?" he asked of the evaluation.

"He fired me."

"You're kidding."

At noon on Wednesday, June 3, Richardson met with Deats; Treese; Professor Jim Fraser, chair of Area C; Lynn Rhodes, the assistant director of field education and chair of STH's affirmative action committee; and Kathryn Johnson, a student who had been active in the Women's Collective. The fourth area chair, Earl Kent Brown, was in Ohio, but they included him in the meeting by phone.

The group decided to compose a letter urging Nesmith to reconsider, and to try to get as many members of the faculty as possible to sign it. The latter task was complicated by the fact that some professors had already left for the summer. One, Harrell Beck, was in Australia. Nevertheless, active telephoning produced the desired response. Despite all the vexations of the last several months, no one had expected Nesmith to fire Nancy Richardson. She was not only popular with the faculty, and widely perceived to be an effective administrator, she was also the one person in administration whom the students trusted. The faculty's letter, dated June 3, reflected these perceptions:

All of us are surprised and dismayed by the news that you intend to terminate Nancy Richardson.

We recognize that this is an administrative, not a faculty decision. As an administrator you can employ and terminate your staff according to different policies and procedures from those specified for faculty. Whatever the legality of the matter, we suggest that there are ethical and procedural problems with the suddenness and lack of warning in this move. There seems to us to be a moral imperative to consult with the person involved and with some of your faculty and administrative colleagues.

Our experience of Nancy, both what we have observed as colleagues and what we have heard from students, has convinced us that in the crucial areas of housing, financial aid, and community-building Nancy's service has been invaluable to you and to all of us.

She has managed to gain student trust through her respect for confidentiality while helping students understand the complexity of life in a university-related seminary. We have serious concern for the welfare of the school and the chaos this decision may precipitate. Without the climate of trust which Nancy has helped to foster, student protest could be more volatile and more destructive.

We are sure that the moral questions involved in your decision will have an adverse impact on the internal life of the school and on our image in the larger church community, in the event that your decision is confirmed and announced. The adverse impact on our teaching and the classroom atmosphere of the school cannot be overstated.

We vigorously urge you to reconsider.

The letter was signed by fourteen of the eighteen full-time faculty members of the School of Theology, including the chairs of all four areas. A fifteenth, Professor of Systematic Theology Robert Nelson, wrote Richardson a short private note indicating that he certainly would have signed the letter had he been reached. A sixteenth, Elizabeth Bettenhausen, had been unreachable and therefore unable to give her assent at the time, but she followed up when she returned to town on June 8 with a statement of her own. Bettenhausen's letter described her response to the news as "one of bafflement, sadness, and fear."

CHAPTER 10

UNUSUAL LIFESTYLES

THE plan was to have Bob Treese deliver the faculty's June 3 letter to Nesmith a few days later at a meeting of the Southern New England Conference of the United Methodist Church. At the conference, however, the dean was not eager to talk about his latest personnel decision. Treese managed only a few words with him over lunch at a crowded cafeteria.

"You know, Bob," Nesmith said, "a dean is supposed to be protected. When I was at MacMurray College, that was my job, to absorb a lot of the student flak. Nancy wasn't doing that, so I got all the student flak."

He added, "Nancy really has betrayed me," and referred to the last of the administrative-team training sessions, at which, according to Nesmith's source, Richardson had made a derogatory remark about his leaving the meeting early. Treese, having been at the session, contested Nesmith's information: "Dick, I did not hear that. You'd better check your sources."

Treese also said, "Dean, you did this without any consultation. I am completely surprised. I thought we had the best year in the administrative team we ever had, and I thought we finally had developed some trust. Here you go ahead and do this."

Nesmith responded, "I did not consult in this because when I consulted on the firing of Nelle Slater I got so much flak that I determined not to do it."

Earl Kent Brown wrote Nesmith a letter from Ohio. As a senior professor who had been Nesmith's confidante on many occasions, Brown felt a sense of personal betrayal, and said so:

Dear Dick:
    I have just heard via the grapevine that Nancy Richardson
is to be dismissed. I do not know the reason for this action, for

I have only heard the fact, not the rationale. It might seem
that I should hesitate to comment, for I am sure there is a rationale, though I cannot for the life of me imagine what it is.
It might be further argued that it is none of my business, since
she is administration, not faculty. I would reply that actions
that bid fair to shake the whole school to its very foundation—
and this one does—are legitimate concern for every citizen of
our community. I am therefore presuming to share my point
of view. It is simple to state.

I am appalled!

I am appalled because I have found her an efficient and
willing administrator of a very difficult and complex operation.

I am appalled because her shop is one of the ones which
students consistently rate highly in the area of helpfulness and
concern. They see her as an ally and friend rather than as an
enemy. This is rare among administrators of scholarship
programs.

I am appalled because you have used her name so freely
this last year when defending yourself against the charge of
running a predominantly white male administration. . . . It is
hard to see how you can have it both ways. If Nancy was a
"major female voice and influence" on your administration,
then how can her dismissal now be so minor a matter as to be
worthy of no advance discussion with any of your faculty
colleagues?

It will not suffice to say that you will replace with a
woman, even if that is your intent. The fact is that you have
fired your only female department chief, if indeed you have
fired her. To do this in an age when sexism is one of the two
or three leading issues in church and society seems to me to be
singularly suicidal.

I am appalled because you are now voluntarily assuming,
indeed flaunting, the label "sexist," and you are pasting that
label across the lintel of the school. I am sure you do not see
this action as sexism. But you will have great trouble convincing anyone else of that fact, given our recent history. I know,
for I have been one who had sought to defend you against that
charge in the Nelle case. It has not been an easy argument
even to get heard—much less to win. It will be an impossible
argument to sustain if Nancy too is dismissed. Through quiet
efforts I had thought we were making progress on some of the

negative fallout in that area that accompanied the Nelle case. This despite the fact that in one year you have replaced both a female registrar and a female Assoc. Dean with white males. This move will confirm a suspicion, which—frankly—you cannot afford at this time or any other time. The School cannot afford it either.

I am appalled because in three years I have never heard Nancy utter an unprofessional or disloyal word in faculty meeting or in private conversation. And in those years I have never heard you utter a word of criticism about the way she runs her shop.

I am appalled because the deed is done in Summer when faculty and students are scattered. Your intent may be to diffuse organized opposition. Your action will be perceived as perfidy and as a betrayal of everything you have said for four years about community.

Finally I am appalled because I feel personally betrayed. You are under no obligation to discuss administrative issues with me; but you have repeatedly honored me with your confidences in matters that affect school life deeply. I had thought we were tuned in to each other fairly well where major issues of school life were concerned. To discover that this is not the case forces me into a lot of reconsideration and reassessment. In the long run, that may be the highest price paid for this action, as far as I am concerned.

I urge you to reconsider and not put yourself and the School through the anguish and division which will inevitably result if you persist. I ask this for the School's sake, for we cannot really afford a major brouhaha about sexism. But even more I ask this for your own sake, for I cannot but believe that you are the one who will suffer most from such an action. I cannot believe that a situation that was not even serious enough to discuss [with] the EXEC or Chairs three weeks ago is now so irreconcilable and impossible to patch up, if the effort is made with a good will.

Sincerely yours,
Earl Kent Brown

Neither the organized approach of the faculty letter nor Earl Kent Brown's impassioned personal plea moved Nesmith to reconsider. All this protest, and much more that was to follow, seemed only to strengthen his resolve. As was to become clear as the controversy progressed, Nesmith saw his critics at STH not so much as a consituency or community to be reckoned with or accommodated but as enemies to be cleaned out, whether by discharge, where he was able to do it, by changing the tenor of the school so that those with a "prophetic" bent would not be so attracted to it, or simply by attrition. It was not merely a question of one independent-minded administrator who would not "protect" him or "take the flak"; it was a question of the nature and direction of STH itself.

At Bob Treese's suggestion, and with Nesmith's assent, Nancy Richardson brought a tape recorder to her Friday, June 8, meeting with the dean. Whether she or anybody else seriously considered a lawsuit at that point, some faculty and staff certainly wanted documentation of Nesmith's actual statement of his reasons for the termination. And although the dean evidently intended the meeting to be brief and businesslike, especially given the extended discussion of issues on May 29, he was easily drawn into a debate over his motives, covering a wide swath of territory from the politically momentous to the most trivial incidents of academic life.

Richardson asked Nesmith to explain the "pedagogical" and "ideological" reasons for his decision. He responded, in more depth than the last time, that by pedagogical he meant her failure both to protect him from student discontent and to communicate with him about strategies for dealing with it. "Most of my other subordinates come in through that door two or three times a week to have some general quick sharing on how things are moving. By and large I find out how I'm moving with student processes when I get clubbed by them."

On the "ideological" issue, Nesmith explained:

You have been on the firing line, for example, say, related to the women's issue, where you quite rightly have very strong objectives. . . . At the same time you are a member of an administrative team that can't always deliver and certainly haven't always delivered in the way that you, with your social ethics hat on here as a woman . . . would want. There is a kind of tension there.

The second illustration—the racism issue. Again, your own personal ethic and your ideological dispositions press you to want to see things move out here on the front of racism and justice. Over here, you are a member of an administration that wins and loses on that score. We lost Stephen Reid, a blunt

fact. Now, in the way you and I carry those other tensions
. . . once again, you and I have tended, sometimes, to work
very well together, other times to fall apart.

This reminded the dean again of the "women's issue," and particularly
Beverly Harrison. "I took a very sharp scolding from the BTI over the
Beverly Harrison proposition, and some of the feedback around the edge
of that meeting came back indicating that you were not supportive of the
BU position."
Richardon responded:

I think you are absolutely right, around issues of affirmative
action, I have been as clear as I can be. I think both justice
and law demand an affirmative action process, and I have tried
to be as clear with you, as clear publicly in the school, as clear
everywhere that I believe that is what we are about, and that's
what I want us to be about, and when we fail to do that, then
I'm upset about that.

Nesmith mentioned the anti-racism work that he described Richardson and Deats as "pushing," and characterized the recommendations as
"being used simply as a way of attacking our own administrative corps."
Summarizing, he said, "You and I have succeeded more, the more it has
been non-ideological, the more it has been detailed and numerical, such
as in something like financial aid, or something like housing. But the
more you take it into an area where there is heat, diversity, and where
in a sense, some of my institutional representing responsibility as dean
will tend at times, in the student definitions, to come off on the conservative side, the more you and I find ourselves less capable of that kind of
easy rapprochement that helps us be clear strategically with each other."
After another half hour of give and take on a number of specific
incidents that Nesmith recounted to illustrate further his theory of ideological incompatibility, he concluded:

The sum issue, it seems to me, is that you and I do not agree
at a number of key points. That out of what you feel to be
your integrity, you are prone to voice that, obviously, in a
way that ultimately does, in fact, then complicate our capacity
to work as an administrative team, and in a way that ultimately keeps the issue of trust, with about three-month regularity, bubbling up and breaking apart between us, all in sum
to say that in the critical area of student relationships, a dean

cannot get the job done when about every three months, he or she has to go back and rebuild that relationship.

This reminded Nesmith of the blistering BUTSA report, which had been read aloud to a full faculty meeting in early May:

> I cannot afford to have the students come back again a year from now with a report to the faculty that in effect castigates the administration from one end to the other with literally no mention of the fact that the key person on the front line on behalf of that administration even exists. When a dean of students or director of student-community affairs, or whatever name, is on the line, for that administration, no matter how successful, there is no way that they can if they are really doing their job, avoid taking some share of that critique, disease, perplexity.

Richardson disagreed: "I felt there was some critique in there, myself [referring to the BUTSA report], as well as in B. J.'s speech [at commencement]. I felt that the references to the administration included me, in some instances."

"No," said the dean, "really the only explicit reference was at the point of the reference to the 'country club' administration to note that you were, in fact, a woman on the other side of the mix. I cannot afford the luxury of someone who isn't more visibly carrying this administrative relationship with students with regularity of contact with BUTSA, with at times, more direct face-off on some of the issues."

"Face-off with BUTSA, is that what you are referring to?"

"With whomever. . . . With that kind of regular communication, so that say, as in the anti-racism stuff, I would not have been as surprised as I was, but would have known from you, a person significantly involved in it, some of what was there."

"What were you surprised about? I'm sorry," said Richardson.

"The drives on, for example, the appraisal of the dean [Nesmith], the appraisal of staff, the hiring of a black after it was already clear that we had hired a white [Simon Parker] . . . Just a number of places, again, we don't need to rehearse all that."

Richardson: "I just am not—I sent you a long, detailed report of that so I am just surprised that you're saying you did not hear from me. I sent you a report about it."

"But what I didn't get," explained the dean, "was the kind of critical, reflective, strategic discussion in advance of it. I got a report on it after it was a *fait accompli* in the same way I was getting a report about the formation of this retreat committee after, for practical purposes, it was a *fait accompli*—"

"Wait a minute—"

"—and I can't operate that way."

At last, the discussion turned to the mechanics of termination. "We need to talk . . . about the severance process," said Nesmith. "Do you want that on tape or not?"

"I want it on tape."

Nesmith now told Richardson he wanted her to leave immediately, instead of at summer's end. She would receive four months' severance pay. Richardson protested this change in terms. She pointed out that "there are some advantages to the school" in terms of administrative efficiency, if she worked over the summer.

"Are you willing to go off the record for a minute?" Nesmith asked.

"No."

"All right. I am prepared to appoint an acting director of student and community affairs." Richardson could take some time to clear out her office, although, Nesmith added, "the mood I detect you've assumed here is one that does not make that probably desirable."

"I'm sorry," said Richardson. "I don't understand what you are saying."

Nesmith: "Well, what I detect is a fairly forensic stance on your part, understandable and fair game."

"Forensic? I don't . . . I understand that as a debate word so I don't understand what you are saying."

"Well, use it that way. There is nothing that suggests that an administrative body needs to keep someone who is debating with it at a critical spot in its operation and in that respect the sooner that you can find yourself clearing out the better. If you were going some other route there would probably be other kinds of time that could be evolved."

Nesmith received well over a hundred letters of protest in the summer and early fall. They came from individual students, groups of students, alumni, ministers, theologians, Methodist Church bureaucrats, and members of an East Boston parish where STH students had done fieldwork. One came from seventy-three female theologians and ministers in the Boston area.

The East Boston group wrote of Richardson's anti-racism workshops in the community (one of the most racially tense of Boston's stubbornly segregated neighborhoods). "Her work has inspired more anti-racism efforts in our community and facilitated a greater awareness of the connections between racism, sexism and classism, which we believe were the same issues Jesus of Nazareth was addressing through his ministry." The theologians and ministers who signed the protest letter included professors at Harvard Divinity School, Andover Newton Theological School, the Episcopal Divinity School, Chicago Theological Seminary, Tufts, Union Theological, and Weston School of Theology.

To most of these the dean responded with a few standard form letters, vague, restrained, polite, sometimes paternalistic, and careful to refrain from countercharges. His explanation was differences in "chemistry," differences in administrative style. To a few of the correspondents he wrote more personal responses, usually stressing the same themes, sometimes adding new ones. To an old friend at the United Methodist Church's Board of Global Ministries (Walter Schenck, director of university and young adult ministries), Nesmith wrote on August 18 that although Richardson was a good, competent, and committed person, she was not an appropriate person for her job. "My decision," he wrote, "in concert with a number of my administrative colleagues [whom he did not identify] is simply that given four years of experience, the last two of which have carried a number of critical discussive moments, I concluded that Nancy was not capable of bringing the measure of balance and excellence essential for the continued building and re-building of our program."

Nesmith specified what "building and re-building of our program" meant:

> Until very recently our context is one wherein more United
> Methodist students are attending Gordon Conwell Seminary
> than Boston University School of Theology. A significant fac-
> tor in this is the students' sense that "Gordon" is more com-
> mitted to the local church while Boston University is more
> committed to specialized ministries or unusual lifestyles. You
> simply must speak to the interest of the parish with greater rel-
> evance. Part of that relevance must be a concern for justice
> and a strategic sense that is also appropriate to the parish.
> Herein lay a second whole concern, for much that we're doing
> in social ethics is more viable for a community organization or
> for a national agency than for a parish and pastor.

Nesmith also mentioned in this letter for the first time a purely administrative matter on which he faulted Richardson. He claimed that "despite considerable press from my office, not a single dollar of the $49,000 distributed to minority students in the northeastern jurisdiction [of the United Methodist Church] last year came to Boston University.

For reasons I still do not understand, Nancy chose to not persist past an initial information gathering problem to a point where she could get results. Instead, she let the matter 'slide.' " Nesmith asserted that as a result, "from $7,000 to 10,000 in scholarship monies for Boston University students" was lost.

It was to turn out that Nesmith's facts were almost entirely in error here. There had never been $49,000 available in any year for minority students from the northeastern jurisdiction of the United Methodist Church. Moreover, requirements of denominational affiliation were attached to what money was available, requirements which most BU minority seminarians did not meet. Those few who did were generally aware of the scholarships and had applied; some had received small stipends. The $7,000 to $10,000 "loss" turned out to be based, at best, on speculative estimates of numbers of eligible students and average award amounts. The entire accusation was a brew of half-remembered comments at church gatherings, combined with Nesmith's own imaginings. At bottom, no doubt, it was true that Nesmith had heard something about some quantity of money being available and was perturbed that Richardson had not, at least not to his knowledge, drawn it to BU's coffers.

What was significant at this point about a supposed $49,000 in ethnic minority scholarships was that Nesmith—for the first time, in August 1981—was beginning to inject into his public recitation of rationales for the firing of Nancy Richardson a non-ideological and non-"pedagogical" motivation—a simple matter of administrative competence. Whether university attorneys had suggested that he begin to do this in order to shore up a "legitimate nondiscriminatory reason" defense to a legal charge of political retaliation by Richardson is a question whose definitive answer will probably remain permanently buried. But the fact is that Nesmith received his first threat of suit—a "demand letter" that I wrote shortly after agreeing to represent Nancy Richardson—on July 17, about a month before his letter to Schenck.

Walter Schenck wrote back, thanking Nesmith for the "additional information which I did not have in hand" at the time of his first letter, but expressing concern nonetheless.

> The thrust of the argument I made in my earlier letter was
> simply that Boston University School of Theology has gar-
> nered its reputation by educating prophetic leadership. These
> persons have provided leadership for the whole church in a va-

riety of ways, both across this country and around the globe. Thankfully, Boston University School of Theology does not yet owe its life to big oil, the cigarette industry or Coca Cola.

While the letters continued to flow in, while students drafted and circulated leaflets and petitions, and three of them kept up two-hour daily vigils outside the dean's office, and while Richardson herself filed grievances with both BU and the Commission on the Status and Role of Women of the United Methodist Church, leaders of the STH faculty began to talk of attempting to oust the dean or vote "no confidence"— the same action that the BU faculty as a whole had taken twice in the 1970s against John Silber in ultimately unsuccessful attempts to depose him. Earl Kent Brown, in a late-June memo to Professors Deats, Treese, Fraser, and Merle Jordan, tried to discourage this line of thought. Still angry over Nesmith's "betrayal," Brown nevertheless defended "the Dean's right to develop the administrative team he can work with effectively. . . . Dick is not the only person dissatisfied with Nancy's work I discover"—not naming names. Furthermore, "my experience of Dick is that he is too canny a politician to have acted primarily on the racial issue, or at least to have admitted it if he had."

I am more than ever convinced of the folly of suspending the Exec. [the executive committee of the faculty]. When Dick acted there was no one with the mandate to speak forcefully to him in those first days when he might conceivably have reversed himself—i.e., before all the issues of pride and position made such reversal all but impossible. The exec. could and did of right call Dick into conference on Nelle and could speak with an authority no individual or group of individuals can now. . . .

I am puzzled by some of the language I hear. In a long list of adjectives one of you shared with me appeared the words "immoral" and "unethical." I think there was much of stupidity and bad procedure in what he did and the way he did it. But I remain unconvinced there was a major failure of ethics or morals either one. Perhaps I am ill informed.

I am also taken aback by the rhetoric of "forcing the Dean to resign" or "voting no confidence." . . . I don't have "no confidence" in the Dean. He does a lot of things well and we as a

school have come a long ways in four years from where we
were at nadir. . . .

No confidence votes are double-edged swords. They may cut
the wielder even more than the object. Put a vote of no confidence up against the real achievement of the last four years,
and you will convince most outsiders—not to say central
administration—that it is the faculty that is deranged, not the
Dean. . . .

The average of the last two Dean search processes has been $2\frac{1}{2}$
years, and that is not far from the story in other schools of the
Univ. Can anyone who lived through the last two Dean search
processes really think there is someone out there upon whom
STH and John S. can agree who could be in harness in any
reasonable time who would be more satisfactory than what we
have? I am reminded of a paper in social ethics I read in the
Philippines in 1970 which began, "The first step is to assassi-
nate the President. Everything will be better then." If I learn
anything from history it is that the rhetoric of the 60s, that
assumed that anything but what we have now will be better, is
almost always in error. . . .

It is probably wise to recall that even votes of no confidence
are limited in possible effect. John S. has survived two of them
quite nicely thank you. They radically worsened interrelations
between admin. and faculty. They did not force his
resignation.

A vote of no confidence puts a tremendous weapon in John's
hands—to use against either Dick or the faculty as he chooses.
It does not give any promise of remaining a weapon under faculty control to achieve faculty ends.

The faculty ultimately, when it reconvened in the autumn, made life
very difficult for Nesmith, but did not vote "no confidence" and did not
campaign in any formal or organized way for his resignation. The student
vigils and leaflets continued, and a "committee for justice" was organized
by a number of faculty, staff, students, former staff, and former students.
Contributions were solicited for a legal fund, a newsletter, *Refocus*, began
publication in Feburary 1982, and buttons reading "We Shall Persist—
Nancy," began to appear.
    Nesmith was called to account shortly after the firing by two United

Methodist Church bishops, Edward Carroll and Dale White. Bishop White later described the meeting to Paul Deats, who in turn reported the discussion to some of his colleagues.

First, the old school-closing issue reared its head: Nesmith expressed his usual concern that the faculty were not supporting him over the Richardson firing, as they had not also over Nelle Slater, and that if the faculty continued to be recalcitrant, it might end in the closing of STH. The bishops warned Nesmith that the school was not his to close; others, in the church, had to be consulted. Nesmith reminded them in turn that "if things fell apart again . . . [Silber] might carry out his oft-repeated threats of closing the school." Since Nesmith clearly had the power to ask Silber to do so, his message to the bishops may have been that they should not or could not second-guess his personnel decisions.

The bishops also confronted the dean "on the dangers of his style of administrative leadership—lack of consultation, insistence on being seen as tough, image of being in charge, suddenness of decisions like terminating Nancy, etc. (The response reported was that Nancy's termination was not a sudden decision, but had been considered for two years, and should have been done two years ago.)"

Of course, not all the reaction to Nesmith's decision was negative. As the early efforts at dialogue became increasingly frustrating, as the Committee for Justice accelerated its attacks, and as Richardson and I, with help from the committee, took steps to initiate litigation, many in the faculty and staff fell into line behind the dean, or maintained a prudent silence in the hardening controversy. Among alumni, the adversary nature of the situation inevitably engendered reaction. One STH alum, pastor of a Methodist congregation in Contoocook, New Hampshire, wrote to the committee that it appeared to be "more an advocate for Nancy Richardson than one who would bring clarity out of a muddle. Indeed, I would like to know what happened, but all I hear is charges and counter-charges, demands and court action. I do not see where any of this will help Nancy Richardson or B.U.S.T." Nesmith, who saw a copy of this letter, responded: "I couldn't agree more. There has been a small group for whom Nancy and anything they could attach to her case has been an issue throughout the year."

A similar letter dated March 16, 1982, from a Reverend Paul Hogue of Jackson, Mississippi, came directly to Nesmith:

Dear Dean Nesmith,
    I received a send out from a group called the COMMIT-TEE FOR JUSTICE. The paper is REFOCUS. On reading it

I believe or ask is the A.C.L.U. behind the Committee for Justice. I replied to them saying that REFOCUS is out for justice only for Nancy Richardson. Since leaving the School of Theology in 1940 almost every year I have seen and often been a part of situations somewhat like yours at BUST. It is so easy to feel the whole world is attacking you. I have worked in most W. European countries and in many African countries. I said to the C. for Justice with all the needs in Boston and elsewhere we want news of the school bringing an answer not news of the school scratching at one another.

In 1940 a few of us students had a faculty gripe. At the senior banquet we students had a show. We put on a faculty meeting in which we were the faculty. We got our points over, had lots of fun, and I think it was helpful. I was Dean Earl Marlatt. Did you know him?

If the A.C.L.U. or some similar organization is running the COMMITTEE FOR JUSTICE I would be glad to know. Even if you made a mistake the answer is not for the students to take over as is shown on page 2 of REFOCUS with the six demands.

Nesmith wrote a reply. "It is not ACLU," he assured the Reverend Hogue. "We have a committee of 25 or so students and faculty for whom this has been an issue because of their identification with Nancy Richardson. . . . I suspect the situation will mellow out with the coming of summer."

The dean could not have known that although I took on the representation of Nancy Richardson while still an attorney at a large private law firm in Boston, I would in fact move to ACLU in September 1982, three months before the case went to trial.

CHAPTER 11

SHARING OF THE BURDEN

THE year after its decision in *University of California v. Bakke*, which resolved so few of the legal questions about affirmative action, the United States Supreme Court faced the issue again. This time the affirmative action plan, challenged in court by a white male, was in industry, not academia. The case of *United Steelworkers of America v. Weber*, decided in June 1979, involved a collectively bargained program designed to increase the number of minority workers in craft apprenticeships at the Kaiser Aluminum plant in Gramercy, Louisiana. Although there were plenty of black workers at the plant, and in the surrounding area from which Kaiser drew, minorities were conspicuously absent from the highly paid craft jobs—a result of the notorious racism that had historically plagued craft unions.

The affirmative action plan reserved for black employees one-half of all openings in the plant's craft training program until the percentage of black craft workers in the factory approximated the percentage of blacks in the local labor pool. Brian Weber and others who felt they were thereby denied access to the training program brought their legal challenge under Title VII of the 1964 Civil Rights Act, not the Fourteenth Amendment to the U.S. Constitution, as in *Bakke*. This was because the Supreme Court, nearly a century before, had interpreted the Equal Protection Clause of the Fourteenth Amendment to prohibit race discrimination only by "state actors," government entities such as the state university in the *Bakke* case. As Kaiser was a private employer, not a state actor, the legal challenge to this race preference by Kaiser and the union was brought under Title VII, the federal employment discrimination law.

William Brennan, writing for a majority of five in *Weber*, upheld the program. The other justices were White, Marshall, Blackmun, and Stewart, who had taken a contrary position in the *Bakke* case the year before. Justices Rehnquist and Burger dissented; Powell and Stevens did not participate.

Barely mentioning the year-old decision in *Bakke*, Justice Brennan's opinion simply demonstrated that Kaiser's affirmative approach to integrating its craft labor force was entirely consistent with the purposes of Title VII, which was intended, at least in part, "as a spur or catalyst to cause 'employers and unions to self-examine and to self-evaluate their employment practices and to endeavor to eliminate, so far as possible, the last vestiges of an unfortunate and ignominious page in this country's history.' " Brennan continued:

> It would be ironic indeed if a law triggered by a Nation's concern over centuries of racial injustice and intended to improve the lot of those who had been "excluded from the American dream for so long," . . . constituted the first legislative prohibition of all voluntary, private, race-conscious efforts to abolish traditional patterns of racial segregation and hierarchy.

The Kaiser program, like the one at UC-Davis that Allan Bakke had challenged, involved a numerical goal or quota to which frustrated white aspirants could point, and which undermined or rearranged the usual "qualifications" for acceptance into the program. (In the Kaiser plant, as in a great many employment settings, decisions on entry to the craft program would ordinarily have been made on the basis of seniority.) It is difficult to believe that the different legal bases for the challenges—in the case of *Bakke*, the Equal Protection Clause of the Fourteenth Amendment; in the case of *Weber*, Title VII of the 1964 Civil Rights Act—really made a difference in the result. What, then, accounted for the solid majority of five, upholding a numerical racial preference in *Weber*?

Justice Stewart (now deceased), whose vote appeared to switch, might have provided the answer. In the absence of such inside knowledge, however, some clues might be gleaned from the narrow, cautious language at the end of Brennan's majority opinion, as well as from a concurrence by Justice Blackmun. Brennan wrote:

> We need not today define in detail the line of demarcation between permissible and impermissible affirmative action plans. It suffices to hold that the challenged Kaiser-USWA affirmative action plan falls on the permissible side of the line. The purposes of the plan mirror those of the statute [Title VII]. Both were designed to break down old patterns of racial segre-

gation and hierarchy. Both were structured to "open employment opportunities for Negroes in occupations which have
been traditionally closed to them."

At the same time the plan does not unnecessarily trammel the
interests of the white employees. The plan does not require
the discharge of white workers and their replacement with new
black hires. . . . Nor does the plan create an absolute bar to
the advancement of white employees; half of those trained in
the program will be white. Moreover, the plan is a temporary
measure; it is not intended to maintain racial balance, but simply to eliminate a manifest racial imbalance. Preferential selection of craft trainees at the Gramercy plant will end as soon as
the percentage of black skilled craft workers in the Gramercy
plant approximates the percentage of blacks in the local labor
force.

Of course, all of this could also have been said of *Bakke*, and the Fourteenth
Amendment's Equal Protection Clause.

Justice Blackmun's concurrence echoed a theme familiar from *Bakke*:
that race-conscious affirmative action was a justifiable remedy for the
nefarious effects of past discrimination. Although Kaiser and the Steelworkers Union had, not surprisingly, refrained from agreeing that either
or both of them had discriminated in the past, and the affirmative action
plan was not the result of any lawsuit that had been tried or settled,
Justice Blackmun believed that, based on the statistics, at least an "arguable violation" of Title VII had been shown, and that this justified the
race preference.

The same sort of attraction for limiting principles, and desire to link
affirmative action to specific past discrimination, was evident the next
year in a case challenging a federal law that required that at least ten
percent of federal funds going to any local public works project be spent
on the services of minority businesses. The case had the unmelodious
title of *Fullilove v. Klutznick*, and this time Chief Justice Burger, joined
by White and Powell, wrote the deciding opinion.

As in *Weber*, where the purposes of Title VII provided the main
justification for upholding the affirmative action plan, so in *Fullilove* the
organizing principle of Burger's opinion was deference to congressional
findings, not only of past discrimination and racial exclusion in the construction industry, but also of the impediments, products of past discrimination, that still plague minority contractors as they compete with
whites for such necessities of the trade as bonding, working capital,

knowledge of bidding procedures, and access to old boy networks. Congress, said the chief justice, had the power and unique ability to make such findings.

Burger had little trouble with the constitutional issues. "As a threshold matter," he said, relying on school desegregation cases, "we reject the contention that in the remedial context the Congress must act in a wholly 'color-blind' fashion." Without mentioning *Bakke*, he went on:

> It is not a constitutional defect in this program that it may disappoint the expectations of nonminority firms. When effectuating a limited and properly tailored remedy to cure the effects of prior discrimination, such a "sharing of the burden" by innocent parties is not impermissible. . . . The actual "burden" shouldered by nonminority firms is relatively light in this connection when we consider the scope of this public works program as compared with overall construction contracting opportunities. Moreover, although we may assume that the complaining parties are innocent of any discriminatory conduct, it was within congressional power to act on the assumption that in the past some nonminority businesses may have reaped competitive benefit over the years from the virtual exclusion of minority firms from those contracting opportunities.

In a long concurring opinion, Justice Powell attempted to reconcile the result in *Fullilove* with the quite different analysis he had offered up in his deciding opinion in *Bakke*. Here, because he assumed that Congress (unlike UC-Davis) was competent to make and had made specific findings of past discrimination, he was willing to accept that redressing such discrimination served a "compelling governmental interest"—according to Powell the necessary standard whenever racial preferences, whether benign or invidious, were in issue. But, he warned,

> The time cannot come too soon when no governmental decision will be based upon immutable characteristics of pigmentation or origin. But in our quest to achieve a society free from racial classification, we cannot ignore the claims of those who still suffer from the effects of identifiable discrimination.

What was one to make of the *Bakke-Weber-Fullilove* trilogy, with their numerous opinions, their shifting judicial coalitions, their fine distinctions? Perhaps all three decisions had been worldly wise compromises.

They neither ruled out voluntary affirmative action plans, nor ruled them all decisively in. There was something in this mass of words for everybody.

Cynical court watchers might suspect that the justices who made the difference in these three cases were simply more moved by the plight of white aspirants to professions, such as Allan Bakke, than they were by the complaints of the blue-collar Webers and Fulliloves. But, these justices might respond in self-defense, in *Weber* and *Fullilove* we were talking about displacing such relatively arbitrary white advantages as seniority, working capital, and connections; in *Bakke* we were talking about *merit*.

CHAPTER 12

THE PICKERING DILEMMA

I was a relatively unseasoned litigation associate at one of Boston's largest commercial law firms, Palmer & Dodge, when Nancy Richardson first walked into my office, referred by an old friend, Emily Hewitt. Emily, who in a previous incarnation had been one of the first women to become an ordained Episcopal priest, was now a real estate lawyer at another big firm in town. Starved as I was at the time for work that seemed politically meaningful, I accepted Richardson's case, despite such apparent legal drawbacks as Nesmith's potential defense that he was entitled to an administrative team that met his personal definition of loyalty.

Among their many virtues, federal and state employment discrimination laws prohibit not only discrimination itself based on race, national origin, religion, or sex, but also retaliation against employees who file discrimination charges, participate in discrimination cases, or otherwise oppose discriminatory practices on the job. After Richard Nesmith fired Nancy Richardson from her position as director of student and community life at the Boston University School of Theology, citing "pedagogical" and "ideological" differences between them, this anti-retaliation provision in the employment discrimination laws became our primary legal hook. As my July 1981 "demand letter" to Nesmith said, the reasons for the firing, "as expressed by you, centered on Ms. Richardson's 'ideological' commitments, specifically her activity in support of women's rights and racial justice at the university, and affirmative action by the university in hiring."

The letter went on:

> Title VII of the 1964 Civil Rights Act . . . specifically prohibits discriminating against employees because of their activ-

ity in opposing unlawful employment practices. (The state anti-discrimination law . . . contains the same prohibition.) Under the relevant case law, the employment practices opposed need not be proven to have been unlawful for liability to attach, so long as the employee reasonably or honestly believed that discriminatory practices existed. Your stated reasons for discharging Ms. Richardson are thus violative of both state and federal statutes.

Your actions also violated a broader proscription, contained in the state civil rights act . . . [which] prohibits any interference or attempted interference, by threat, intimidation, or coercion, with the exercise of constitutional rights. . . . Ms. Richardson's participation in anti-racism workshops, in the women's caucus, and in opposition to some of the university's hiring practices, all criticized by you and mentioned as causes of your discontent, were First Amendment–protected activities. Your statements establish a violation of the state civil rights law as well as of the applicable employment discrimination statutes.

Finally, under the common law of this state, a duty to act in good faith inheres in every contract, including employment contracts that are terminable "at will." Your failure to provide Ms. Richardson with any semblance of warning or due process, your statements attempting to blame her for not deflecting criticism of you, and your decision to punish her for her opposition to perceived discrimination and for her exercise of her First Amendment rights, all demonstrate bad faith.

The three "legal theories" ticked off in this letter were novel—hardly garden-variety claims in employment law. The first claim, grounded in the legal bans on "retaliation" against employees who oppose discriminatory practices, had had an uneven career in the courts. For one thing, the complaining employee had to prove two cases: first, that she "reasonably" or "honestly" believed that the employment practices she opposed were discriminatory, and second, that the boss retaliated against her for her opposition and not some other reason. On top of this, most courts had built into the retaliation claim a balancing test that weighed the employer's interest in worker loyalty, efficient operation, and management prerogatives against the employee's free speech rights. Since Richardson had been a member of the administrative team, with special obligations, at least in Nesmith's view, to "represent" the administration, he would have a strong defense based on the balancing test.

Retaliation cases were almost by definition natural casualties of the balancing test. While the reasons for protecting whistle-blowers and other gadflies from retaliation in employment settings should be plain enough (without such protection, discrimination and other wrongdoing might never come to light), almost any employee who contemplates such action knows the risk. To a great extent the law cannot prevent retaliation. Supervisors and bosses feel betrayed, and begin to sense that the outspoken employee is less trustworthy and efficient, even if she has not really done any damage to the operation.

If Nancy Richardson's retaliation claim under Title VII and the analogous state anti-discrimination law (known as Massachusetts General Laws, chapter 151B) was somewhat speculative, the Massachusetts civil rights act was an even more uncertain proposition. The scope of that broadly worded and relatively new statute was at the time virtually untested. It had been passed in late 1979 as a response to the horrifying racial violence that accompanied court-ordered school desegregation in Boston. Unlike most of the Reconstruction-era federal civil rights laws on which it was partially modeled, the Massachusetts "baby civil rights act" specifically applied to the actions of private individuals or organizations as well as to those of government agents. Its only limitation was that the interference with constitutional or civil rights had to be accompanied by "threats, intimidation, or coercion."

It was unclear whether this language applied to employment discharges. If so, that would have a dramatic and probably unanticipated impact on employment relations in Massachusetts, for whistle-blowers who exercised free speech rights in bringing the derelictions of their employers to public attention could, among many others, claim protection. But here, too, even if the civil rights law were ultimately determined to apply to employment terminations, a balancing test weighing employee rights against employer prerogatives and "efficiency" would most likely also be developed.

This would be necessary especially given that the baby civil rights act governed the conduct of private parties, not just the state. What did the constitutional right of free expression mean, anyway, in the context of a private university, a private company—or a private club or private home? When a child is told not to tease his sister, he may respond in time-honored fashion, "It's a free country," but if his parents punish or restrain his conduct, the baby civil rights act doesn't mean he can sue for interference with his constitutional rights.

What were Nancy Richardson's free speech rights in the context of her job at Boston University? Did they have to be traded off against

Nesmith's or the university's rights to express themselves, and to hire employees who would do it for them?

The advantage of the baby civil rights act claim—count two of the complaint in the lawsuit that was filed in state court in October 1981—was that it encompassed the entire spectrum of Nesmith's objections to Richardson's "pedagogy" and "ideology," not only that part dealing with employment discrimination. Thus, for example, the discussion of homelessness, and Nesmith's criticism of Richardson's "warm" response to injustice, could possibly be turned to advantage.

The corresponding disadvantage of suing BU and Nesmith under the civil rights act was that, like the First Amendment to the U.S. Constitution, the state law would probably be interpreted to present a *Pickering* dilemma, so named after *Pickering v. Board of Education*, a 1968 Supreme Court decision. In *Pickering* the court struck a balance, or at least attempted to articulate one, between the free speech rights of public employees and the administrative or policy needs of their employers. Pickering, a schoolteacher, had been fired for having had the audacity to contribute publicly, in the form of a letter to the local newspaper, to an ongoing debate in the community about school administration.

When *Pickering* reached the Supreme Court, a majority of the justices ruled that in each case where such a government employee claims that he has been punished for speaking freely, judges must weigh and balance a variety of factors before deciding if the employee's First Amendment rights have indeed been infringed. Those factors include the employee's interest in discussing issues of public concern, the public's interest in hearing the discussion, and the state's interest as employer in the "efficiency" of the public service. Thus in *Pickering* the Supreme Court read into the First Amendment a balancing test quite similar to that courts were later to use in attempting to apply the anti-retaliation provisions of the discrimination laws to the difficult realities of institutional employment.

Employees of private universities such as BU, unlike their colleagues in the public sector, are not ordinarily protected by the First Amendment against punishment for their exercise of free speech, even within the shifting limits articulated by the Supreme Court in *Pickering*. But the state civil rights law, as noted, protects private employees from retaliation for their exercise of free speech. Thus the question under this baby civil rights act, just as in a First Amendment–public employee case like *Pickering*, can be posed in lawyerlike terms as: When does an individual's speech so materially interfere with her performance of the essential elements of her job that she ceases being an effective employee?

To give a stark example, if the BU public relations director had appeared on a local television talk show, defending the university in the *Richardson* case, and expressed his considered view that Dean Nesmith was a liar, the university could legitimately claim that his effectiveness was so badly impaired that corrective action of some sort was justified, regardless of the public's interest in learning about this raging controversy.

The *Pickering* inquiry is necessarily colored by the inquirer's notions of how much autonomy an employer should have to determine what is effective job performance and how deeply laws or courts should intrude into personnel decisions. In Richard Nesmith's view, it is fair to say, any conscientious advocacy by one of his administrative underlings, whether on affirmative action generally or on a particular political decision like the failure of the university to hire the feminist scholar Beverly Harrison, would and did interfere with the employee's job effectiveness and therefore with the employer's efficiency. This was particularly the case, so he frequently said, with respect to the sensitive, flak-catching dean of students job.

Likewise, however, a racist employer could probably argue that any employee—at least any employee in a supervisory or managerial position—was not doing his job if he protested race discrimination. This is obviously not a situation that the authors of the discrimination laws meant to leave unremedied. The argument, like so many arguments based on balancing tests, can ultimately collapse. Just as the *Pickering* balance, if weighted too heavily toward employer efficiency, will swallow free speech entirely, so the protections against retaliation in the discrimination laws are drained of meaning if managers may define job performance to include total loyalty on discrimination issues.

Richard Nesmith's decision to fire Nancy Richardson raised all of the *Pickering* issues in classic form. As the dean had frequently said, and as he summarized in a December 1981 letter to an STH contributor, the dispute over Richardson,

> while initially around a person, is fundamentally around the issue of the direction of the School. . . .
>
> In the development of a sense of direction and the consequent building of faculty, I'm quite determined that we emphasize excellence and identification with the center of the church.
> There are some who would have us more deeply committed to [a] particular political ideology.
> Therein lay the fundamental ground of debate. . . .

My July 1981 demand letter did not result in any serious negotiations with BU, so not long afterward Richardson filed a complaint with the federal government's Equal Employment Opportunity Commission, or EEOC, as it is known in the trade. She alleged that the university had retaliated against her, in violation of Title VII of the 1964 federal Civil Rights Act. This was a necessary prerequisite under Title VII to filing a suit in court. In response, BU's attorneys submitted to the EEOC a lengthy document, generously supplemented by copies of memos from Nesmith's file, detailing Richardson's four-year history of evidently abysmal job performance. Nesmith had written, for example, that because of inattention to her administrative responsibilities, Richardson had failed to follow through on information regarding "some $49,000" in Methodist Church scholarship funds for minority students, which he asserted had been distributed in the fall of 1980. This accusation had first surfaced about a month after the July demand letter. Nesmith now elaborated: Richardson's "preoccupation with other things across the summer of 1980, a period under which she was under regular contractual employment, cost us from $7,000–$10,000 in student scholarships."

Richardson was also responsible, according to Dean Nesmith, for the university housing department's failure to eradicate insects and rodents from BU apartments rented to STH students. She had insisted on switching management of certain theology student housing from one branch of BU's sprawling real estate bureaucracy to another, resulting in higher costs to the students.

She was unable to get along with other administrators. She was virtually insubordinate in scheduling a meeting of a planning committee for a September 1981 all-school retreat without consulting and strategizing with the dean in advance. And she refused to clean up the student lounge after meetings.

Nesmith enlarged upon these complaints at a long, informal "conciliation" session at the Boston offices of the EEOC in December 1981. Here, accompanied by a labor lawyer from the large Boston law firm of Nutter, McClennen & Fish, the dean attacked virtually every aspect of Richardson's administrative work. He described his discontent over her role in the politically sensitive debates about affirmative action, but buried the essence of the subject with nearly impenetrable administrative jargon that accused her, for example, of lacking "strategic communicative accountability."

He also defended his, and BU's, actions in each of the employment controversies that we claimed had led to his decision to fire Richardson. It was here at the EEOC that Nesmith, describing the famous Beverly Harrison interview, opined that Professor Harrison had simply "not cut the mustard."

The EEOC, not an agency known for speedy or particularly aggressive investigation of discrimination claims, sent the case to its Washington office for the resolution of a "jurisdictional" legal question, and was not heard from again for several years.

That jurisdictional issue had to do with the School of Theology's status as a religious institution, and it persisted as one of the more intellectually interesting red herrings in the Richardson case. BU argued that applying the employment discrimination prohibitions of the secular world to a seminary would violate religious liberty; and therefore that the School of Theology, or at least the school's employment relation with Nancy Richardson, must be exempt from state and federal anti-discrimination laws as a matter of constitutional right.

On the facts this claim was weak, and a poor investment of BU's litigation budget. A basic rule in religious freedom cases is that the person or institution claiming an interference with its "free exercise" of religion, in the words of the First Amendment, must show that some actual religious belief or practice is being imposed upon. A church has no claim to exemption from ordinary secular laws—sanitation or zoning laws, for example—simply because it is a church. It must have some religiously based objection before it can get its First Amendment foot in the courthouse door.

In the Richardson case, there was no evidence that Nesmith's decision was motivated by religious belief. Nevertheless, about a year later, and a week before the Richardson trial began, BU's lawyers again raised their religious "jursidictional" defense by attempting to persuade a state superior court judge that Richardson's lawsuit should be dismissed because the United Methodist Church's way of dealing with political issues like affirmative action—through gentle persuasion and prayer—precluded application of the coarser methods of secular law to the disputes that led to Richardson's departure.

This argument relied in part on a theory that churches as institutions are constitutionally entitled to a good deal of organizational autonomy, especially in dealing with their employees. Some courts in fact have carved out an exception to the strictures of federal employment discrimination law for a church's employment relations with its ministers. That is, Title VII and most analogous state laws already exempt religious institutions from the ban on *religious* discrimination in employment. But the courts went beyond this and said that when it comes to the hiring of a minister, to ban discrimination of any kind would interfere with the church's constitutional rights. If a church wants to be racist or sexist in its choice of ministers, that can be no business of the secular law.

But Nancy Richardson, although ordained, had not been employed by BU as a minister when she was fired. Nor had she been working for a church. The School of Theology, though tied to United Methodism, accepted students of all denominations, hired teachers and administrators of many denominations, and, most important, was ruled not by a church but by John Silber and the Trustees of Boston University. STH, like every other branch of BU, was subject to and had for years complied without objection, at least on paper, with the affirmative action review procedures of the federal government.

When Nancy Richardson's case came to trial in Suffolk County Superior Court in December 1982, the state judge assigned to preside, Paul Garrity (no relation to the federal judge, W. Arthur Garrity, of school desegregation fame), rejected BU's "free exercise of religion" defense. He said that despite the voluminous materials submitted by Nutter, Mc-Clennen & Fish in support of their theory, including a lengthy affidavit from Nesmith and doctrinal excerpts from *The Book of Discipline* of the United Methodist Church, there was no factual basis for concluding that the Richardson termination had been religiously motivated in the least.

The state court suit was filed in October 1981. It alleged the three legal violations that I had sketched out in the July 1981 letter to Nesmith. Because we chose to file in state court, we relied for count one upon the state anti-discrimination statute, chapter 151B of the General Laws of Massachusetts, which is more or less a state analogue of Title VII.

We chose this state court route for a number of reasons. Under chapter 151B, as interpreted by the Massachusetts courts, an individual wronged by employment discrimination (or, in Richardson's case, retaliation for opposing discriminatory practices), might be able to recover money damages for the emotional distress she had suffered. Such a result was forbidden under Title VII, which permitted back pay awards as the only form of financial compensation.

Under 151B, additionally, we could claim a trial by jury; Title VII did not permit jury trials. Thus, in Title VII cases judges decided the facts and made the crucial decisions about witnesses' credibility. Years of Title VII experience nationwide suggested that judges often identified with management witnesses or tended to accept their recitation of "legitimate nondiscriminatory reasons" for terminating employees. A jury might be more skeptical, or might even identify with the employee's point of view.

Finally, a Boston jury was likely to have at least a few members of racial minorities. The federal district court drew from a broader, and whiter, population. We wanted an integrated jury.

Strategic considerations like these are at best only educated guesses. In the Richardson case the choice of state court may have backfired. The jury we ultimately drew was conservative, and more deferential in its attitudes toward authority than was Paul Garrity, the feisty judge.

As in most civil lawsuits, the filing of the complaint in *Richardson v. the Trustees of Boston University* was followed by discovery, a process of exchanging relevant documents and information. It was in the course of this discovery that we first received the lengthy document, detailing Richardson's countless inadequacies on the job, that BU had originally submitted in confidence to the EEOC.

Nothing in that bill of particulars should have been surprising. In race and sex discrimination cases, defendant-employers commonly assert that their real reason for taking an action against an employee was not race or sex at all, but poor job performance. This defense can easily be transposed to a case like Nancy Richardson's, involving retaliation for the exercise of free speech. By the time the discovery phase of the litigation is over, the employee or former employee has been dragged through so much mud that she may have little spirit left for the final encounter at trial. And since employers, or the managers through whom they make their personnel decisions, are the best—frequently the only—witnesses to their own states of mind, it is notoriously difficult for a plaintiff to rebut her supervisor's claims that he believed her job performance was substandard, and fired her for that reason.

Indeed, few managers, given the well-known existence of Title VII and its state analogues, are likely to express discriminatory motivations directly. And since no employee is perfect, everyone is vulnerable to the poor job performance defense.

In Nancy Richardson's case, we did have remarkable evidence on tape of Nesmith's actual reasons for his decision, as stated on June 8, 1981. But the tape was long, rambling, difficult to hear, and at times even more difficult to comprehend, with its liberal use of academic and church bureaucratese. On the positive side, the tape was distinctly silent on the housing–financial aid job performance matters upon which BU apparently intended to rely in defending the case. But it was also, to Richardson's detriment, less than perfectly explicit or single-minded in its allusions to the ideological motivations that formed the basis for the plaintiff's case. Was Nesmith punishing Richardson for actual opposition to employment discrimination—in the words of Title VII and Chapter 151B of Massachusetts law—or simply for failing affirmatively to campaign for his views? If the punishment was for silence, for omission, was that sufficient to state a claim under the Chapter 151B anti-retaliation clause? And what of the overlap between Richardson's activities on behalf of affirmative action (which is not required by Chapter 151B) and her activities in opposition to actual unlawful discrimination that she perceived in such situations as the failures of BU to hire feminist theologians like Professor Beverly Harrison or new black scholars like Stephen Breck Reid? Nesmith's motives were so messy and convoluted, and described in such intricate jargon, that they resisted easy insertion into legal pigeonholes.

Nesmith was not careful about the details of many of his accusations against Richardson, and with effort his credibility could probably be impugned at trial. But in employment discrimination law this business of trying to show that the employer's "articulated nondiscriminatory reasons" are pretextual is a legal landmine. The plaintiff gets sucked into litigating a collection of often phony factual disputes created by defendants and their attorneys instead of focusing on the real issues in the case. The Richardson legal team did not avoid this pitfall, and we ended up spending much time and energy, both during the eighteen-month pretrial phase of the case, and at the trial itself, attempting to rebut, cast doubt upon, or prove pretextual, the often trivial and still more often irrelevant examples of poor job performance that Nesmith had described. Irrelevant because it didn't matter, ultimately, whether Richardson had been negligent and failed to procure $49,000, $7,000, or $0 for BU or its minority students, since the evidence seemed clear that Nesmith did not fire her for her handling of this and like matters. As he had said on June 8, the pedagogical and ideological issues were paramount: "[W]e have succeeded more the more it has been detailed and numerical, such as in something like financial aid, or something like housing."

CHAPTER 13

THE LAWYERS' CREATION

IT is doubtful that any of the scores of books written about celebrated American trials render a true impression of the sheer tedium and inefficiency of the process. These works glean the highlights of the testimony, the best or worst examples of the cross-examiner's art, the skillful, clumsy, or condescending rhetoric of final arguments. Rarely do they offer even a glimpse of the unending delays and interruptions; the slow pace of testimony as attorneys flip through papers or clear their throats, jurors cough, and witnesses review documents; the frequent bench conferences with the judge, unheard by curious jurors and spectators, over technical questions of the admissibility of evidence, or the arguments on legal points or niceties of wording that govern what instructions will ultimately be given to the jury.

Trial books, too, either assume bottomless physical and mental resources on the part of the drama's participants, or ignore the stupendous physical and mental drain exacted by preparations whose fruits may consume only minutes of courtroom time. Lawyers "on trial," especially unseasoned ones, commonly encounter a species of simultaneous hyperactivity and exhaustion, triggered by equal doses of adrenalin and nerves. By the time a major trial commences, the weeks of preparation have taken their toll. The pretrial maneuverings sap energy. Then there are the nightly ruminations over the admissibility of evidence, affidavits, documents; the preparation of arguments on such legal points; the late-night rehearsals of testimony. In the daytime, the attorney worries whether one witness will arrive from out of town, or whether another, a novice at legal conventions, will withstand the sarcasm, trap-setting, and verbal one-upmanship of cross-examination.

Then, on the more bluntly physical level, there is the sheer weight of the litigation bags, loaded with deposition transcripts, documents, memos on points of evidence, trial notebooks containing outlines of anticipated testimony, the fat paperback containing the rules of court, and in Massachusetts the obligatory text, Leach and Liacos's *Handbook of Massachusetts Evidence*. All of these are lugged to court daily, and back to the office (where piles of mail and phone messages wait) at the end of the day.

Yet the trial attorney's nervousness, and nervous exhaustion, are mixed with exhilaration as the spectacle, scripted and directed by the lawyers, unfolds. It is undoubtedly less than the whole truth, indeed, at best can only be a slim slice of the multifaceted truth, but it is the lawyers' creation. The challenge of moving the creation forward every day, and the turmoil of the contest, produce soaring spirits and apparently limitless supplies of energy even while the stomach churns with butterflies.

The trial in *Nancy Richardson versus the Trustees of Boston University and Richard Nesmith* unfolded for three weeks at the old Suffolk County Courthouse in what is left of historic downtown Boston. The judge, Paul Garrity, dominated the proceedings, as judges with powerful personalities invariably do. Temperamental, unpredictable, folksy, and known for his sympathy with the underdog, Garrity had achieved at least a local variety of immortality early in his judicial career for his handling of a massive class-action lawsuit brought by legal services attorneys on behalf of the impecunious tenants of Boston's public housing, and challenging the legality of the deplorable conditions in which these tenants were compelled to live. After years of frustration with the defendant Boston Housing Authority's inability or unwillingness to carry out his orders, Judge Garrity took the drastic step of putting the entire system into what turned out to be a lengthy court-supervised receivership.

In his less celebrated day-to-day work on the superior court, Garrity had been called on the carpet by the appellate courts more often than many of his colleagues for intemperate remarks or rulings; yet on legal issues he was often creative and intelligent. His first ruling in the Nancy Richardson case, the week before the trial was scheduled to begin in December 1982, was to throw out the university's complicated "summary judgment" motion arguing that because Richardson had worked in its School of Theology, and her claim of unlawful employment termination arose there, the constitutional freedom of religion prevented secular courts from adjudicating the dispute. Impatient with the last-minute nature of the university's maneuverings on this issue, and also probably dubious of the merits of this "freedom-of-religion" defense, Garrity ruled that it would have to be raised at trial.

The plaintiff's case was by necessity complex and multilayered. Most of it focused on the reasonableness of Nancy Richardson's belief that Boston University's employment decisions over the years, particularly in the year leading up to her dismissal, had been tainted by discrimination. This was a necessary element of her ultimate claim: that BU School of Theology Dean Richard Nesmith had fired her in retaliation for her freely expressing herself and opposing what she believed were discriminatory employment practices at the school.

Thus the case centered around a number of faceless, absent victims. Among them were Union Theological Seminary Professor Beverly Harrison; the young black scholar, Stephen Breck Reid; and Nelle Slater, STH's former associate dean. To add to the confusion, testimony would be necessary about the hiring in 1981 of the noted sociologist Peter Berger and the administrator Simon Parker as Nelle Slater's replacement, over the opposition of Richardson and many others on the STH faculty.

Given the necessity of all these subplots, it would be difficult to rivet the jury's attention to the ultimate issue in the plaintiff's case—the lawfulness of Dean Nesmith's motives for firing Richardson from her job as director of student and community life at STH—and at the same time persuade them, as under the law the plaintiff must, that she was sincere and reasonable in viewing all these subsidiary events as examples of employment discrimination.

Probably three-quarters of the battle was to be waged on this preliminary turf. The testimony of the plaintiff's witnesses—STH field education director Bob Treese, Richardson herself, her friend and colleague Lynn Rhodes, social ethics professor Paul Deats, two former BUSTH student activists, and two other professors who made brief appearances—concentrated heavily on their perceptions of the Harrison, Slater, Reid, Berger, and Parker episodes.

Another strategic difficulty for the plaintiff's side—this one common to the great majority of employment discrimination cases—was how to handle the poor job performance defense. Eighteen months of pretrial discovery had made clear that despite Dean Nesmith's statements to Richardson at the time he fired her, statements focusing on the pedagogical and ideological differences they had, BU intended to defend based on a morass of complaints about the plaintiff's execution of her non-ideological duties. These ranged from major responsibilities like student housing and financial aid to such apparently trivial differences with Nesmith as whether she or the janitorial staff was responsible for straightening up the student lounge after meetings.

One strategic approach for the plaintiff's side would have been to ignore, and not try to impeach or rebut, the dean's testimony regarding these dissatisfactions with Richardson's job performance, then simply argue to the jury that the chronology of their articulation, compared with what he said to her and others at the time of the firing, showed they were pretexts. This had at least two advantages: not dignifying the poor job performance defense with a rebuttal that would inevitably look defensive, and not further complicating and prolonging an already difficult case.

There was risk here, though. Silence could be taken for concession. And the plaintiff's side had amassed some tempting evidence that Nesmith had been at best sloppy, at worst untruthful, with respect to many details of his belated critique of Richardson's performance. After some research, for example, it became evident that Nesmith's complaint that Richardson's negligence had caused the loss in one year of some $7,000 to $10,000 in scholarships for minority students (out of an available total of $49,000) was inaccurate in several respects. First, records of the Multi-Ethnic Center of Drew University, which handled these minority scholarships for the northeastern jurisdiction of the United Methodist Church, indicated that only $13,800, not $49,000, had been made available in the year in question. Second, these records showed that the few eligible BU students had received the stipends. Third, Nesmith's account of where he had gotten his information was contradicted not only by minutes of Multi-Ethnic Center meetings, which did not indicate his presence, but by the person in question, former center director William B. (Bob) McClain.

McClain, who had left Drew and was now teaching in Washington, D.C., told Richardson by phone that he and three other black BUSTH graduates had met with Nesmith not at Drew but at an Eastern Pennsylvania annual conference in 1979. The blacks lit into the dean about minority recruitment, said there was money in the jurisdiction yet BU was not attracting many black students. Nesmith responded with ambitious recruitment plans, to which one of the four said, "Dick, that sounds like a lot of bullshit to me." Nesmith left the meeting quite upset. No amount of scholarship money was mentioned.

Where Nesmith came upon his figure of $49,000 remained a mystery. As for the $7,000 to $10,000 that he originally claimed Richardson had lost in 1980 because of her "preoccupation with other things," the dean explained at his deposition that this had merely been a "guesstimate."

Yet ultimately, who cared about these details? And would testimony about them simply create more confusion than enlightenment for the Suffolk County jury that was to decide the case?

We ended up compromising. We did not clutter Richardson's direct testimony with this material, but after she had been questioned, at length if obliquely, on these matters on cross-examination, we spent the better part of an afternoon, during Richardson's redirect examination, filling the record with testimony and the court clerk's table with documents evidencing her administrative competence and, we hoped, undermining whatever damaging effect Nesmith's anticipated testimony would have. Ultimately, all this evidence about the intricacies of financial aid, the varieties of student housing arrangements, the billing procedures of BU's real estate bureaucracy, and the rodent and insect problem at 515 Park Drive, a BU-owned apartment building, may indeed have hopelessly cluttered our case.

It did, however, inspire one juror, Ada Arthur, to comment to Richardson, apropos of student housing, as she passed the witness box on her way out at the end of the day, "Did the cockroaches play leapfrog?" Although the defense thought this mysterious remark revealed a prejudice in favor of the plaintiff, Judge Garrity was not so sure, and after questioning Ms. Arthur the next morning, and scolding her for having improperly communicated with the plaintiff, he permitted her to remain.

In contrast to the complexities that beset the plaintiff's litigation choices, Boston University's defense was relatively simple and elegant. Dean Nesmith was presented as an upstanding man of the cloth and a benevolent authority figure who tolerated Richardson's poor job performance for years, gave her the benefit of every doubt, even tried to offer her a new position, before reaching the end of his Christian patience. Moreover, he was a sincere proponent of racial justice who had endured prison in his commitment to the civil rights cause, had hired many women and minorities, and had been unfairly maligned by chronic malcontents such as Professor Paul Deats, instructor and affirmative action committee chairperson Lynn Rhodes, and of course, Nancy Richardson herself.

In accordance, one might have suspected, with this approach, Nesmith came to court on about one day out of every two wearing his clerical collar. Almost all the principals in the case, of course, were ministers and owned such collars, but they did not wear them except to preach, and certainly did not wear them in court. Nobody in the plaintiff's circle could remember ever having seen Nesmith in a collar. Plaintiff's counsel therefore asked Judge Garrity to enjoin the dean from continuing to parade before the jury in this reverential garb, lest they be unduly prejudiced in his favor. Garrity considered opposing affidavits, quickly composed at his command, then denied the motion without comment.

The trial was perhaps too much about affirmative action for victory to be anything but a long shot in the city of Boston, which had weathered more than its share of racist outpourings—or, perhaps, in any American city that had a predominantly white population. Even among minorities, affirmative action was hardly a matter of universal approbation. Indeed, given the frequent equation of affirmative action with hiring the "less qualified," and the obvious stigma that such a characterization embodies, it would not be surprising if numerous minority people opposed what they understood it to mean. And for both whites and minorities, women and men, whatever their attitudes toward civil rights remedies in general, it was probable that their notions about the by-now much embattled concept of affirmative action were confused and fragmentary.

To deal with that issue, the plaintiff's side asked Judge Garrity at the opening of trial to permit individual *voir dire*, questioning of potential jurors, about their attitudes toward affirmative action. This was a procedure not often allowed in Massachusetts although common in some other states. San Francisco's veteran left-wing attorney Charles Garry had shown the effectiveness of individual *voir dire* in unearthing hidden juror prejudices during his brilliant defense of Huey P. Newton and other members of the Black Panther Party some fifteen years before.

The defense opposed the *voir dire* motion. Its chief attorney, a dapper, graying trial veteran named Charles Parrott, argued that since violating affirmative action guidelines or requirements was not the same as actually violating the state employment discrimination law, the university's possible deficiencies in the affirmative action realm, and Richardson's beliefs about them, were irrelevant to her legal claim that BU, through Dean Nesmith, had unlawfully retaliated against her because of her opposition to discriminatory employment practices.

Judge Garrity allowed our motion, but the individual *voir dires* were not an unmitigated success. The inquiry, as designed by the judge, was truncated, and confined to a few predetermined questions. The questions had to be asked in such a way that most potential jurors, sensing that the appropriate answer should be positive, generally responded that they accepted affirmative action, or had no objection to it. Thus, the *voir dire*, whether as structured or as executed, or both, did not elicit much of the jurors' own impressions and views. To add to the difficulty, lead attorney Parrott had persuaded the judge that the *voir dire* should be framed in terms of an assumed, rather than an acknowledged, legal requirement that Boston University observe affirmative action. This cast doubt on the justice of the plaintiff's entire enterprise, and led potential jurors into understandable confusion. Some gave answers that were likewise tentative: if it's a requirement, well then, I guess, sure, the university ought to comply.

Despite all this, the *voir dire* was useful in introducing the jurors to the concept of affirmative action, and giving them an idea of what the case was about. On one occasion when a juror asked for a description of affirmative action, I replied that:

> The basic idea is that there need to be some affirmative kinds of steps taken to remedy the discrimination and injustice that's gone on in the past in the employment market against women and minority group people. The ultimate goal is to try to have a workforce that is a little more diverse and representative, especially in the higher echelons such as a university, graduate school, professors, administrators . . .

Then, getting to the heart of the matter:

> There is a variety of steps that have been devised to try to accomplish that, all the way from a simple kind of openness in the search process and advertising for jobs so everybody will be aware there is something available rather than going by word of mouth; and going beyond that to more affirmative measures, such as actually recruiting among women and in a minority community to try to get the applications in. . . . Another thing that affirmative action usually involves is looking at what the qualifications are. Are they really necessary? Are they having an impact that is keeping women and minority people out of these jobs? And if they are not really necessary, why do we have them?

As in any jury trial, civil or criminal, each side had the right to challenge, or try to unseat, jurors, both peremptorily (without explanation) and "for cause." Defense attorney Charles Parrott's first peremptory challenge was to a decorator who lived on Beacon Hill; his second was to a black postal worker, married to a teacher. When, for his third challenge, Parrott eliminated another black person, a woman who worked for the voluntary school urban-suburban racial integration program called METCO, I protested. Parrot's assistant, attorney Alan Rose, explained:

> The basis for our challenge has nothing to do with race.
> Rather, it has to do with a particular occupation of this person.

She is working for METCO. It's a program that clearly and strongly promotes the concept of affirmative action. That's its whole purpose. We believe that because of this particular juror's close affiliation with the METCO program and the source of her livelihood, our peremptory challenge is on that basis.

THE COURT: Why don't you challenge her for cause on that basis, as opposed to challenging her peremptorily?

MR. ROSE: All right.

THE COURT: All right. Counsel has made a challenge for cause. What is your response?

MS. HEINS: My response is that we specifically made a motion to be allowed to interview prospective jurors to see if they had any objection to affirmative action. They did not ask to be entitled to challenge jurors who favor affirmative action or accept it as a legal obligation. And I don't think that such a motion would have been granted. That's essentially what they're asking for now. They want the people who agree with affirmative action off the jury.

THE COURT: I note very pointedly that when the two persons who happen to have black skin were called [actually, two of three], you specifically indicated that you had no questions. One might possibly make the point that *Soares* [a state supreme court decision prohibiting peremptory challenges based on race] . . . is applicable to you as well as it is applicable to the other side, and I permit your challenge for cause.

Judge Garrity's logic here was impenetrable. If, as he implied, I had demonstrated an impermissible reverse bias by failing to question two of the black potential jurors about affirmative action, thus essentially deciding they were acceptable solely on the basis of skin color, it did not follow that the punishment for this transgression should be the judicial error of allowing a wholly untenable challenge for cause by the other side. In presiding at trial, one ought not be governed by the dubious principle that two wrongs make a right. But Garrity had a point to make, and he undoubtedly knew that this type of judicial caprice was not the stuff of which reversible errors, as defined by appellate courts, are made.

The twelve jurors and four alternates were a representative Boston group, minus virtually the city's entire middle class. The defense had eliminated the few venire members who appeared to have education beyond high school. Nearly all of the jurors resided in one of Boston's racially balkanized neighborhoods—South Boston, East Boston, Hyde Park, or Dorchester—or in one of the almost equally segregated working class cities adjacent to Boston proper and also included in Suffolk County: Chelsea and Revere. Of the eleven whites, three had recognizably Italian surnames; three, recognizably Irish. There were no Hispanics.

The four white men, two elderly and two quite young, were employed as, respectively, a supervisor at a realty firm (Naumann Bassick), a laborer for Boston Edison (Anthony Petrillo), a welder at the General Dynamics shipyard in Quincy (Michael Hastings), and a shipping receiver for an engravings supply company (John Hynes). Of the eight women who survived the length of the trial to participate in deliberations, the two blacks were Eara James, a group leader for Polaroid, and Mabel Walker, a nursing technician at Tufts-New England Medical Center. Of the six white women one, Linda Ranaudo, appeared to be the youngest of the entire group, while the other five—Jane Murphy, Margaret MacDonald, Ada Arthur, Martina Herzog, and Janet Galante—were well into middle age or beyond. All except MacDonald had clerical or switchboard jobs. MacDonald described herself as "just at home . . . a housewife," to which Judge Garrity gamely rejoined: "You're not just a housewife. . . . Domestic engineer."

Boston is a working-class city and this jury certainly had a working-class complexion. But the defense team's jury selection strategy, and the laws governing jury duty in Massachusetts, also contributed to the conspicuous absence of professionals, managers (with the possible exception of Mr. Bassick), or others likely to have college educations. Under then-prevailing Massachusetts law, numerous exemptions and excuses from jury service were available in Suffolk County, especially to those in the professional classes.

A disadvantage of this type of jury became evident early in the trial, during the testimony of STH Field Education Director Bob Treese. Treese was describing to the jury an event critical to the plaintiff's case—the formulation of the various anti-racism recommendations, mostly designed to enhance STH's ethnic diversity, that the faculty had made in May of 1981, a few weeks before Richardson was fired. A section on credentialing had suggested, in the context of faculty hiring, "taking into account that in a professional school other criteria than the Ph.D. . . . might be acceptable or preferable." Treese explained what was meant by credentialing.

It means to find criteria which would make it possible to have a more inclusive faculty than almost all white males with a few white females. It means that to take into account professional competence in religious leadership, along with academic competence, that perhaps there are some instances where professional competence and achievement in the ministry may be more important criteria for selecting a faculty member than simply a research academic degree. Although that's not to put down a research academic degree. In the world in which we live, and in the churches for which we're preparing ministers, they need to experience a wider variety of faculty representing our culture, a more inclusive kind of faculty. So that there need to be other criteria for the selection of faculty and administrators than the academic community normally has, which is research and a Ph.D., which is a Doctor of Philosophy degree.

Was it more than a little anomalous to put these abstruse issues to a jury of welders, telephone operators, shipping clerks, and "domestic engineers"? It will not do to eschew intellectual snobbery in approaching such matters, since they are at the heart of trial strategy, and trials are what our legal system ultimately depends upon to resolve disputes when all else fails.

A jury is always risky, but then so is a judge. If the testimony in *Richardson v. BU*, as it unfolded, awash in the memoranda and documentation that are the stuff of academia, made little sense to this jury of working men and women, at least most of them were not likely to identify automatically with the boss. Whether they would identify with an employee who had evidently been compassionate, independent, and not generally responsive to the politics of academia at least as the dean perceived them, remained an open question.

December 6, 1982. The *Boston Globe*'s veteran courtroom reporter, Joe Harvey, covered the opening day of trial:

Trial began yesterday in Suffolk Superior Court in a suit by a member of the Boston University theology school faculty who charges she was fired because of her activist role in seeking to have the school put an affirmative action program into effect.

Nancy Richardson "was illegally terminated because she followed her conscience," her lawyer, Marjorie Heins, told Judge Paul G. Garrity and a jury in opening the case against the uni-

versity trustees and Richard Nesmith, dean of the School of
Theology. . . .

Heins told the judge and jury of 11 women and five men that
Nesmith said Richardson was being dismissed for "ideological
and pedagogical reasons."

In the suit, Richardson said she was "abruptly terminated because of her active opposition to employment practices that she
considered unlawful and her constitutionally protected participation with students and faculty in social and political issues
on campus." . . .

Heins said Richardson strongly supported a "young black Old
Testament professor" who unsuccessfully sought appointment
to the theology school faculty. . . .

The suit asks the court to order Richardson reinstated to her
job with back pay and also to award her damages for alleged
civil rights and job discrimination violations.

CHAPTER 14

THE NECESSITY OF CAPITALISM

Pᴙᴏғᴇssᴏʀ Bob Treese was the plaintiff's leadoff witness. Small, gray-haired, avuncular, smiling, a touch rotund, beloved by generations of BU seminarians, Treese simply exuded sincerity and good nature. Treese had been Richardson's nominal supervisor in her first two years at STH, knew about the responsibilities of her job, and could describe for the jury, none of whose members had within his or her personal experience the structure or function of a graduate school of theology, some of its bureaucratic intricacies.

He did all this creditably; then direct examination turned to the various employment incidents that formed the core of the case. Regarding the rejection of Beverly Harrison, Treese testified that Richardson had commented to him at the time, "[t]his was a typical male response to a competent woman." Nesmith, in turn, had resented Richardson's protest, and more than a year later, in a meeting of the three of them, had complained that "students were still criticizing him about the fact that Beverly Harrison had not been employed, and he was blaming Nancy for student criticism."

Treese recounted the dean's explanation for firing his associate dean, Nelle Slater:

Q: [D]id Richard Nesmith ever state any reasons for that decision?

A: Well, he had a way of coining metaphors. He said they couldn't dance together. . . .

Q: When you say that Nancy Richardson remonstrated with Richard Nesmith, can you describe what she said to express her state of mind about the termination of Nelle Slater?

A: She said, "This is an example of the fact that Richard has difficulty working with strong and competent women."

Q: Now, was there a point during the '79–80 school year when the BUTSA Council [the student government association] held a forum on the subject of the discharge of Nelle Slater?

A: Yes.

Q: And can you describe to the best of your recollection what was said at that time?

A: The thing that is most vivid in my memory is the fact that Richard, in response to protests, talked about the fact that it wasn't his inability to work with strong women because he could work with Nancy. . . . who was strong, who often disagreed with him, and he could work with her, and therefore that proved he could work with competent women.

And he ended by saying that he and Nancy could ride in the saddle together.

Treese described a charged meeting of the STH administrative team in January 1981, an event to which Nesmith had also pointed, during the discovery phase of the litigation, in justification of his firing Richardson. A consultant, hired by STH to help the administrators improve their ability to communicate with each other, had assigned the group several readings, including the Parable of the Pounds from the Gospel according to Luke. Treese testified:

The Parable of the Pounds is the parable where the people . . . were given one, five, and ten pounds, and those who doubled the pounds and gave it back to the master were given five or ten cities as a reward.

When we came back and we were discussing this around the table, Nancy . . . said that she didn't particularly like that parable, because it reminded her of capitalism, that those who have, get, and the more you have, the more you get.

And in the process she also went on to discuss how that might relate to housing, because she reminded us of something we all were feeling at the time when the [Boston] *Globe* had just published a series of articles on two thousand homeless women in the city of Boston, and this was in January, and they had no place to sleep. So she was contrasting the ambivalent feelings we all felt, because the university and the School of Theology needed to buy housing and have housing for students, and at the same time there were all these homeless women; and in the process of that, Nancy got wet. That didn't keep her from continuing to talk about it, and also the necessity for finding student housing in spite of that ambivalent feeling.

Q: Did Richard Nesmith say anything in response?

A: Mr. Nesmith's response was something to the effect that there was a conflict in Nancy between ideology and administration.

I wasn't sure what that meant, so I said, "Dean Nesmith, are you saying that Nancy is not an effective administrator because of this feeling of ambivalence?" And he said no, that wasn't what he meant. . . .

[T]he other members of the administrative team were very supportive of Nancy, and expressed the fact that we all felt ambivalent about this business of housing in the situation of many homeless women. . . .

Then at the end of the meeting, . . . Richard asked Nancy and me to stay after the meeting to talk with him.

Q: What happened at that meeting after the meeting?

A: Richard launched into a long discussion, almost a diatribe, I guess, about the value of capitalism. He was angry at Nancy for her mentioning her feeling that the Parable of the Pounds reminded her of some aspects of capitalism. He talked about the necessity of capitalism.

I wasn't sure what was going on. . . .

Finally, Treese recounted how he had approached Dean Nesmith the weekend after he fired Richardson, at a meeting of the Methodist Church's Southern New England Conference. He delivered a letter from most of the faculty urging reconsideration. Judge Garrity would not permit the letter itself into evidence, since it contained hearsay statements about Richardson's competence and value to the school. The dean took the letter and then, said Treese, recounted his reasons for firing Richardson:

Nancy had not protected him as a dean of students, which he equated her position with. . . . [W]hen he was at MacMurray College he had taken the flak as a dean of students, so that the dean of the school did not get a lot of student criticism. . . . Nancy had failed to do this. He felt that she was responsible for the fact that at the graduation ceremony the student speaker had made a serious critique of the leadership at the school.

Defense attorney Charles Parrott, although graying like Treese, presented a marked contrast in style. With his perfectly tailored suits, Bostonian bow ties, and slightly unctuous manner, Parrott was physically at ease in the courtroom.

Parrott's cross-examination of Professor Treese focused on the hiring history of the School of Theology. Parrott tried to get Treese to agree, one by one, that every hiring of a black or female employee at STH over the years had been an "accomplishment of affirmative action." Since many people had come and gone over the years, this was a lengthy process. Trial lawyers, like other dramatists, know that repetition of almost any litany has cumulative dramatic effect, and so it was, or was hoped, evidently, with this element of the defense.

Treese for his part tried to explain that not only bottom-line results, but also procedures, were important. This led to retorts from Mr. Parrott: "I'm sorry, did you not understand my question?" or, "[D]o you have trouble answering yes or no to a question that calls for it, sir?" When Treese rejoined that he did not particularly consider it an "accomplishment" of affirmative action when a black person or a woman of any color was hired as a secretary, the cross-examiner pounced on him thus: "So you distinguish in your mind, that you would interpret this position taken by the faculty on affirmative action to draw some kind of a line between what you call an administrator such as Nancy Richardson and a black secretary?"

Or, in the same vein, moments later, referring to a black woman who had been hired, and subsequently fired, as a secretary: "Are you drawing some line of discrimination between Nancy Richardson, a woman hired originally to be associate director of student affairs and community life, and later as director, and Eleanor Robinson, the black woman?"

I objected to this question as argumentative, misleading, and mischaracterizing the testimony. Judge Garrity snapped: "Overruled. It's very clear. It goes to this witness's credibility and his opinions."

In fact, Judge Garrity consistently overruled the plaintiff's evidentiary objections that BUSTH's hiring record as to candidates other than Beverly Harrison, Nelle Slater, Peter Berger, or Stephen Breck Reid was irrelevant to the point that Parrott appeared to be driving at in his cross-examination: that Nancy Richardson's beliefs that BU had discriminated in those situations were unreasonable or even dishonest. Garrity in fact opined, in front of the jury, that this information about other employment decisions was "highly relevant."

Willard Rose was a tall, husky young black man with, already, a somewhat imposing and ministerial air. He had headed the BUTSH's student government (BUTSA Council) the previous academic year, and had corresponded with Stephen Breck Reid about the events that led to Reid's decision to accept a job at Pacific School of Religion and abandon his ill-fated application to BU. Now an associate pastor at the Metropolitan Community Church in New York City, Rose felt that he was testifying at some personal risk, as he still had credits to complete toward his Master of Divinity at BUSTH. He thus needed to remain in the relatively good graces of the administration, and did not doubt that Nesmith, Silber, or some other actor in the drama could make the completion of that degree difficult if he chose to do so.

Rose testified that Nancy Richardson was a skilled administrator, much appreciated among the students. He explained by describing one incident in which he, only black member of BUTSA Council, felt that he had implicitly been expected by the others single-handedly to produce additional black names for appointments to student government committees. At his request, Richardson came to a council meeting,

and we sort of had a session where we dealt with how the insistence of the BUTSA Council to rely on me as a black person for all the black appointments was institutionally racist,
and that we should strive to move beyond it. I think her role
was one of calming waters, of smoothing ruffled feelings, and I
think her participation led to the continued existence and
strength of the BUTSA Council.

Rose detailed BUTSA's communications with the dean over the hiring of Simon Parker in 1981. Back in 1980 the students had repeatedly requested a job description, which was not forthcoming from Nesmith till many months after he had decided to hire Parker. They were never asked to interview other candidates. In a memo to Nesmith the students asked, "How would Dr. Parker's appointment appear in light of the School of Theology's commitment to the hiring of ethnic minorities and women faculty and administration? The Council had reservations over the interview process that made Dr. Parker the only candidate for the associate dean position that was interviewed. Thus, there was no basis for comparison."

Nesmith's response, according to Rose, was "that there was difficulty in finding qualified blacks and women for this particular position."

At a meeting in February 1981, said Rose, the dean told the BUTSA Council members of his intention to appoint Peter Berger to the faculty. The students questioned Nesmith about "the charges of sexism in not treating women equally in the classroom . . . that had been raised against Peter Berger." They also asked, what about affirmative action, and do we need another sociology of religion specialist in the first place? Nesmith was "visibly agitated at the severity of the questions that were being raised."

Rose gave his perceptions of the Stephen Reid fiasco. Although Reid had withdrawn his application early in March 1981, the student body was not informed. So, "[a]fter not hearing any official notification that Mr. Reid had been appointed as Old Testament professor, I took it upon myself to call Mr. Reid and ask him what was the holdup, why wasn't he appointed. I called him on March 31, 1981." Because it was hearsay, Rose could not tell the jury what Reid had said to him in this conversation. He was able to say, however, because it went to the issue of Nancy Richardson's state of mind, that he informed her that "the response that I got from Mr. Reid didn't coincide with the rumors I had been hearing about why he was not appointed to the Boston University School of Theology from administration sources."

Finally, Rose recounted a conversation with Nesmith in June 1981 in which, as representative of the student body, he had asked the dean to explain his reasons for discharging Nancy Richardson. Nesmith categorized the reasons, as he had for Richardson herself, as "ideological and pedagogical." An example of unacceptable pedagogy was her failure to prevent or soften the 1980–81 year-end BUTSA report, which had castigated the STH administration in a number of areas. Nesmith was perturbed that "Nancy didn't receive any of the criticism that some other people in the administration received. He felt that if Nancy had been around when the report had been written, then it would be more critical of her or less critical of the administration."

Rose added that Nesmith did not mention any dissatisfaction with Richardson's handling of housing or financial affairs, so that he was surprised some months later at a September 1981 student forum when Nesmith asserted that these were reasons for his decision.

Rose paraphrased the "ideological reasons," which, he said, Nesmith had told him

> stem from Dean Nesmith's understanding of the difference between an administrator and a person on faculty. He felt that a social consciousness or awareness was good for an administrator, but it wasn't primary. The primary role for an administrator should be in support of the administration's policy. He gave an incident in the past that I had not known about, about Nancy's intercession with a prior appointment of a woman faculty to the School of Theology, of Beverly Harrison, and he said that she might—she went overboard on that sort of thing, and that wasn't in tune with what he understood an administrator should be.

*****

> My name is Nancy Richardson. I currently have two part-time jobs, and am a graduate student. One of my part-time jobs is the consultant of women's concerns at the Episcopal Divinity School and [the other is] co-director of Women's Theological Center in Boston.

> I am a graduate student in social ethics and education.

Nancy Richardson took the witness stand toward the end of the third day of trial. The jury had watched her now for two days, sitting at plaintiff's counsel table, an average-sized middle-aged woman with short graying hair, no makeup, and clothing mostly borrowed for the occasion. Comfortable as the leader of countless small discussion groups, Richardson turned out to be somewhat awkward on the more imposing courtroom stage.

> I entered the University of Richmond, in Richmond, Virginia, in 1958. . . . I graduated from that school in 1962 with a B.A. degree in psychology and mathematics. . . . After that, I taught high school math for a year. Then I entered a Baptist seminary in North Carolina to prepare for a career in campus ministry. . . .

> I received a grant from the Danforth Foundation to be a campus ministry intern at San Diego State College in San Diego, California. I worked there . . . for one year, doing . . . different kinds of on-campus programs and working with a variety of kinds of social justice issues. . . .

At the end of that year I had intended to return to the seminary and complete my third year . . . but . . . I was invited to apply for a position as the associate director of religious activities, as assistant to the chaplain at Duke University. . . . So I began working there at that time and going to school part-time at Duke Divinity School. . . .

I worked at Duke University for four years as associate director of religious activities. The other part of my responsibilities was the director of the YWCA. While I was working there, one of the things that happened is that Martin Luther King was shot, and the outcry both at Duke and around the country . . . had a very important impact on me and on the way I saw my work there. . . . I became aware of some more dimensions of what was happening in terms of racial injustice in the country.

Our goal was to make Richardson's history, her personality, and her demanding conscience attractive to the jury yet avoid the image of an obstreperous or uppity woman. This was a predominantly female jury, but it was far from a feminist one.

Although our case depended on proving that Richardson opposed certain employment practices, the irony was that her opposition had always been subdued, limited for the most part to faculty discussions. Charles Parrott, on cross-examination, was to make much of the fact that she did not complain about the employment practices that she apparently thought so shoddy to Boston University's general counsel or its affirmative action office. The implication was that she couldn't have been very serious about her beliefs. But Parrott here was trading on the jury's innocence of politics and practices within a university. It would have been disloyal, if not very bad politics, to take such decisive, public, and inevitably pointless steps.

The furthest Richardson had ever gone, in fact, was to sign the Boston Theological Institute letter protesting BU's rejection of Beverly Harrison. In 1978, as Richardson recounted it, Beverly Harrison had been interviewed by the faculty, "and it was generally announced that the faculty had voted to recommend her to the university central administration for appointment as a tenured professor."

[However,] I knew that immediately after she made her presentation . . . Mr. Nesmith asked the person who was chairing the search committee to get out the dossiers for the second candidate. . . .

What happened next was that I heard . . . that Beverly Harrison was coming back for an interview with President Silber regarding her appointment, and Richard Nesmith asked me . . . if I would be the person who would sort of guide her around and see to it that she had lunch and that sort of thing, which I did. So I talked with her before the interview, and I spoke with her again after the interview . . .

She told me that the interview had been quite difficult. She said that she felt that President Silber and Dr. [Alasdair] MacIntyre had been rude. . . .

She said that while Mr. Silber was interviewing her, that they were shuffling through paper, and that when she began to talk, they just seemed disinterested and then began sort of an attack and began firing questions at her and would not let her present her material . . . and she felt that it was a very hostile setting.

She said that at one point Dr. [Nelle] Slater [then the associate dean] . . . intervened and tried to focus the situation so that Dr. Harrison could present her material as she had written it, and that was the only point at which there was ever any attempted intervention, and that she had been very disappointed that Mr. Nesmith had in no way represented her as his candidate, that she had felt that she had been basically taken in, and dumped, and had not been presented as a candidate that the School of Theology was behind.

Q: Did you ever have occasion to speak to Mr. Nesmith about this interview of Beverly Harrison?

A: Yes I did. . . . Mr. Nesmith asked Dr. Slater and me to have lunch with him, and at lunch . . . he told us that Dr. Silber had not approved the appointment, and we talked about that for some time. . . .

I told him that Dr. Harrison had told me about the interview and that I felt she had not been treated properly and that I felt that had the School of Theology faculty, he, and the other people on the faculty, been committed to hiring her, that they would have presented her in a different way, that they would have presented her as their candidate and they would have in some way indicated their support of her in that setting when she was under fire.

And he replied that that was the way things are done in academia, and that he didn't feel it was his responsibility to intervene in that because that was part of the academic game, to see if people could stand it.

And so I said I thought it was a very unfortunate way of proceeding, and that I really did not believe that all candidates were treated with that kind of rudeness.

Then . . . he said, "What we're going to have to do is to deal with people about this," and wanted to know how we were going to communicate this to students and to other people . . . who had been very enthusiastic about the possibility of her being at BU.

Q: Did you reply?

A: Yes I did. I said that I thought that Beverly had been screwed. . . . I said that I thought it was unfair treatment, that a man would not have been treated in the same way, and that I was going to say that, that I did not feel that it was appropriate for me to say something I didn't believe about that.

Q: What did he respond, if anything, to your comments?

A: He said he was not surprised to hear me respond that way, that he knew that I would be upset and he knew other women would be upset, and that a lot of men would be upset, and he would not ask me to do something that was a violation of my integrity about that, and that he knew it was going to be a hard time coming when people learned that Dr. Harrison had not been appointed.

Q: What happened next with respect to the failure to appoint Beverly Harrison?

A: Well, there was a faculty meeting. . . .

[T]here was a very heated discussion. At that time Lynn Rhodes and I were the only two women on the faculty, so we were raising concerns that we felt were particularly important to women. A lot of people were raising concerns about what had happened. Because Dr. Harrison is a well-known essayist and highly respected in the field and had lost the opportunity, people were quite concerned. Both Reverend Rhodes and I talked about the information that we had received about the meeting with President Silber. One of the faculty members who was present at that meeting, Leroy Rouner, indicated that indeed it was a difficult meeting. His words were that President Silber had gone for the jugular. . . .

Q: [C]an you give me your state of mind, your state of belief, as to the Beverly Harrison situation . . . ?

A: Well, I believed that she had been discriminated against. I believed that what had happened, in fact, was that she had not been taken seriously because of the work that she does and the way that she attempts to bring women's perspective into her ethics work. . . . I felt she had not been treated with respect that other candidates have been treated, and particularly—I mean, Dr. Rouner's statement seemed to me to say clearly what had happened, that they had gone after her, . . . and were not intending to hire her. . . .

The following year, Richardson testified, Dean Nesmith complained to her that the Women's Collective at the School of Theology was still criticizing him about the failure of BU to hire Beverly Harrison.

Q: Did you respond to him?

A: Yes I did. I told him that I had not organized that criticism and that I didn't feel it was my responsibility to try to stop it, that women were speaking their views, and I felt that they had a right to express their opinions, and it was not my responsibility to try to keep them from expressing their opinion.

In December 1980, Richardson testified, she, Lynn Rhodes, and a part-time black faculty woman named Dolores Williams, met with Nesmith about hiring in general and Peter Berger in particular.

We went to talk with him because members of Area B had told us . . . that the dean had said that there would be an appointment of a . . . big-name theologian in the department; and we went to talk to him about that, suggesting that to categorize an appointment that way in terms of big-name theologian was very likely to be setting up a situation in which the people who would qualify for it would be white males, and that it would therefore not be open to women or men of color. . . .

[Nesmith] responded in a very favorable way, I think, to the possibility of shifting the theology appointment to a junior-level appointment, and defining that in a broader way. He said that the money, that the Peter Berger appointment was an appointment that had been set up by the president, and that the money was for Peter Berger, it was attached to Peter Berger.

Q: By that point can you describe what your state of mind was with respect to the process by which Peter Berger was being put on the faculty?

A: Well, it just seemed to be a blatant disregard for affirmative action procedures.

Q: Did you ever express that opinion?

A: Yes. . . . I expressed it to the dean, saying that to have money that was designated for a special person seemed to be a blatant disregard.

Nesmith, Richardson recounted, had told a BUTSA forum in February, in response to pointed questions about the proposed hirings of Peter Berger and Simon Parker, that Stephen Breck Reid had also been hired; "that the appointment had cleared through the central administration and it was simply a matter of formal approval by the board of trustees which would happen at their next meeting."

He could not use this technique again, however, in April at the faculty retreat, by which time it was generally known that the Reid appointment had not "cleared through the central administration." So in April, in rebuttal to the same grumblings about Berger and Parker, Nesmith pointed to Richardson, among others, as examples of successful affirmative action at STH.

As to the Reid situation itself, Richardson described how Nesmith had attributed the candidate's withdrawal in favor of the Pacific School of Religion to opportunism, without mentioning the salient fact that Reid had not received an offer from BU and was not likely to. Richardson thought the public relations ploy was hardly candid. Then, at the faculty meeting,

One of the questions that Mr. Nesmith asked was how would we deal with the students about this? How would we explain it. . . .

I said that I thought it was inappropriate to make comments about Mr. Reid, such as an opportunist as he had said; and if he had gotten a better offer I thought that he should take it. And he should tell them [the students] that he got a better offer. . . .

Q: Do you remember anything else that was said with respect to Mr. Reid at that meeting?

A: Yes. Mr. Nesmith said that . . . there were a lot of questions about exactly what had happened, . . . that when Mr. Reid was in the process of being interviewed at the other school, . . . [a] person in central administration asked for a copy of Mr. Reid's dissertation. And he said that President Silber wanted to be very careful about making an appointment of a young black scholar . . . if he was not clear at the time of the appointment that he would be accepted for tenure.

Richardson described to the jury the May 29 and June 8, 1981, conversations in which Dean Nesmith had fired her. Although the tape was to be played for the jury, it was lengthy and often difficult to follow, and, because of the best evidence rule, we would not be able to put the transcript in evidence. (The rule's name explains its substance: the original of a document, tape, or photograph is the best evidence of its contents, and other evidence usually will not be accepted.) Thus, the tape would go into evidence while the transcript would be entered as an exhibit for identification. The jury could use it to follow along as the tape played; but they would not be able to take it with them to their deliberations.

Richardson was allowed to read the transcript to "refresh her recollection" of the exact words of the June 8 conversation, then paraphrase those words to the jury. In between, she could put that sometimes delphic discussion into context. So, for example, after describing the evolution of the anti-racism recommendations, and the controversy surrounding the dubious process that led to the hiring of Simon Parker, Richardson was able to explain Dean Nesmith's reference in their June 8 conversation to the anti-racism workshop: "he thought it was inappropriate for the anti-racism workshop to recommend the appointment of . . . an ethnic minority associate dean after an appointment had already been made."

Richardson's direct testimony concluded with an expression of her feelings about the termination. This was necessary to support our request for damages to compensate for the emotional distress she had suffered. The testimony also shed some light on the ambiguities of her role at

STH, and indeed on the ambiguities in Dean Nesmith's own complex and tortured approach to the issues of diversity, academic freedom, loyalty and commitment in his administration. "I was . . . very upset," Richardson explained,

> because in criticizing me, he had . . . essentially said that it was not possible for me to [participate] in a faculty meeting. I was a member. I had a vote on the faculty. And . . . what he meant was if I disagreed with him I could not vote at a faculty meeting. . . . He said he wanted diversity on his staff. He had encouraged me to speak out. He encouraged me to say what I believed to be true.

CHAPTER 15

LACK OF FOUNDATION

CHARLES Parrott's cross-examination of Nancy Richardson pounded away on the poor job performance defense. After questioning the plaintiff, for example, about persistent repair and maintenance problems at 515 Park Drive, one of the university-owned dormitories that had been reserved for seminary students, defense attorney Parrott asked:

Q: During the time that you had the job as assistant director of community and student living and thereafter when you were director of the same, did you ever solve those problems for the School of Theology students as to housing at 515 Park Drive?

A: Did I ever solve them? It was not my responsibility to solve them.

Q: Please.

A: No, I never solved them.

After testimony about a memo, signed by Richardson, Lynn Rhodes, and another professor, Norman Thomas, regarding their ambivalent feelings about crossing a picket line during a strike, Parrott asked:

Q: You indicated in the first sentence of the third paragraph: "As per your instructions, we are required to report for work but we were unhappy in doing so." Do you remember that?

A: Yes.

Q: So you were unhappy about reporting to work during the spring and April of 1979, is that correct? . . .

A: I was unhappy about having to cross the picket line, yes.

After an involved exchange about the United Methodist Church's scholarships for minority students:

Q: At the time of [Nesmith's] September [1980] memo when he asked Art Richardson [STH development director] to do pretty much the same thing he had asked you to do two years before; is that correct, a year and a half? . . .

A: I think he was asking him to assist in that, yes.

Q: Because you had done a magnificent job and got at that money?

MS. HEINS: Objection, argumentative.

THE COURT: Sustained, argumentative.

After a colloquy about Dean Nesmith's attempts to persuade Richardson to violate the financial aid policy guidelines that she, he, and the rest of the administration had labored over and approved:

Q: So he didn't like that policy, is that correct, the policy you suggested?

A: No, he approved it, sir.

Q: And then he wanted to change it?

A: Yes, sir.

Q: Do you think he had a right to do that?

A: In that particular instance, I didn't, sir. . . .

Q: In fact, you told him that you thought what he wanted to do wasn't legally acceptable?

A: That's correct, sir, I did.

Q: Is it part of your job to give him legal opinions on his policies?

Or, on Richardson's vocal opposition to employment decisions:

Q: [Y]ou opposed the hiring process of Stephen Breck Reid, did you not?

A: Yes, I did. . . .

Q: And you opposed the termination of . . . Nelle Slater?

A: Yes, I did. . . .

Q: And you spoke out against the hiring by Boston University of Professor Peter Berger, did you not?

A: Yes, I did.

Q: Were you hired by Dean Nesmith to be a spokesman on committee practices at Boston University?

A: No . . .

Q: Did it get to be part of your job training when you went to the sessions [of the administrative team] to directly oppose the policies, the hiring policies of Boston University?

A: No, that was not part of my training.

Although this type of thing at first blush might have seemed helpful to the plaintiff's case, in the sense of reinforcing it, Mr. Parrott presumably felt it served a purpose in suggesting two things to the jury: first, that Richardson was the type of nagging and obstreperous woman who plagues authorities wherever they may be; and second, that she was running off at the ideological mouth instead of concentrating on doing her job.

Then, perhaps not with the greatest of logical consistency, Parrott began to imply inadequacies in Richardson's method of protesting employment decisions. Campus map in hand, he asked her how far it was from the School of Theology to BU's affirmative action office, its legal counsel's office. Presumably the jurors would get the message: that a sincere critic of discriminatory employment practices would have walked this route. Or, in the same vein:

Q: Now, were you upset because Professor Berger was not qualified in your view to be hired by the university as a professor?

A: There was no job description. So I didn't know whether he was qualified or not.

Q: It's your honest belief that a job description is required in the hiring of a nationally known scholar such as Dr. Berger?

MS. HEINS: Object to the form, containing an assumption that I don't think she's testified to.

THE COURT: Sustained. Lack of foundation.

Q: At the time the process was going on with regard to the hiring of Dr. Berger, did you come to the knowledge that he was a scholar with a reputation?

A: I knew this before then, yes, sir.

Q: Yes, and his reputation was nationally known, was it not?

A: Yes.

Q: As a scholar in the field of sociology, is he not?

A: Yes.

Q: Published many books, has he not?

A: Yes.

Q: You've probably read some of them?

A: Yes, I have, sir.

Q: Is it your honest or was it your honest belief that the university was required to publish a job description to hire the likes of Dr. Berger to a position known as the University Professors Program?

A: To publish an opening of a job, yes, yes.

Q: Ma'am, I am sorry if I am not making myself clear. The question was and may I have it back, your Honor?

THE COURT: Yes.
(Whereupon, the record was read as requested by the court reporter.)

MS. HEINS: I believe she answered it, your Honor.

THE COURT: Objection overruled.

THE WITNESS: Yes.

Q: And did you base that honest belief on any discussions that you had with Sister Madonna [Sister Madonna Murphy, who had at the time been director of affirmative action for all of BU]?

A: No, I did not.

Q: Did you base that honest belief on your reading of the University Affirmative Action Program?

MS. HEINS: I object, your Honor, to the foundation. It's not in evidence that she read it. In fact, she said she never saw it. [Richardson had testified that she had asked her secretary to obtain a copy of this document from the affirmative action office but had not received one.]

THE COURT: Objection overruled.

THE WITNESS: No.

Q: Did you base your honest belief on any discussion with the . . . Equal Opportunity Employment Office at Boston University?

A: No.

Q: Did you base your honest belief on any discussions with legal counsel at Boston University while you were there?

A: No.

Parrott repeated this litany when cross-examining Richardson about her opposition to the other employment processes that were at issue in the case.

He attacked her credibility and sincerity with respect to the Harrison incident. In the years since, STH had hired two women professors in the tenure track, Elizabeth Bettenhausen and Linda Clark. I protested that this was irrelevant, "because she opposed what happened to Beverly Harrison. In 1978 she wrote a letter. That's what he blamed her for. . . . What may have happened to her state of mind a year or two later is not really relevant."

Judge Garrity testily disagreed, just as he had when the same issue arose on Bob Treese's cross-examination, "I think this is highly pertinent to the witness's credibility," he snapped.

Another example of the cross-examiner's art emerged during the brief testimony of Professor Linda Clark. She had written a letter to the members of her department at BUSTH, Area C, protesting the proposed appointment of the sociologist Peter Berger to the faculty. I called Clark to testify solely because Judge Garrity had refused to admit this memo into evidence. It was not offered, as trial lawyers arguing evidentiary issues would say, "for the truth of the matter asserted," but for its effect on the plaintiff's state of mind, and to bolster the claim that her state of mind was reasonable. The judge accepted the point, but still refused to allow the memo in without giving the defense an opportunity to cross-examine its author.

Even with Clark on the stand, the judge was at first reluctant to admit the memo into evidence. After a sidebar colloquy, he relented, but cautioned the jury:

> That particular document . . . does make several assumptions and the assumptions in that document [are] not being presented to you for their truthfulness or falsity. The document is being introduced to you as claimed by plaintiff, Ms. Richardson, came to the state of mind she claims to have [*sic*].

Clark then read aloud portions of the memo, referring to Berger's known "deep hostility to feminism" and the "farce" that she felt was being made of affirmative action by Dean Nesmith's insistence on the appointment. The memo continued: "Hiring someone holding his views about feminism seems to me to fly in the face of the commitment of the school to struggle with issues of sexism."

In preparation for cross-examining Clark the defense team had checked all, or a good number, of Professor Berger's many books out of the public library and, when the time came, drew them dramatically out of a litigation briefcase and placed them on the counsel table. As attorney Alan Rose asked the witness, one by one, if she had read each of the books, he picked up and then dropped on the table, with a satisfying thud, what presumably was the appropriate title. Because there were more than a dozen books, and Rose went slowly, this colloquy took some time.

"And did you read *Movement and Revolution* by Peter Berger?"
Slam!
"No."
"You did not. And how about Peter Berger's book called *Protocol of Damnation?*"
Bang!
"No."
"That's *damnation* one word not *damn nation*, two words. And how about Peter Berger's book, *Facing up to Modernity*, did you read that?"
Thump!
"No."
"Now, you have heard of the principle of academic freedom, have you not?"

"Yes."

"What is academic freedom?"

Clark hardly paused.

Q: Does the question give you trouble?

A: It is the right to espouse certain viewpoints and to teach in certain ways without being called into question about it.

Q: Isn't it a fact, ma'am, that in writing this letter to the members of Area C, you called into question—to use your words—his views?

A: Yes.

Q: No further questions.

One might have noted here a difference between sexist views and sexist behavior; Berger's reputation was not confined to the abstract airing of anti-feminist opinions.

The defense team's approach to the Peter Berger episode had the virtue of candor. The message, communicated through the cross-examination of Linda Clark and others, was that affirmative action procedural objections, or high-minded talk about diversity or credentialling, were so much meaningless noise when it came to "the likes of" a big name like Peter Berger.

What was consistently interesting about Dean Nesmith is that he did not, at least explicitly, take this approach. His social ethics hat may have been gathering dust, but it was in the closet somewhere. Thus his indignation, back in May 1981, at Professor Deats's imputation to him of a lack of civil rights commitment, an indignation that seemed genuine, if relying on somewhat rusty credentials. And thus his tortured dialogues with Richardson and others over capitalism, ambivalence, and the moral ambiguity of it all.

Professor Jim Fraser's testimony covered his knowledge of the Simon Parker and Peter Berger affairs, including a discussion with the dean as early as summer 1980 about the possibility of snagging Berger for Boston University. Nesmith had asked Fraser to keep that discussion confidential at the time.

In the fall, Nesmith began sounding out others on the faculty, particularly in Fraser's department, Area C. "He felt that Peter Berger would make an important contribution to the school and would also gain us some sympathy in central administration."

Fraser had additional evidence on Nesmith's reasons for terminating Richardson. The discharge had been debated at the September 1981 faculty meeting. There, said Fraser, "the reason [Nesmith] gave was the fact that Nancy had rallied the faculty against him on the Peter Berger appointment." He added, "It's my judgment that that was not correct, that the faculty made up their own minds."

The witness had heard one further comment on the subject from Nesmith, made during a meeting later in the 1980–81 year when Fraser was questioning the basis for his own termination.

Q: Professor Fraser, do you know at this time whether or not you will be continuing at Boston University?

MR. ROSE: Objection, your Honor.

THE COURT: Sustained.

Q: Let me ask you this. At any time in the current school year has Mr. Nesmith made any statement in your presence with respect to his reasons for terminating Nancy Richardson?

A: Yes, he has.

Q: Can you tell us briefly the circumstances of that conversation and what he said?

A: It was—this is in October of this year. I was having a grievance hearing appealing my termination from Boston University. I asked Dean Nesmith the reasons why I had been terminated, and he said that he would not give me those reasons . . . and later in the same conversation he said to me the last time I gave the reasons for termination, I ended up in court with it.

Garrity blew his top.

MR. ROSE: Your Honor, may that go out?

THE COURT: Absolutely. The witness slipped in a response to a question that I had sustained your objection to and the jury is to totally disregard any evidence of this witness's purported termination.

You can, of course, accept what he said—the witness said as indicating what the defendant said about Ms. Richardson.

Janet Burdewik, a former student, followed. It was late on Wednesday December 13, a day that had already seen the completion of Richardson's testimony, plus Fraser's and Clark's. Burdewik had been a member of BUTSA Council in the eventful 1980–81 year and was now working as coordinator of a refugee sponsorship program for the Massachusetts Council of Churches. She testified that at a February 1981 meeting with BUTSA Council, already described in part by Willard Rose, the dean "got agitated and announced at the end of the meeting or shortly before it was closed that he was determined to hire Peter Berger, no matter what anyone said." Later the same day, at a gathering of the school's affirmative action committee, Nesmith took another approach.

He said, "I am sick of people spreading innuendoes about Peter Berger's sex life. I happen to know . . . I think that these rumors are being spread by white males on the faculty who are threatened and also by women who do not want to see Peter Berger come here."

At which time he said to Lynn Rhodes, a faculty member, "I am sick of you spreaking these rumors."

And Lynn replied that she had not spread any rumors . . . and the dean said she was a liar.

Q: Did you have any subsequent conversation with Mr. Nesmith about Peter Berger?

A: Yes. In a chapel setting or worship setting that is regularly held by the seminary community, Dean Nesmith pulled me aside and said that he thought that the women at the School of Theology had misunderstood Peter Berger and that he would like me to get a group of women students together so that we could go out to dinner with him to discuss the Peter Berger matter further.

Q: This was said in the chapel?

A: Yes, it was.

Q: And what was your response?

A: Being it was a worship service, I really didn't—I was there to worship and I really—I answered that I would talk about it after the worship service but that I really—my feelings were that I did not want my worship experience to be interrupted by such conversations.

Thursday, December 16, 1982. This was the eighth day of trial. Judge Garrity was getting restless; the jurors were getting restless. Christmas was approaching. The plaintiff's case had three witnesses to go.

The first, Professor Earl Kent Brown, was, like Linda Clark, called because the judge had refused on hearsay grounds to permit Brown's lengthy memo summarizing the ins and outs of the Peter Berger controversy into evidence without an appearance by its author. This was despite its admissibility, under the hearsay rules, given its relevance to both Richardson's and Nesmith's states of mind.

Brown read parts of the memo to the jury. On cross-examination he was asked to read other portions, that praised Nesmith; he also readily acknowledged that despite all the doubts expressed, he had ultimately come around to support the Berger appointment. Brown's response to the Berger episode thus resembled his role during the summer 1982 interfaculty rumblings about trying to force Nesmith's resignation: he had ranged from hotly eloquent in his condemnation of injustice to coolly statesmanlike as he counseled moderation and self-preservation for the school.

Lynn Rhodes was called to fill in the history of the STH affirmative action committee, the struggle to make it permanent, and the genesis of a set of affirmative action principles that had been approved by the faculty in the spring of 1980. She had, she said, resigned from her leadership of the committee that same spring because "[m]y position was both as faculty and administrator and I was untenured, and I had been told that some of my actions were disloyal to the dean of the school."

"Who told you that?"

"Richard Nesmith. And therefore I considered I could not be an effective chairperson of his committee, both because I did not have tenured status and because I was in both positions as administrator and faculty person."

Our last witness was Paul Deats, the renegade Texan who had been driven out of that state's university some thirty years before for organizing an interracial student congregation. By describing the May 1981 executive committee blowup, Deats could perhaps leave the jury with a vivid picture of an angry, sputtering, self-justifying Nesmith, angry enough at Deats to take out his frustration on the more vulnerable Richardson.

Q: Was there any discussion of affirmative action at that meeting?

A: Yes.

Q: Can you tell us what was said?

A: I expressed to the executive committee my progressive loss of confidence in the central administration of Boston University's commitment to affirmative action and I indicated that I was tempted to extend the same loss of confidence to the administration of the School of Theology, which meant Dean Nesmith.

Q: What was said after that?

A: Dean Nesmith said he did not intend to be called a racist and told us of his involvement with the civil rights movement in the fifties in Mississippi.

Q: Did you observe anything about his demeanor?

A: He was angry.

Q: Do you remember anything else that was said at that early May or mid-May executive committee meeting?

A: I told him I was not attacking him as a racist. I was attacking the process and the commitment to affirmative action. Before the meeting adjourned, my action was explained by the dean as being my fear of having a person of the quality and caliber of Peter Berger on the faculty.

And I am afraid at that point, if not before, I became angry, said I didn't propose to be psychoanalyzed by a person who was not qualified as an analyst, and I had my own reasons for objecting to Peter Berger's appointment, which were not fear but were the objection to the process by which he was named.

CHAPTER 16

THE CONDUCTOR OF AN ORCHESTRA

THE defense team decided to stake its entire case on the credibility of the lead actor in this drama, Dean Richard Nesmith. And it was, all things considered, a wise choice. Although Nesmith had a few rough moments on cross-examination, he was overall a glib, smooth, and well-rehearsed witness for himself.

Nesmith's testimony was divided into three parts. In the first, he talked at length, and occasionally with some eloquence, about his job, Christian ministry, and the United Methodist Church's relation with STH, its first seminary. In attempting to set the stage, and also to suggest that the church really had an important influence in the school, attorney Parrott asked the dean what the Methodist Church's expectations for the training of its ministers were. This gave Nesmith a chance to expound with some conviction about the seminary:

> Expectations regarding, for example, academic understanding and competence. Do you have a knowledge of the faith? Do you know what the faith is about? Secondly, professional skill. Do you know how to preach? Do you know how to counsel with people? Do you know how to organize a church? And also, we speak of gifts and graces. Do you have that personal demeanor, that personal quality that will represent the church in the Christian faith as well?

The dean spoke with similar eloquence of his own job:

> To be one who would understand and work with and develop faculty because the heart of the enterprise is a teaching process that occurs around faculty and staff. . . .

It involves a normal coordinating management function in-
house, like the conductor of an orchestra that keeps the wood-
winds and the strings roughly playing on the same chord. . . .

In the second part of the testimony Nesmith described a gradual
process of observation of, and gradual disappointment in, Nancy Richardson's job performance. In the first evaluative conversations, he was
not yet "dissatisfied" with Richardson, but as to various issues, "I wasn't
sure we were quite getting on top of that."

In the course of tracing his mounting dissatisfaction, Nesmith worked
the ideological disputes into a framework that also included the more
quotidian matters of financial aid and housing. He and Parrott (who kept
a discreet distance and addressed the dean with exaggerated respect)
together tried to unfold before the jury the dilemma of a sympathetic
administrator watching his subordinate stray further and further from
her role, and into an agenda of her own. Thus Nesmith, describing his
second evaluation session with Richardson, stated:

[O]ne of the lead issues we worked on in that conversation was
the communication issue. . . .

[T]he background of this was some of the turmoil that has
been discussed here around the BTI [Boston Theological Insti-
tute]. A letter that came to me and I tried to talk through and
to articulate my sense of how staff works.

Q: What did you tell her?

A: Well, I reviewed how . . . we had talked about the Beverly Harrison appointment. I recognized her feelings along
with Nelle Slater and Lynn Rhodes and indicated that I would
not put them on the spot publicly. In a sense, I said I will
cover that. And then I was a bit surprised when I had the BTI
letter come to me in the mail, and I said simply at that juncture, the place for us to do our staff critiquing of each other
and to take care of our differences is here at this table, not to
come around the horn through some other entities.

At the next evaluation, according to Nesmith, "I pressed the importance of our getting turf . . . housing units . . ." But he was also disturbed by her working with the STH women's collective: "[M]y first
thought was to support that, underline the value of that, but to also note
a couple of cautions here."

Q: What were the cautions you noted?

A: One was the issue of time. Every pastor gets caught, so much pressure, and every administrator, and it is easy to get tacked on the end of your job description instead of centered, and I tried to reinforce the importance, making sure we have the discussion of housing and our working student government, and financial and personnel working at the heart of the matter before we get too far into too many areas, even though I support some of those areas. . . .

[Y]ou have got to do the center of the job in order to stay legitimate, keep people happy before you get too far out on the fringes of the job. I was trying to outline that administrative insight. . . .

I didn't feel we were getting it together yet in housing and the normal student government and hence, was trying to simply voice a word of caution at that juncture. . . .

Every student personnel officer is the arm in the everyday work with students of the dean's office. And for example, in an area like student government or an area such as a women's collective, she is a spokesperson for my office. And at a number of points, I felt that the students were not in a sense being — again talking about the teaching function . . . given an understanding of the administrative realities of a school of theology.

By the next year, Nesmith acknowledged, Richardson had succeeded on the housing front. "To Nancy's credit, we had worked together finally to get 515 Park," the Boston apartment building owned by BU. But the representation issue, said Nesmith, continued to fester. This time it was activated by her sympathy for a BU workers' strike, and the memo she had signed expressing ambivalence about having to cross a picket line. They discussed "the connecting role between the dean's office and the student functioning. . . . [S]trikes were not easy for church and our community really had to wrestle through that and her memo cited her ambivalence of being an administrator. . . . And I saw some of that ambivalence, not only displayed there, but when we were trying to communicate with students."

Q: And in your mind, did that affect her performance on the job?

A: Yes.

Q: And how?

A: I think . . . she had difficulty in taking students and in representing . . . an administrative point of view.

Nesmith now recounted a lengthy series of defects, as he perceived them, in Richardson's job performance: maintenance problems at 515 Park Drive; permitting the administration of that building to be transferred from one branch of the university's housing bureaucracy to another; failing to assure that a sum of Methodist Church scholarship money for minority students found its way to BU; finally, her calling together a planning committee for the September 1981 all-school retreat:

> In the faculty meeting, a fairly tense meeting, it was a lot of those kinds of political dynamics that occasionally get stirred in a faculty discussion. Action was taken for an all-school retreat. Some of the faculty volunteered to share in some of the planning of that retreat . . .

> We needed to talk to some people on the Board of Advisors (an advisory Methodist Church body), some of the alumni, and hence . . .—my recollection, we couldn't just build on the basis of volunteers. . . .

> Hence, the faculty asked me to conduct a meeting for the planning of this retreat. At that juncture, I left campus to visit several of the United Methodist annual conferences. . . .

> I returned to find that Ms. Richardson had already called and named a group to this and without any consultation with me.

Q: And how did you react to that?

A: Frankly, quite angrily.

Q: Why?

A: Because there was a good bit of political sensitivity in that meeting. She is an intelligent person. She could read that; she knew this was of a consequence that the dean normally appointed committees and that in this instance, it was particularly essential since we were talking about off-campus people as well.

Cross-examination of the dean inevitably drew the Richardson team into the quagmire of rebutting the poor job performance defense. Yet it yielded occasional fruits. The first subject was Nesmith's claim that Richardson's negligence had lost the school a substantial sum in scholarship aid for minority students.

Q: In this document that's filed with the court, in answer to my interrogatories, you made reference to this question of scholarships from jurisdictions of the United Methodist Church for ethnic minority students, did you not?

A: I believe so.

Q: Now there were some errors in that, were there not . . . ?

A: I don't know. Let me review it. . . . There was not an error in accordance with the information I had at that time. . . . I know, for example, that source I had for the comment about the $49,000, the chair of the committee distributing the monies, is an accurate report of a conversation I had at that time.

Q: To your knowledge, it's still true there was $49,000 distributed by the northeastern jurisdiction in the fall of 1980? . . .

A: I am telling you that's a figure that was used on the jurisdictional floor.

Q: You know that's not true, don't you, Mr. Nesmith?

A: No, I do not.

Q: Don't you know, in fact, that the actual amount distributed by the Multi-Ethnic Center in the fall of 1980 was more like $13,800, not $49,000? . . .

A: I only know the figure used in the two places I have identified. [One was Drew University; the other, a meeting in Pennsylvania.]

Q: You never bothered checking, did you? . . .

A: Beyond that, no.

Q: Would it surprise you to learn that there was only $13,800 available and distributed by the northeastern jurisdiction in the fall of 1980? . . .

A: Yes.

Q: Did you ever bother asking for a list of the people who had received scholarships from the northeastern jurisdiction for ethnic minority students in 1980?

A: In two consecutive years I had been instructed by the chair that [Boston University] had not received them.

Q: Answer my question. Did you ever bother to check with the records at the Multi-Ethnic Center to find out who had received scholarships and what amounts?

A: No, I did not ask that question. . . .

Q: Now, were you aware . . . that in the 1979–80 year, Mr. Willard Rose had a jurisdictional scholarship from the northeastern jurisdiction?

A: I was not aware of that . . . but he testified to that here and I have no reason to doubt that.

Q: And were you aware . . . that Mr. Rose received such a scholarship in the '80–81 year?

A: No. I noticed his name on that listing you had. [Plaintiff's counsel had received a listing via affidavit from an administrator at Drew University's Multi-Ethnic Center.]

Q: Yes. And therefore, you were incorrect to state in your deposition that no students at Boston University received these jurisdictional funds during Nancy Richardson's tenure, weren't you? . . .

A: I was in error in terms of being adequately informed, as in fact, obviously, was Ms. Richardson.

Q: You are in error?

A: In information at that juncture, yes.

Q: You testified in your deposition in error, did you not?

A: You have that copy?

Q: I certainly do.

A: Can we check it?

Q: Can you remember it?

A: I don't recall that specific testimony, that's why I asked to check it.

Q: You just told me a minute ago that you were in error that some jurisdictional students received scholarships, isn't that correct?

A: In my comment here against the factors, for example, the Willard Rose testimony the other day, yes.

Q: And you didn't bother to check that before you went in for your deposition, did you?

A: No.

Questioned further about the $49,000, Nesmith testified that he had heard the number both at a jurisdictional conference in Eastern Pennsylvania and in spring 1980 at Drew University, from Bob McClain, then head of the Multi-Ethnic Center there.

Q: In fact, . . . you were never at Drew in the spring of 1980, were you sir?

A: I believe I was.

Q: And were minutes taken of the meeting?

A: I do not know.

Q: I point you to the May 12, 1980 minutes at the Multi-Ethnic Center at Drew and ask if your name is listed among those in attendance. [This was the only spring 1980 meeting of the Multi-Ethnic Center board.] . . .

A: My name is not listed there.

Q: You still maintain you were there at that meeting?

A: I was there in two successive years. I thought that I was clearly there in that year. . . .

Q: And it's your testimony, you are quite sure that it was Mr. Bob McClain who told you that there was $49,000 available for jurisdictional scholarships for the northeastern jurisdiction in '80–81 . . . ?

A: I am quite clear that Bob McClain told me that. . . .

Q: Now you mentioned a while ago in response to one of my

questions [that] on further thought you remembered first hearing something about jurisdictional scholarships at an Eastern Pennsylvania conference, correct?

A: Yes, Eastern Pennsylvania college campus.

Q: . . . [W]hen you were deposed by me earlier this year . . . you didn't mention anything about a Pennsylvania conference, did you?

A: I don't know.

Q: You said you first heard about it at the Multi-Ethnic Center at Drew, didn't you?

A: May I check the deposition?

Q: [Reading from the deposition] ". . . Where did you get this $49,000 figure? Answer: In a meeting of a board . . . for the evolution of a Multi-Ethnic program at Drew Seminary."

Was that your deposition testimony under oath?

A: I believe so.

Q: But now, you recall that you first heard about this in Eastern Pennsylvania, correct?

A: I suspect that's the truer testimony.

Q: The deposition?

A: I would think so; it's a fresher memory.

Q: So you would like to revise your testimony of about a half hour ago that you heard about the jurisdictional money when you were at a conference in Eastern Pennsylvania?

A: I think that's probably refreshed my mind if you want it revised, indeed.

Q: I am asking you what you want to do. What would you want your testimony to be for the jury, that you heard about it at Drew or that you heard about it in Pennsylvania?

A: I think the Drew recollection is the freshest recollection.

Q: Which is true and which is false sir?

A: I think probably the deposition . . .

Q: Is true?

A: Is closest to the fact.

Q: I see.

A: A fresher memory.

Q: And your testimony here is false?

A: I noted at a half . . .

Q: It's one or the other.

A: Yes.

On cross-examination, Nesmith occasionally slipped from the pose of moderation, the benevolent giver of credit where credit was due. He began to fence.

Q: Now sir, you testified, I believe, under questioning by Mr. Parrott, that at the end of the '79–80 year you were not satisfied with the level of grace and decorum at the community lunch program, is that right?

A: Yes.

Q: And I think you testified that Ms. Richardson essentially agreed with you about that, didn't you?

A: Yes.

Q: Now, she attempted to make improvements in the lunch program in the '80–81 year, didn't she?

A: I believe she made some attempts, yes.

Q: And the lunch program was highly praised by BUTSA in their report, which is in evidence in this case?

A: I believe that would be an overstatement.

Q: Well, let's look at it, sir. Exhibit 8 . . . "Forum and the community lunch program has been widely supported by the student body. First-year students, in particular, have remarked that they have appreciated the structure which the community lunch program has provided. The program offers a viable method for new students to become acclimated to seminary life." You remember reading that or hearing that, do you not?

A: Yes.

Q: And that was praise for the lunch program, wasn't it?

A: A measure of praise, yes. Especially related to first-year students.

Q: And that was actually one of the few items in your administration that was praised by the students in the BUTSA report, wasn't it?

A: I don't recall the full measure of praise or blame in that report.

Q: You don't?

A: I don't.

Q: Do you recall on your direct testimony that you thought it showed that you were in the red?

A: Yes. Student personnel.

Q: You weren't in the red on the lunch program according to that report, were you?

A: In terms of my judgment, we were still not . . .

Q: I'm asking you if you were in the red. . . .

MR. PARROTT: Don't interrupt him.

MS. HEINS: He's not answering the question. . . .

MR. PARROTT: Then move to strike, but don't interrupt him.

MS. HEINS: Well, I think I'm entitled to an answer to my question.

Q: According to that report, you were not in the red on the lunch program, were you?

A: The report focuses on first-year students.

Q: Can you give me a yes or no answer?

A: In my judgment we were in the red on the lunch program.

Q: According to that report?

A: Well, I said, in my judgment.

Q: I asked you according to that report, sir.

A: That report gives it more of a plus, yes.

Having testified to the propriety of various hiring processes that the plaintiff had opposed, Nesmith was now cross-examined, for example, about the appointment of Simon Parker as the Associate Dean in 1981.

Q: Now . . . let me direct your attention to paragraph 4 on page 1 of this exhibit [an affirmative action report, completed by Nesmith, regarding Parker's appointment], where you write, "Interviewed by the executive committee of the faculty and recommended by same." Now you heard Professor Deats and Professor Fraser both testify in this case that that was not so. Do you think you stretched the truth a little on this?

A: The reality was that they recommended Simon Parker as the strongest of the three interviewed.

Q: Do you think you stretched the truth a little on this?

A: No. . . . I have simply indicated that he was recommended as the best among the three they had interviewed. That's what this says.

Q: And they also asked you to interview some other candidates, and they gave you specific names of minority candidates, didn't they?

A: They encouraged further search . . .

Q: Yes.

A: . . . and I made further search on the names they suggested.

Q: And you don't think it's stretching the truth to have written here, "recommended by same"? . . .

A: I said what they said. They recommended him among those they interviewed.

Q: They said he was the best of the three, and they wanted you to search further, didn't they?

A: Yes.

*****

Q: Now, you wanted Nancy Richardson to express the administration line on the Reid affair, didn't you? . . .

A: I would think she'd at least have a responsibility to understand the facts of the case.

Q: That's not my question. You remember my question.

A: Restate it.

Q: You expected Nancy Richardson to express the administration position on the Reid incident, didn't you?

A: I hoped she'd certainly be informed on the Reid incident, yes.

Q: That's not my question. You expected her to state the administrative position, did you not?

A: Yes.

Nesmith, however, now insisted that he and Richardson did not have strong disagreement on BU's treatment of Stephen Breck Reid. In fact, he said, "I don't recall her representation on the Reid situation." This prompted a reading of his deposition testimony:

"Question [relating to Nesmith's statements, tape-recorded, at his June 8, 1981, meeting with Richardson]: What specifically did she do or not do with reference to the disappointment over Stephen Breck Reid and the expressions of disappointment that followed in the School of Theology community that led you to refer to that in your termination discussions with her? . . .

Answer: Director of student community affairs is an arm of the administration, an arm of the dean's office, and in that vein, ought to help translate for students, for example, the tensions, the dilemmas that you face on these kinds of issues. The critique at that juncture is not at the point of shared objectives. It is at the point of our capacity to work as a team and to feel that in terms of my office's responsibility, Nancy was adequately representing that office. . . .

Question: And what again, I ask, specifically did she do or not do with reference to the Reid disappointment and the tensions that followed that you can tell me about as an example of this communication problem or this inability or failure to be an arm of the dean's office?

Answer: On the constructive side, she was a party to some of the discussion that helped us evolve some learnings.

Question: Some?

Answer: Learnings. On the problem side it was a problem with the sense of identification of the administration and of the communication and translation of the reality of a good faith effort.

Question: You did not think she adequately communicated and translated to the student body the reality of a good faith effort with respect to Mr. Reid?

Answer: Right."

Back to the present testimony:

Q: Now you felt . . . that if Nancy Richardson had been doing her job, the BUTSA report would not have been so critical about the failure of BU to hire Mr. Reid, didn't you? . . .

A: Yes. I think it would have had a better understanding of administration.

Q: And this was one of the reasons you fired her, wasn't it?

A: One of the reasons.

Similarly, regarding Peter Berger:

Q: [A]s in the Beverly Harrison and Stephen Breck Reid situation, you wished that she would have taken a different position, didn't you?

A: As in those instances, I would wish that she would be a responsible administrator and help the community understand some of the problems of working through these kinds of problem areas.

Q: And you wished she would have taken a different position, didn't you?

A: As an arm of the administration, yes.

Regarding the dissolution of the faculty's executive committee in May 1981:

Q: You were uncomfortable seeing the faculty moving toward the committee of the whole with what you viewed as factionalism that might result? . . .

A: Yes.

Q: And that was because you saw that in the process that you thought was emerging, Nancy Richardson had closer identity with others than with you, right? . . .

A: In the issues of governance in the factional process, Nancy would be a minor point. . . .

Q: You were concerned in this factional process that we spoke about that Nancy Richardson would not identify with you, correct?

A: My prime concern was the faculty itself. Secondly, indeed, I would be concerned about her administrative office in relation to it, including Nancy.

Q: Can you just answer it yes?

A: Yes.

Q: And you were afraid that she would not necessarily and unquestioningly explain the administrative decisions as you wanted them explained, isn't that right?

A: No.

Q: Part of the pattern of divisiveness that you feared resulted from controversies over employment decisions in the '80–81 school year, wasn't it? . . .

A: That would be one major part of the divisiveness.

Q: And the major employment decisions in that year were the Simon Parker, Peter Berger, and Stephen Breck Reid decisions, weren't they?

A: I believe so.

Q: Now, another event in that series in May of '81 was the BUTSA report, wasn't it?

A: In that series, meaning?

Q: The series of events that you've described [in deposition] dispelled any doubts that you had about terminating Nancy Richardson.

A: It was an event in that period. It was not necessarily in that series. . . .

Q: It was not an event that moved you closer to a decision to fire Nancy Richardson?

A: If you preface it that way, yes, I've already indicated it was an event and one I took seriously. Yes.

Q: And that moved you closer to your decision to fire Nancy Richardson?

A: Indeed.

The very last event preceding the firing had been Richardson's scheduling of a meeting to plan a September 1981 all-school retreat. In his submision to the EEOC, Nesmith had described Richardson's administrative act in scheduling the meeting as "insubordination." At trial he was more circumspect but still swore that this was an important factor in his final decision because Richardson, as an "intelligent person," should have understood the political importance of the dean's calling the meeting himself. Cross-examination pursued the nature of his concern.

Q: Now, your concern was to have a good balance of people on the committee planning the retreat, wasn't it?

A: Yes.

Q: Were you afraid somebody might stack the committee?

A: Stacking is not an appropriate point. I was concerned to get some outside people in the discussion since it was to be all-school.

Q: Deposition, volume 5, page 95, line 13. "Question: When you mean a good balance, were you afraid that somebody was going to stack the planning committee? Answer: That sometimes happens if you get into a highly factionalized situation." That was your testimony, wasn't it?

A: I gather, yes. . . .

Q: So your concern was not who set up the meeting but who was on the planning committee, wasn't it, sir? . . .

A: I assume it would be the same thing.

Q: Your concern was not who sent out the memo to set up a meeting, the time and place, but who was invited, right?

A: My concern was with the composition of the committee.

Q: Right. Now, the faculty members that Nancy Richardson invited to the meeting had already volunteered, didn't they, at the faculty meeting?

A: There was a group of volunteers, yes.

Q: And it was understood, wasn't it, that the student members would be those who were already planning orientation?

A: That was never noted. . . .

Q: The students she invited were in fact students who were involved in planning orientation, weren't they?

A: I don't recall. There were several categories, I believe, among students she invited.

Q: You don't recall. Now, that leaves the church people, the Board of Visitors, and you wanted to suggest some names, right?

A: Right.

Q: And Nancy Richardson sent you a memo on May 21 asking you to suggest some names, didn't she?

A: On May 21?

There followed a lengthy colloquy in which it was finally established that Nesmith received this May 21 memo some time before he fired Richardson on May 29, if not before he left Boston to conference-hop on May 23.

Q: And the meeting that she set for the retreat planning committee was on June 9, right?

A: Somewhere in that period, yes.

Q: And you don't think that gave you enough time to submit names?

A: That ignores the fundamental issue that I wanted to constitute . . .

Q: Answer my question. . . . Didn't you have enough time
between when you received that memo before May 29 and
June 9 when the meeting was set to invite all the people you
wanted?

A: Indeed, had I wanted her to constitute the committee. I
hadn't planned to do so.

The conclusion of Nesmith's cross-examination was an unanticipated
anticlimax. After the defense's strong promotion of Nesmith as a civil
rights martyr, the somewhat more lukewarm approach that he had taken
to the interests of minorities in a 1980 letter to a white male job applicant
might have provided an interesting counterpoint. The letter, which had
been produced by BU during the discovery phase of the case, opined
that "faculty appointments are now so hedged about with requirements
regarding distribution in accordance with race, sex, and age, that it is
extremely unlikely that your interest can be honored here."
    Nesmith claimed not to recognize the letter, and would not admit
that he had written or dictated it. As the plaintiff therefore lacked adequate foundation for its admission (in the judge's view), the jury never
got to see it.

CHAPTER 17

WORDS AND DEEDS

MONDAY, December 20. Nesmith's cross-examination ended. The plaintiff's team decided to forgo rebuttal evidence. Two out-of-town witnesses who could have contradicted certain of the dean's assertions, it turned out, were not exactly eager to testify. Dr. Julius Scott, formerly of Paine College, could have clarified what he'd told Nesmith regarding his availability for the associate dean's job; and Bob McClain, formerly of the Multi-Ethnic Center, could have contradicted Nesmith's assertions about the apocryphal $49,000 that Nancy Richardson had failed to get for BU's minority students. Neither testimony was crucial, and since the witnesses were out of state and therefore could not be subpoenaed, neither was attainable at this stage.

A last possible rebuttal witness, a resident of 515 Park Drive who could have attested to Richardson's competence in securing the attentions of the BU housing maintenance bureaucracy, did not seem to represent the proper note on which to end the case. Nesmith's motivations for firing Richardson, the last major focus of the cross-examination, seemed a better subject for the jury to remember.

Tuesday afternoon Charles Parrott began his summation. He started out explaining why he had called only one witness. "[W]e . . . decided that through Dean Nesmith and through a number of the plaintiff's witnesses we have provided you with all the information you need to find against Miss Richardson and for Boston University and Dean Nesmith.

Professor Treese . . . testified that Dean Nesmith encouraged discussion among his staff, which included Nancy Richardson. . . . [H]e encouraged debate and dissent. Those things came from Professor Treese, so we didn't think it necessary to bring anybody on from our side of the case . . . to tell you those same things. Her witness told you those things, and that's good.

You would hope that a dean and a minister in charge of a School of Theology would encourage discussion and dissent where it's important on issues that ministers and theologians are supposed to deal with, not just theology but questions or problems of racial discrimination, questions of discrimination against women.

Also, Professor Treese helped you in that he told you about all of these wonderful people on both sides of this blackboard . . . all these wonderful people that Dean Nesmith either hired or tried to hire, some of whom were white males, some of them were white females, some of them were black males, and some were black females.

And again you would hope that a minister and a dean of a School of Theology would do those sorts of things. He told you that his religion compelled him to do it, the Methodist teaching, and he told you that he had a commitment to affirmative action and civil rights. . . .

Now, another one of Miss Richardson's witnesses, a faculty member of long standing, Professor Deats, . . . he told you some things that we might otherwise have had to tell you in our case had he not come along. But he very forthrightly told you of Dean Nesmith's involvement over the years in support of the civil rights movement; that is, that he went into the South at a time when it wasn't particularly popular to go into the South and speak for the black cause; and like others, Martin Luther King and others who did it, he got arrested, and he was tried, and he was incarcerated until an appellate system got him out of jail, so to speak. . . .

Now, the two very nice young students who came on to testify—Willard Rose in the first week and then a nice young lady, Miss Burdewik last week—what did they tell you about the dean in so many words? Didn't they tell you that the dean met with them, that he discussed things with them? He discussed the student government. He discussed their concerns about anti-racism. He discussed their concerns about affirmative action with the hiring of Simon Parker and Peter Berger.

Now, we didn't think it was necessary to bring anybody else
on in our case to tell you those things. You would expect Dean
Nesmith's witnesses to tell you those things if we brought
them along. But when the plaintiff's witnesses came on, we
were so delighted they appeared to be telling the truth about
those issues. . . .

Now, as I said at the outset, in order to find for Miss Richardson, you really have to find in your own minds that Dean
Nesmith was a liar as he sat there for two and a half days testifying both on direct and cross. . . . And it may be a difficult task because the man is a minister. He preached and
worked in the civil rights movement. He worked in the inner
city establishing parishes. . . . Now, it is solely your function
to determine whether he was telling the truth or whether he
was a liar, but you should consider those things about him.

In discussing the various employment disputes that dominated so
much of the trial testimony, Parrott chose a well-worn rhetorical dis-
tinction between Richardson's "words" of constant complaint and Nesmith's "deeds" in support of affirmative action:
Nesmith supported Stephen Reid, according to the defense attorney.
"He forwarded his application to the central administration with his
approval after the faculty had acted. . . . Unfortunately, . . . the young
man withdrew his application before the appointment process was
completed."
Richardson and others objected to the process by which Simon Parker
was hired. "By *process*, they seem to have indicated that either the job
wasn't advertised or there wasn't a job description, and so you heard a
lot of testimony about that. But when it came to what really happened,
there were two deeds accomplished by Dean Nesmith: first . . . Dean
Nesmith . . . filled out . . . the Boston University affirmative action
report. . . . He accomplished the deed. He filled out this paper, sent it
forward, and there was no question but that the process was followed."
Parrott did not explain why filling out a paper proved that a process was
followed. He did not mention what the second "deed" was.
"With regard to Professor Berger, again you heard charges that [Nancy
Richardson] felt it was a discriminatory practice not in conformance with
affirmative action because process wasn't followed. Well, after a little
discussion we were able to get before you a document which should prove
to you that Dean Nesmith not only was a man of his word, but he did
a deed in accordance with affirmative action. He filled out this form. . . .

"Now," continued Mr. Parrott, "you should also consider in your deliberations that in these many words that Miss Richardson used she has brought the most serious charges that one could bring against a teacher, a minister, a dean . . ."

> And so, when you view who was telling the truth or who honestly and reasonably believed what they said on the witness stand, you should keep in mind those serious charges that have been made against Dean Nesmith and Boston University, and you should keep very much in mind the many words that were said but the few deeds that were demonstrated by the plaintiff.

Parrott now went over Nesmith's testimony about his growing dissatisfaction with Richardson's job performance, making use of the March 1981 memo, which Richardson said she had not received, in which the dean had written: "We are near a breaking point in our relationship once again, Nancy."

"Now the judge will instruct you," Parrott wound up,

> that it really isn't for you to determine whether Dean Nesmith was right or whether he was wrong in evaluating Richardson's performance. Your job is solely to decide on that issue: Did he believe that he was right? That is, did he believe that her job performance was not adequate and that she could not continue? That's really all you have to find . . .

Even if they found for Richardson, he cautioned, they certainly should not recommend reinstatement:

> [Y]ou have to consider what happens if she is going to be reinstated; that is, you heard testimony that a young black minister by the name of John Scott has been in that job as the director of student and community affairs since Miss Richardson was discharged, so what happens to him if you decide that she should be reinstated? . . .

But I suggest to you that you probably don't have to get to that question. If you will look at the words but consider the deeds of Dean Nesmith and what he reasonably believed in May of 1981 when he terminated her, I believe that you will come back with a true verdict for the defendants: that he did not terminate her wrongfully, but he did it because he believed she was not performing her job adequately.

Having been half-buried through much of the trial in minutiae of the poor job performance defense, I naturally tried during summation to focus the jury once more on what Richard Nesmith had actually said at the time he fired Nancy Richardson.

Ladies and gentlemen, I think in the past two and a half weeks you have probably learned more about BU School of Theology than you ever wanted to know, and I thank you for your patience and attention. It's not a simple case on the facts, but I suggest to you that the fundamental issue is really quite simple: Why did Richard Nesmith fire Nancy Richardson? Were his motives illegal? . . . And when you think about his motives, you will notice something very strange about his testimony in this case.

Richard Nesmith got on the witness stand, and he told you a tale about some reasons he had for firing Nancy Richardson. The funny thing is he never once mentioned social justice or ideology, those words that he repeated so much in their June 8 conversation. . . . He never once mentioned the anti-racism recommendations, and those were a theme of his on June 8. No mention of Stephen Breck Reid or the search for the associate dean, the position Simon Parker finally got, both important concerns of Richard Nesmith's on June 8.

Instead, he got on the stand and told you about a handful of complaints he had dredged up through four years of memos and files: finding out about a scholarship that in fact, as it turns out, he didn't really have his facts straight; the few BU students who were eligible got that scholarship; something about repair problems at 515 Park Drive, a building managed by Boston University; his claims about these things weren't even accurate, as we have shown you. . . .

[T]hese issues of her administrative performance are red herrings. They are classic pretexts, things he came up with afterward, after he knew he would be sued, things he never mentioned to Nancy Richardson when he fired her or to Professor Bob Treese or to Willard Rose. . . .

[W]hy did he go on for an hour and a half on June 8 about "the factor of cause," about the pedagogical and ideological differences? Why did he tell Bob Treese he fired Nancy Richardson because she didn't control BUTSA's criticisms? Why didn't he talk about financial aid or housing or poor job performance to Bob Treese?

And why did he tell Willard Rose his reasons were ideological and pedagogical and give as examples the BUTSA report, the women's collective, the Beverly Harrison letter? Why didn't he talk about financial aid and housing and poor job performance to Willard Rose?

Poor job performance—it's the standard refuge for an employer charged with unlawful motives. But it doesn't get him off the hook. He can't erase the tape. He can't erase the May 29 conversation that Nancy Richardson told you about. He can't erase the conversation with Bob Treese or Willard Rose or his complaint to the faculty, described to you by Professor Jim Fraser, that Nancy Richardson opposed him on the Peter Berger issue. . . .

What did he say to her on June 8, when he went on and on about her commitments to social justice preventing her from defending his point of view on the critical employment decisions that created such controversy in the spring of '81? Only once in that conversation did he talk about housing or financial aid, and then, if you recall, it was to praise her, and I quote: "You and I have succeeded more, the more it has been nonideological, the more it has been detailed and numerical, such as in something like financial aid or something like housing. But the more you take it into an area where there is heat, diversity, and where in a sense some of my institution-representing responsibility as dean will tend at times in the student definitions to come off on the conservative side, the more you and I find ourselves less capable of that kind of easy rapprochement that helps us to be clear strategically."

What does he mean, "be clear strategically"? I suggest to you that he means strategize about how to persuade students and faculty of his line on the issues where there will be heat and diversity. And what were the areas of heat and diversity where Richard Nesmith thought he came off on the conservative side? He admitted it on cross-examination. The areas of heat and diversity were the controversy over the failure to make an offer to Stephen Breck Reid, over the way the Peter Berger appointment was pushed through, over the question of affirmative action in the appointment of Simon Parker as associate dean, and that heat and diversity were reflected in several of the anti-racism recommendations that Professor Paul Deats and Nancy Richardson prepared. . . .

And, if his statements on . . . June 8 were not enough, recall Professor Treese's testimony about what Richard Nesmith said in January when Richard Nesmith got so angry because Nancy Richardson was concerned about homeless people, and Bob Treese asked him, "Are you saying she's not a good administrator?" And Richard Nesmith answered, "No." . . .

And consider, too, these very interesting facts: Richard Nesmith himself testified, and Mr. Parrott reminded you, he tried to interest Nancy Richardson in two other administrative jobs. Would he do that if she were such a poor administrator, if he fired her, as he now claims, for poor job performance?

Having addressed the poor job performance issue as best I could, I now tried to respond to the defense's somewhat sanctimonious emphasis throughout the trial on its great good faith—"deeds" rather than "words"— when it came to affirmative action hiring. "[T]hey say, 'Well, after all, he hired some minority people and some women.' Well, I suggest to you that those other hirings, whether they are secretaries, administrators, junior faculty, or part-time people who weren't on the tenure track, are of very little relevance."

Look at the decisions that she did oppose. . . . And if you think about the testimony of Nancy Richardson, Bob Treese, Willard Rose, Lynn Rhodes, Jim Fraser, Paul Deats, Jan Burdewik, and if you examine some of the evidence that counts in this case, I think you will agree she had an abundantly good reason for her beliefs. . . .

She was hardly alone in questioning what was done to Beverly Harrison. Nelle Slater and Lynn Rhodes agreed with her. Much of the faculty questioned it at their September '78 meeting. . . . Professor Lee Rouner admitted at that meeting that John Silber had "gone for the jugular" against Beverly Harrison. . . .

And Nancy Richardson was in equally good company in opposing the firing of Nelle Slater. . . . Nancy Richardson thought Richard Nesmith hadn't yet learned how to work with women. She opposed Richard Nesmith's decision, and many on the faculty agreed with her, as Bob Treese and James Fraser testified. So did students, who specifically accused Richard Nesmith of sex discrimination at a forum held to discuss Nelle Slater's termination. Richard Nesmith's response, very typical: "I can work with Nancy Richardson. We are in the saddle together."

Notice how, when he fires Nancy Richardson and is charged with illegal motives, he points to other women he has hired, many of whom are now also gone. . . .

Stephen Breck Reid, I have already mentioned. The defense in this case has tried to tell you he just withdrew to take a better job, but the evidence is clear, and you heard it yesterday, President Silber did not want to hire Stephen Breck Reid, and you can read Exhibit 77, written in March of '81, five months after Mr. Reid was on campus to be interviewed. John Silber bounces his file back to the provost's office and writes, "I am at a loss to know what you were approving in approving this appointment." . . .

And Richard Nesmith tells you that affirmative action was followed before Peter Berger was hired. Is he serious? The job description fit Peter Berger like a glove, and only Peter Berger. There was only one applicant and one interview. The ad was published in April 1981, after Richard Nesmith sent Peter Berger's name to the appointments committee. Nancy Richardson had good reason to oppose that appointment. . . .

Ladies and gentlemen, there are two major characters in this courtroom drama. Nancy Richardson is a woman who did her job well, was highly regarded by students and faculty, was consistently committed and expressed her commitment to social justice . . . and, as she said to Richard Nesmith, she never made any secret about this.

Richard Nesmith is a man whose idea of absolute loyalty goes far beyond the legitimate needs of any university administration. He wasn't forthright in his statement to students and faculty about his or BU's employment decisions. He wasn't forthright in his expressed desire to strategize about who should be on the retreat planning committee when people had already volunteered, about making adjustments in the anti-racism recommendations that the faculty had already agreed to, and I suggest to you that he wasn't completely forthright in this case.

And I suggest that, after you have discussed and reviewed all of the testimony and looked at the significant exhibits, you will conclude that Nancy Richardson deserves a verdict in her favor on all three of her claims.

CHAPTER 18

THE FLAG OF POPULISM

BEFORE the summations, Judge Garrity shared with the attorneys the special interrogatories that he had drafted for the jury to answer. These would comprise the verdict form, on which the jurors had to check "yes" or "no" in response to a series of often convoluted legal questions. In some instances, a "no" answer meant that they could go no further. The lengthy verdict form looked and read as follows:

I. Re: Plaintiff's First Claim that Her Employment was Terminated as a Consequence of Actions She Took in Good Faith Because of Her Reasonable Belief the Defendants Were Engaging in Discriminatory Employment Practices.

1. Did Nancy Richardson reasonably believe that Richard Nesmith and the Boston University School of Theology were engaging in discriminatory employment practices?

Yes ＿＿＿＿＿ No ＿＿＿＿＿

2. If your answer to this Question #1 is Yes, were actions Nancy Richardson took as a consequence of her reasonable belief that Richard Nesmith and the Boston University School of Theology were engaging in discriminatory employment practices taken by her in good faith?

Yes ＿＿＿＿＿ No ＿＿＿＿＿

3. If your answer to Question #2 is Yes, did Richard Nesmith terminate Nancy Richardson's employment because of the ac-

tions she took in good faith as a consequence of her reasonable belief that Richard Nesmith and the Boston University School of Theology were engaging in discriminatory employment practices?

Yes _____ No _____

4. If your answer to Question #3 is Yes, please indicate in figures and words the amount of money, if any, which will fairly and adequately provide compensation to Nancy Richardson for any emotional and/or mental suffering and for humiliation and/or for any diminution of earning capacity she sustained as a proximate result of her termination from employment.

$_____

_____
Words

II. Re: Plaintiff's Second Claim that her Civil Rights were Violated as a Consequece of Defendants' Interference with and/or Attempts to Interfere with Statements She Made and/or Opinions She Held in Good Faith Because of Her Reasonable Belief that Defendants' [*sic*] Were Not Complying with Affirmative Action Requirements and/or Engaging in Discriminatory Employment Practices.

1. If your answers to Questions 1, 2 and 3 in I above are Yes did Richard Nesmith's termination of Nancy Richardson's employment violate her civil rights?

Yes _____ No _____

2. If your answer to Question 1 is Yes, please indicate in figures and words the amount of money if any, which will fairly and adequately provide compensation to Nancy Richardson for damages she sustained as a proximate result of her civil rights having been violated?

$_____

_____
Words

III. Re: Plaintiff's Third Claim that Her Employment was Terminated in Contravention of a Clear Public Policy (Against Discrimination in Employment on Account of Race and/or Sex and/or for Affirmative Action) which Thereby Violated the Implied Duty of Good Faith and Fair Dealing in Employment Relationships?

1. If your answers to Questions 1, 2 and 3 in I above are Yes was Nancy Richardson's employment terminated in contravention of a clear public policy?

Yes _____ No _____

2. If your answer to Question 1 is Yes, please indicate the amount of money, if any, which will fairly and adequately provide compensation to Nancy Richardson for damages she sustained as a proximate result of her employment having been terminated in contravention of a clear public policy?

$_____

_____
Words

IV. If your Answer to Questions 1, 2, and 3 in I Above are Yes, Should Nancy Richardson be Reinstated to the Position from Which She was Terminated?

Yes _____ No _____

Date:

_____
Signature of Foreperson

There were a number of serious problems with this complicated set of special questions that Judge Garrity had drafted. The first, and perhaps the most serious, was the way in which the judge was prohibiting the jurors from even reaching the second and third counts in Richardson's complaint (the "baby civil rights act" and common law covenant of good faith claims) unless they found for her at the first count, retaliation in violation of the employment discrimination law. We argued vociferously that the second and third counts were independent of the first: the baby civil rights act claim was premised on Richardson's free speech in general, which included but wasn't limited to her protest of BU's employment practices. In particular, her sympathy for homeless women and, as Richard Nesmith perceived it, her antipathy to capitalism, had indisputably triggered a negative reaction in the dean, and a letter from him to Richardson suggesting that these views of hers loomed large in his mind as he contemplated the final step of termination.

Likewise, Richardson's common law claim, based on the theory that affirmative action was a public policy in Massachusetts, and that firing someone for supporting that public policy was illegal, overlapped with but went beyond the retaliation theory of count one. This was because failing to follow affirmative action was not in itself generally viewed as a violation of the discrimination laws. If the jury found that Richardson was terminated for supporting affirmative action but not for protesting employment decisions that she reasonably believed to be discriminatory, she could win under count three but not count one.

Judge Garrity's special question form ignored these distinctions and, in essence, made the second two counts in the case superfluous. When I first brought this point to the judge's attention, however, he refused to make any change in the special questions as he had drafted them.

A reason for his refusal emerged a day into the deliberations. The jury had requested clarification of a procedural issue. In the course of answering its question the judge apparently decided to correct the previous day's directions, which had premised any consideration of counts two and three upon a plaintiff's verdict under count one. Taking the foreperson's copy of the special question form, the judge scribbled an "or No" after the "Yes" in questions II.1 and III.1, so that the form now read, "If your answers to Questions 1, 2 and 3 in I above are Yes or No . . ." But the judge refused to have these conditional clauses, which were now meaningless and could only sow confusion, deleted from the form. His explanation for this refusal: that the inadequacy of clerical help in the superior court made it impossible to get the questions retyped:

> The only difficulty was—again, if I could just give a cry of
> "Help" to the Supreme Judicial Court—I had to be more
> concerned about getting this damned thing typed than I was
> about the substance. That's how bad it is.

A second problem with the special questions had to do with the elusive legal concept of causation. In the Richardson case, as in human affairs generally, there was evidence of many different factors that motivated Nesmith's decision. Discrimination law—indeed most law that has to do with human motivation—recognized that single causes are rare. The prevailing standard in discrimination cases involving such "mixed motives" was whether an unlawful motive was a "determinative factor" in the decision. Under First Amendment jurisprudence, the standard is the more liberal "substantial factor."

I argued to Judge Garrity that his instructions to the jury, and most importantly his special questions, which unlike the several hours of oral instructions were in writing and would go with the jurors into their deliberations, should incorporate the "substantial factor" standard, since this was in essence a free speech case. At worst, the special questions ought to incorporate the "determinative factor" standard familiar in employment discrimination cases, instead of simply asking the jury whether Nesmith fired Richardson "because of" her voiced opposition to certain dubious hiring practices.

Garrity rejected the request: "That would be delightful if we were dealing with lawyers on the jury, and I guess we are not."

This judicial reaction may or may not have had the common-sense virtue that Judge Garrity attributed to it, but it did leave a certain inconsistency between the written special questions, which the jurors would have with them during deliberations, and the more evanescent oral instructions on the law, which the judge would deliver. Garrity may have simply been reflecting here the common wisdom that very little of that legal goobledygook in the oral instructions to juries penetrates, is remembered, or could be expected to. But the result of using simple "because of" language, with its implication that if Nesmith had any legitimate reasons he was off the hook, may have been disastrous for the plaintiff's chances. And Garrity's instructions to the jury on a related question of "but for" causation were to be equally distressing.

In arguing over count III, the common law–public policy claim defendants' counsel urged that they were entitled to an instruction that affirmative action was *not* clear public policy, while plaintiff's counsel of course urged just the reverse. Judge Garrity chose the middle ground, although he sided with the defense to the extent that, despite the legal existence of federally mandated affirmative action requirements, he was going to tell the jury "that the plaintiff has the burden of showing that there is a clear public policy in favor of affirmative action." When my co-counsel, Heidi Urich (from Palmer & Dodge), objected that "ultimately it is a legal question," not a question for the jury, whether "affirmative action is in and of itself a clear public policy in this state," Judge Garrity offered this bit of folk wisdom:

> You know something? It isn't a legal question. It is a political
> question, and affirmative action is not moral. It's not legal. It's

political, and it's going to be ultimately decided by the folk out there. And I hate to wave the flag of populism here, but that's pretty much the way to sort it out, is to give it to the jury.

Tuesday afternoon, December 21, 1982. Judge Garrity got his jury instructions off to a friendly start.

I am not waving the flag or anything, but when I say your responsibility begins and ends at doing justice, I really mean it. And what does justice mean here? Justice means essentially two things. It means that, when you deliberate this case and you reflect upon the evidence that was presented to you, you have to sort it all out, and you have to do it fairly, honestly, reasonably, without any bias or prejudice, without any emotions or sympathy. You have to call the shots as you see them. You have to call it the way it is.

When I was a little kid, Thursday nights my mom and dad used to let me stay up until nine o'clock and let me watch *Dragnet* and there was this wonderful character who was named Sergeant Friday, played by Jack Webb. And I see some of you older folks smile when I tell you about Sergeant Friday. And Sergeant Friday used to say about eight or nine or ten times during that television show, "I want nothing but the facts, ma'am." Do you remember that? Sure. That got some of you younger ones smiling.

And that's what we want from you. We want nothing but the facts. We want you to decide the case on the facts before you. That's half of your responsibility of doing justice. The other half of your responsibility of doing justice is to take the law as I give it to you, whether you like it or not, and there is no particular reason for you to like or dislike in any strong way the law that I am going to tell you you have to follow here.

[T]he issue is: Why was she fired? And that's what you have to decide, and that's at once easy to state, but it's very complicated; and I suggest it will be extremely difficult, as most cases are, when you deliberate them. . . .

Did Dean Nesmith terminate her for what she said, . . . or did, in opposition to what she claimed were discriminatory activities by the School of Theology and/or its failure to live up to affirmative action requirements? Was she fired for that, or was she fired because she didn't do her job? . . .

During this trial both counsel made lots of objections. It was a hotly contested case. But that's to be expected. There are some very deeply felt emotional positions here to consider on both sides, and on occasion counsel got angry, but that's what a trial is all about. Don't think that trials take place in a test tube. Don't think that trials take place as characterized on television. You've got real people, human beings, actively and vigorously and effectively representing their clients, and they are going to object, and that's their job to object. And they didn't over-object. They weren't obnoxious. They didn't under-object. They weren't pussycats. They objected, I think, precisely when they should have, and I made my rulings. . . .

Don't talk about the case during lunch. You will get indigestion. Wait until you finish. . . .

Let's get back to the witnesses for a second. . . . You can believe everything a witness testified to, you can disbelieve everything a witness testified to, or you can pick and choose. It's totally up to you. . . .

How do you do it? Well, you look at the witness. You size the witness up. You look at their demeanor. That doesn't mean how well they are dressed or whether or not they have absolutely horrible bow ties like mine. That has nothing to do with the person's credibility.

I am sure you all realize that the race or sex of a person, the articulateness of a person has nothing to do with a person's credibility. It doesn't mean a darn whether or not a person is white or black or happens to have red-colored skin like mine. That has nothing to do with believability of a witness.

After more down-to-earth advice of this sort, covering usual subjects, such as preponderance of the evidence (the standard of proof in a civil case), Judge Garrity moved on to the special questions.

[I]f you answer number 1 and number 2 yes, you have already found she was reasonable, and you have already found she was in good faith. The question now is: Why was she fired? Was she fired because of what she said and/or did in good faith and upon reasonable belief, or was she fired because she wasn't doing her job? What caused Dean Nesmith to decide to terminate Nancy Richardson? That's the gut question. . . .

[I]f you decide that he fired her for a lot of reasons, including what she said in writing, orally, and/or did as well, if that was the reason that he terminated her, the question then becomes: If she hadn't done that stuff, if she hadn't said or done things in opposition to what she reasonably and in good faith believed to be the BU School of Theology's discriminatory practices, if she hadn't done that, would she still have been fired? If the answer to that is no, then she has been fired because of what she said or did. Do you understand that? Is that clear? Most of you aren't shaking your heads. Do you want me to do it again? Okay. . . .

If you decide he fired her for a lot of reasons, including because she didn't do her job and because she said and/or did things in opposition to what she reasonably believed to be the School of Theology's discriminatory practices, and she did so in good faith, if she was fired for, if I could say, good reasons and bad reasons—I am sure the lawyers will pick on me for using that language, but I don't care because that's the way I speak, and that's the way you speak—if she was fired for good and bad reasons, then you have to determine whether or not she would have been fired if she hadn't done anything or said anything about what she reasonably believed, as you have already found if you answer the first two questions, yes, to be BU's discriminatory employment practices. Do you understand that now? Why was she fired? Why? Okay?

This second attempt at explaining the notion of "but for" causation was clear as mud. In fairness, however, this is a notoriously difficult concept to get across to juries, and a counterintuitive one. Human motives can rarely be so surgically sliced.

Garrity instructed the jury on damages, and then explained that even though legally he was the only one who could make a decision on injunctive relief (reinstatement), he could take their advice: "You may decide that, even though she is entitled to damages because she is right and he is wrong, there's just too much bad blood and it's dumb to have her reinstated, or you may decide it's only right that she be reinstated. . . . And I can tell you that it's going to be like Ivory soap. There is going to be a 99.44 percent chance that I will follow your guidance on that.

"Now let me check my notes," the judge continued. "Let me get into II. In order to consider Ms. Richardson's second claim, you have to answer all the questions in I, yes—reasonableness, good faith, and she was fired because she engaged in activity, spoken or written opposition again to what she reasonably believed to be Boston University engaging in discriminatory employment practices and/or failure to comply with affirmative action requirements.

"If you say yes to all that stuff, the question then becomes, if she was wrongfully discharged . . . is that a violation of her civil rights? . . .

"Now let me tell you what civil rights are. . . . What's a right here that Ms. Richardson claimed was threatened, intimidated, and/or coerced or attempted to be threatened, intimidated, and/or coerced? Freedom of speech. . . .

"Let me sum it up." Garrity now repeated the mistaken instruction that counts two and three depended entirely upon a plaintiff's verdict under count one. "Her second claim is that she reasonably believed that Boston University was both engaging in discrimination in employment on account of race and/or sex and was not complying with affirmative action requirements and that her good-faith activity by word and/or deed in opposition thereto caused her to be terminated, and that her termination violated her civil rights. . . ."

> Now, you note in question number 2 I don't speak to emotional distress, trauma, or dimunition in earning capacity. You don't get to II unless you find for Ms. Richardson under I, and I assume you will have, if you found for her under I, awarded her money under I. . . .

The instructions now became incoherent. Having mistakenly told the jury it could not find for Richardson on count II without also having found for her on count I, the judge proceeded to instruct differently on the burden of proof under count II. On count I, he'd told the jury, Richardson had to prove that "but for" Nesmith's retaliatory motive, she would not have been fired. As to count II, however:

> Miss Richardson has to show that her exercise of her civil rights played a substantial role in the decision to fire her. Once she shows that, the defendants have to show that they would have reached the same decision to fire her even in the absence of her protected conduct. In other words, if Nancy Richardson shows that her protected conduct—free speech, opinion—was a substantial factor in Dean Nesmith's decision and . . . the

defendants do not show that he would have made the same decision anyway, then Miss Richardson has carried her burden
with respect to her civil rights claim.

We had urged Judge Garrity to instruct the jury that the burden of
proof on this issue of "but-for causation" shifted to the defendants for
purposes of both counts I and II, once Richardson had shown that retaliation was a "substantial factor" in Nesmith's decision. After initially
rejecting our argument entirely, he apparently decided to accept it—for
count II only. But since the jury could not even reach count II without
having found for Richardson on count I (where she bore the entire burden
of proof), this instruction, to the extent that the jurors may have absorbed
it, was useless.

Moving to count III, Garrity again confounded it with count I, specifically telling the jurors that they could reach it only if they answered
all three subparts of question I affirmatively. Thus, instead of providing
an independent basis for a jury finding that BU had fired Richardson for
advocating what was clear public policy, affirmative action, the only
remaining issue under III was whether conduct by the defendants in
violation of the employment discrimination law was also "in contravention
of a clear public policy" (a tautology, at least). To make the circle complete, Garrity said, "Clear public policies are being against discrimination
in employment on account of race and/or sex and/or for affirmative action."

Are you with me? Now it becomes interesting: the issue of
damages. Should you award any damages if you decide that
Dean Nesmith was wrong in III? Yes, only if your award of
damages is different from any damages that you have previously awarded if you had decided previously to award damages. You have heard the term "double dipping" or "triple
dipping." My mother is a triple dipper: veteran's benefits,
MBTA pension, and social security. Nancy Richardson is not
entitled to triple dipping or double dipping. She is only entitled to one award of damages for the same thing. Do you understand that? Okay.

A short bench conference followed, to enable counsel to place on the
record any specific objections to the instructions that had just been delivered. I pointed out here that instead of referring to discrimination by
Boston University or Dean Nesmith in the special questions, Garrity had
at points limited his references to BU School of Theology or Dean Nesmith, thereby eliminating from consideration what Richardson's beliefs

may have been about arguably discriminatory acts by President Silber. These included the attack on Beverly Harrison and the erection of a higher entry standard for black tenure-track candidates like Stephen Reid. Judge Garrity's response was illuminating if contradictory:

> THE COURT: I disagree. I think you are absolutely right in terms of that, but, if you think I am going to change it in terms of the hassle I had in getting that typed—and I say this for the edification of the S.J.C. [the state Supreme Judicial Court]; it is awful here at the Superior Court; you have no idea; in case this case gets appealed—but I just cannot go through the hassle of getting that typed again, and I just refuse. Anything else?

Defendants' counsel now made a variety of objections, the last of which struck the judge as sufficiently frivolous to merit a response in kind.

> MR. PARROTT: May I just add two points, Your Honor? I think, as to your test on using the woman and the Scales of Justice, that it is not wholly fair to the defendant to only tip them one way, but to add what I understand is the full explanation: If she doesn't tip them or if they are tipped the other way, she hasn't carried her burden of proof.

> THE COURT: There is one question I have been dying to ask you during this trial. Where do you get those wonderful bow ties, and do you tie them yourself?

> MR. PARROTT: To the latter question, yes, sir.

> THE COURT: If you tie them yourself, forget it. You are much more competent than me legally, and now I find out you are much more competent than me in terms of your manual dexterity. I am jealous.

Richardson's attorneys, being female and thus tieless, had little to contribute to this exchange, and so remained awkwardly silent.

Returning to the jury, Judge Garrity sent them off to deliberate by explaining that "in a civil case, unlike a criminal case, you have to make your decisions by what we call a plurality as opposed to unanimously in a criminal case. A plurality verdict in a civil case is ten, eleven, or twelve of you. If ten, eleven, or twelve of you agree, you have got a verdict, one way or the other. . . . If less than ten of you agree, you are a hung jury. But don't worry. We won't do what they used to do in 1695, down at the Common, with juries that were hung in the courtroom, became hung on Beacon Hill. So that's not a problem."

The jury retired at 1:40 P.M. and was not heard from for the rest of the afternoon. The judge dismissed them at about 3:45, with compliments for their conscientiousness and restraint.

Late the next morning they requested their first bit of added judicial guidance. The question was a general surprise, and offered the first glimpse of how this group of twelve was handling the legal concepts in the case. The request read: "Instruction on the law as regards reasonable doubt when answering a yes or no question."

Garrity seemed amazed. "What do you mean by that? Are you asking me to redefine preponderance of the evidence? Because reasonable doubt has nothing to do with a civil trial. I thought I made that clear. . . . "

JUROR: Well, reasonable doubt—

THE COURT: I know I said it's not like a criminal case, where somebody—

JUROR: I think maybe we misconstrued that.

THE COURT: You didn't misconstrue anything. It's impossible for you people to misconstrue. I misstated it.

He went at it again. "In a civil case the plaintiff has to prove its case . . . by a fair preponderance of the credible evidence, which is fifty-one versus forty-nine, more likely than less likely, or the scale stuff. Does that clear that up?"

Juror Naumann Bassick, an elderly man who had apparently been the author of the confusion, said, "In the month of March we ran into a yes or no thing in which I was foreman of the jury. The judge instructed us—it was a patent case, it wouldn't be criminal, would it?"

Garrity: "No, civil."

"If it's civil, he instructed us that if you had a reasonable doubt on any yes or no questions, the answer should be no."

THE COURT: That's not exactly correct. The judge was wrong. It doesn't work that way. If it's fifty-fifty, if you can't make up your mind either way . . . then the plaintiff has not proved his, her, its, their case. Do you understand?

JURORS: Yes.

THE COURT: Okay. It's subtle. In fact, it's so subtle that you spend three years of law school figuring out these concepts, and I state this to the Supreme Judicial Court if they ever read the transcript: I think the charges in this state are out of it, that there is absolutely no appreciation for how people communicate with each other in 1982 on the part of the judiciary. We provide instructions at the conclusion of a jury trial, using to some extent archaic language, and we're typically unable, because we're not trained in communication skills, at least in sophisticated communication skills, to provide those kinds of concepts to you.

"Now," the judge continued, "Clarification of questionnaires that were handed to each member in the courtroom—"

MS. HEINS: Can we go to the sidebar for a minute?

THE COURT: No. . . . The question is: 1. If under Section I, Question 1 is answered no by a member, does he or she participate in the decision of the rest of the questions?

Yes. If you answer Roman number I, Question 1, no, if 10 or 11 or 12 of you answer that question no—right?—then you go to Roman numeral II. Do you understand that? Because that's the ball game as far as I is concerned.

Let's pick it up a little bit further. If you answer Roman numeral I, no, you go to Roman numeral II. I think I made a mistake on number I. I think that number I should read, "If your answer to Questions 1, 2 and 3 in I above are yes or no"—okay? Have you got that?—did the termination violate Miss Richardson's civil rights?

Okay? Let me see the original back and I'll put yes or no on that, over counsel for the defendants' objection.

The same as to Roman numeral III. Yes or no. Do you understand?

Are you with me so far?

JURORS: No.

THE COURT: Okay. No matter what you answer Roman numeral I, you have to independently determine—remember I said during my instructions, you have to consider each claim separately. Do you remember that?

Now, let's assume you decide that Nancy—let's assume that you decide number 1, Roman numeral I, no, you then go to Roman numeral II, number 1. Is that right?

JURORS: Yes.

THE COURT: And what you have to decide is—you've already decided that Nancy Richardson was unreasonable in her belief; if you answer I, 1, no, you've decided that she is unreasonable. Is that right?

THE JURORS: Right.

THE COURT: Then you go to Roman II, 1, and you have to decide, even though she was unreasonable, did her firing deprive her of her civil rights? Is that clear now?

THE JURORS: Yes.

Judge Garrity had thus decided, on the second day of deliberations, to rectify the error he had compounded many times over the previous day. Was this colloquy sufficient for the correction to sink in? Was it "clear now"?

Unlikely, for several reasons. First, even though the judge had now technically told them they could reach count II even if they found against Richardson on count I, the instructions of the day before had so keyed the elements of claims II and III to those of I that the latter two had no independent substance. The only kind of free speech Judge Garrity mentioned in his charge had to do with opposition to employment practices.

Further, even in his attempt at corrective instructions, Garrity undermined the free speech claim by assuming that to have said no to claim I the jury would have found Richardson's speech or beliefs unreasonable. This was wrong as a matter of fact; the jury could have found her reasonable but refused to find that Nesmith terminated her "because of" her opposition to discriminatory practices. Garrity's unfortunate example could also infect their thinking on count II. If Richardson was unreasonable, how could her civil rights have been violated? Or even if they were, who cares?

Third, the jury may have missed the import of this exchange entirely. When, the following day, the verdict was read by the clerk in open court, the yes or no correction was incorporated into count III but read only as a yes in count II. Any confusion on this score would have been understandable, since the "if" question was needless and made no sense once an "or no" had been added to the "yes."

Finally, there was no telling what questions on the verdict slip the jurors had already discussed and decided by the time the correction was made. If they had reached question II, their deliberations had been tainted by the improper condition.

After the jury resumed deliberations, plaintiff's counsel requested that the written special questions be retyped or else the entire "if" clause be deleted. Given Garrity's oral correction, it was now superfluous, and could only confuse the jury. It was here that the judge, acknowledging this mistake, nevertheless refused to do more about it because of inadequate secretarial help: "I had to be more concerned about getting this damned thing typed than I was about the substance. That's how bad it is."

December 23. At 11:20 A.M., the jurors had reached a verdict. The clerk read the special questions and answers:

In the case of Nancy Richardson versus Trustees of Boston University and Richard Nesmith, I, the plaintiff's first claim that her employment was terminated as a consequence of actions she took in good faith because of her reasonable belief that the defendants were engaging in discriminatory employment practices:

1. Did Nancy Richardson reasonably believe that Richard Nesmith and the Boston University School of Theology were engaging in discriminatory employment practices?

The answer is yes.

2. If your answer to question number 1 is yes, were actions Nancy Richardson took as a consequence of her reasonable belief that Richard Nesmith and the Boston University School of Theology were engaging in discriminatory employment practices taken by her in good faith?

The answer is yes.

3. If your answer to question number 2 is yes, did Richard Nesmith terminate Nancy Richardson's employment because of the actions she took in good faith as a consequence of her reasonable belief that Richard Nesmith and the Boston University School of Theology were engaging in discriminatory employment practices?

The answer is no.

The next question, question 4 [damages], they never answered.

THE COURT: That's appropriate.

THE CLERK: The plaintiff's second claim, that her civil rights were violated as a consequence of the defendants' interference with and/or attempts to interfere with statements she made and/or opinions she held in good faith because of her reasonable belief that the defendants were not complying with affirmative action requirements and/or engaging in discriminatory employment practices:

1. If your answer to questions 1, 2, and 3 above are yes, did Richard Nesmith's termination of Nancy Richardson's employment violate her civil rights?

The answer is no.

THE COURT: Why don't you just, to save time, read this right here, which is under Roman numeral III.

THE CLERK: If you answer the questions number 1, 2, and 3 in I above yes or no, was Nancy Richardson's employment terminated in contravention of a clear policy?

The answer is no.

THE COURT: Clear public policy.

THE CLERK: Clear public policy.

4. If your answer to questions number 1, 2, and 3 in I above are yes, should Nancy Richardson be reinstated to the position from which she was terminated?

The answer is no.

Garrity thanked the jurors. "It was a tough case for both sides. It was ably presented by both sides. I am satisfied that you did your job ably and well. You did justice.

"Thank you very much. I guess you can go off Christmas shopping right now, if you want, or you can go home."

The trial had been a close one; the deliberations harsh and exhausting. A glance at the verdict slip afterward revealed that on the crucial causation question (number 3 in part I) the answer yes had been checked, then erased.

CHAPTER 19

IT'S A POLITICAL QUESTION

THE jury found that Nancy Richardson was reasonable to believe that Boston University had engaged in illegal employment discrimination; but then they let the defendants off the hook by refusing to find that the dean fired her because of her opposition. Was this their idea of a compromise verdict? Had they cut the baby in half?

Of all the possible explanations for the jury verdict, perhaps Judge Garrity's had the most truth when he opined that "[i]t isn't a legal question. It's a political question, and affirmative action is not moral. It's not legal. It's political, and it's going to be ultimately decided by the folk out there."

We had understood this, of course, from the start, which accounted for the attempt to educate the jurors on affirmative action during *voir dire*, and for the careful efforts throughout to have plaintiff's witnesses testify to the reasons for affirmative action, the principles behind it, the meaning of "inclusiveness," the re-evaluation of "credentialing." And the irony was that the jurors in their verdict did seem to accept Richardson's analysis of events, and to reject the defense's attempts at self-justification through a more-liberal-than-thou approach of blackboards full of minority and female names, assertions of the old BU defenses (Reid withdrew his application; Harrison couldn't take the heat), and canonization of Nesmith the civil rights fighter.

Why then did the jurors refuse to find that the dean fired Richardson for her opposition, in the face of substantial evidence that this was exactly what he did? Had Parrott and company succeeded in muddying the waters of causation sufficiently by merging into the generalized defense of poor job performance elements both of Nesmith's strictly administrative beefs and of his fundamental dissatisfaction over Richardson's refusal to be an arm of the dean's office? Had the defense so skillfully merged the two and buried the retaliation factors in language about "representation" and "accountability," that the jurors could not distill the suspect from the nonsuspect motives in the case?

Had the defense persuaded the jury, *Pickering*-style, that because of the importance of Richardson's job in the administrative scheme, her free speech rights, including her protection against retaliation for opposing employment discrimination, had to give way to the institution's policy needs, as defined by Nesmith?

Were Judge Garrity's instructions on causation hopelessly confusing, or did the emphasis in the special interrogatories on a single cause (the "because of" language) lead them to believe that if *any* lawful motives were involved the defendants were off the hook?

Finally, had the jury simply failed to follow the admittedly complicated theory of the plaintiff's case, whose convolutions were made even more mystifying by Nesmith's indirect speaking style? Were all those memos and recommendations—the juice of academic life—meaningless to the rest of the working world? In short, was this just not a jury case?

Politics, theatrics, and confusion all played their part in this verdict.

Theatrics is of course the essence of a jury trial and if both the attorneys and witnesses are not skilled as actors no quantity of intellectual brilliance or legal acumen will go far toward achieving the just result. Richardson was quoted by one newspaper midway in the proceedings to the effect that a trial was about theater, not justice; and it was evident that in this department the Parrott-Nesmith team really had the upper hand. Parrott was a dapper, impeccably dressed, graying veteran trial lawyer. Nesmith was an experienced preacher, with a mellifluous voice and metaphorical style. Both were authoritative-looking males, well into middle age. They *looked* like people who hold power and speak with authority in the world.

Richardson was not a performer. Her speech did not flow eloquently, was full of the "sort ofs" and "kind ofs" that pepper ordinary talk. I had been practicing law for three years and had handled only one previous jury trial—a minor criminal case that took half a day to try. I had not mastered the rhetoric of words versus deeds and other venerable chestnuts of jury trial work.

On the other hand, the performance gap may not have been critical. One of the two young men on the jury, Michael Hastings, a welder at General Dynamics, later told Richardson that he and the other jurors were impressed with the "hotshot lawyers" on both sides.

If acting is crucial, the script is no less so. To the extent that our plot was difficult to follow, and the jurors got lost in a mass of memos and a semi-incomprehensible tape, we suffered. After all, we had the burden of proof.

The defense presented a simple, short case, for which the jury, after eight days, had to be grateful. There was one witness, the boss, who simply testified that, although he was the soul of patience, after four years and innumerable warnings, he finally had to admit that this employee didn't make the grade. The testimony was well orchestrated, easy to understand. As one juror, Margaret MacDonald, later told me:

> The dean said she didn't perform her duties as he wanted her to. He was her boss and she didn't do as he wanted. All the other charges seemed liked making a case to discredit him. We discussed the law, but our talk always came back to [the fact that] she didn't comply with his wishes.

Richardson may not have been a sympathetic enough plaintiff. She was not herself a victim of race or sex discrimination. The victims— Reid, Harrison, Nelle Slater, Julius Scott—were absent. Did the jury perceive Richardson, as Judge Garrity phrased it in his comments outside the presence of the jury, as just "griping"?

And griping, to boot, about difficult questions such as the dean's ability to work with "strong women." How many of the eight female jurors considered themselves "strong women," or even liked "strong women"? Again, juror MacDonald's comments are revealing:

> Maybe if she'd been more discreet she would have won. She just went a little overboard. She took the initiative on her own. She was very poised, very sure of herself, maybe too sure of herself. If she'd just shown some nervousness. She appeared very strong. She just didn't come across right. Maybe if she shed a few tears. She should've put down that veil.

Ada Arthur, when asked later by Richardson why the jury thought Nesmith had fired her, replied, "Because you were a rabble-rouser?"

Confusion—whether because of the judge's instructions or the inherent complexity of the case or both—characterized the jury deliberations. This was clear early on from their initial question regarding reasonable doubt, a standard of proof that is wholly inapplicable to civil cases. Likewise, Eara James, one of the two black women who deliberated, reflected a misunderstanding of the basic theory of the plaintiff's case when she said afterward:

The school did practice discrimination, but she wasn't discriminated against. If they [the victims of discrimination, Reid, Harrison, etc.] had been there too, she would have won, but it wasn't against her. . . .

He violated others' civil rights, not hers.

If, after all was said and done, the jurors thought this was a discrimination case rather than a free speech case, that was truly a level of confusion beyond anyone's anticipation.

There was no question that the judge's instructions and special questions were confusing. "It was confusing the way he [the judge] had set it up," Eara James said. " 'If you answer yes . . .'—very confusing to me."

A few people did want to award her money. Afterwards, we decided the school wasn't guilty, so we couldn't. She should have at least gotten some money. We felt bad about it.

I thought she should have been reinstated to a different job, and compensated for the time in between. But we couldn't do it because of the way the paper set it up.

Margaret MacDonald confirmed this:

The judge gave us the papers; we were a little bit confused. Then we looked back at the papers and got clear. The special questions were very confusing. Everybody interpreted it a different way. Without the questions we would have come out differently. They confused us no end. . . .

We couldn't decide for her on two or three; we had to follow number one. That's the way we thought we had to. That's the way the judge wanted it.

Michael Hastings agreed, saying that the forms dominated the deliberations, forced the jury to put aside the affirmative action issue and focus simply on whether Richardson should have been more supportive of her boss. The forms "took everything away from the whole case."

At least one juror, Ada Arthur, thought that a verdict for Richardson would have required her reinstatement at BUSTH—probably an unpalatable result for all concerned. Arthur was sorry about the verdict but felt that the odds were against Richardson: "To tell the truth, you are an individual and you're fighting a whole school. You had a lot of courage but it was against you. . . . Believe me, my dear, I wouldn't want to go back to a job like that. They would make you very, very, unhappy."

Juror MacDonald also expressed regret:

Some of us were on the border; I happened to be one of them. I fought it tooth and nail. Then I got convinced. Believe me, it was a very fine line. We really battled it around. I didn't sleep a couple of nights. It really felt bad afterwards.

Hastings thought the outcome sad and unjustified, and emerged from the experience feeling guilty. But the majority of jurors, he said, simply felt that Richardson should have been more deferential to her supervisor. The "middle and high class people" supported Nesmith. Hastings differed with them: working for a living shouldn't mean that people "can't stand up for what they believe."

To the extent that the jurors did understand that the case was about free speech, it seems that a majority of them bought the poor job performance defense. Eara James said, "Parrott took the mistakes she made and he used it against her. That was very effective."

About the building [515 Park Drive], she never paid a visit to the building; she tried to solve the problems without visiting. And then there were two black students who didn't come because of the financial aid. She went against trying to help them.

Ms. James was responding here to testimony regarding two separate events. There was a memo in evidence regarding three black applicants who had been accepted but had not come to STH, apparently for financial reasons. Richardson had also testified, in response to cross-examination, that she had objected to the dean's desire to deviate from the financial aid policy formula in order to attract favored applicants to the school. But this disagreement did not relate to race, and Richardson had not been "against trying to help" black students. The defense had succeeded in combining the two events in this juror's mind through Richard Nesmith's testimony that Richardson was not "flexible" in "perceiv[ing] some unique situations that moved you beyond policy."

Juror James also had difficulty deciding where she stood on the dean's veracity, which, as Parrott had emphasized in his summation, was crucial to the defense case. "Nobody thought he was lying, as far as I could see," James said to me at one point. "Supposedly religious people, you'd think he'd try to speak the truth. She also believed she was doing what was right. He wanted her out of there. The students trusted her more than they trusted him." But her comments revealed ambivalence:

> I think that he was well instructed by his lawyer. I would watch his eyes. Some things he said weren't the truth. He didn't tell the whole truth. It was reflected in his face. Truth is in a person's eyes.

> But the evidence was there on paper. He used the documents against her.

> We knew some mistakes were made. This guy [Nesmith] was really terrible. But we felt that school will be more cautious now.

Michael Hastings was less self-contradictory on this point. He did not like the dean, "could see right through him."

On the crucial question of causation, the dean's articulation of "legitimate nondiscriminatory reasons" for firing Richardson apparently had the desired effect. They supplied those on the jury who already leaned toward Nesmith with ready ammunition to argue that, given his feelings about these matters, plaintiff simply had not proven, indeed could not prove, that the disputes about affirmative action and employment discrimination "caused" his decision. Even if we had proved him wrong in various of his assumptions about her handling of financial aid and housing, even if he never bothered to get his facts straight, he was still within his rights as long as he fired her "because of" these mistaken assumptions, not "because of" retaliation.

The phrasing of the special questions to the jury (*"because of* the actions she took in good faith") assisted the defense, too, for they suggested that we had to prove that a single motive caused the dean to do what he did. Thus, just as Parrott had said in summation, we had to prove that the dean was a consistent, calculating liar; we had to eliminate almost all of the reasons he had articulated from the case. Whatever the jury might have made—or retained—of the bewildering instructions on mixed motives and "but for" causation, their verdict slip asked only whether Nesmith had fired Richardson "because of" her free speech on employment matters. The law's sophisticated comprehension of multiple human motives, embraced however inadequately in the determinative or substantial factor standards, was not put to the jury in the Richardson case.

Ultimately, as the parties and the judge knew, political predilections were the driving force in this jury verdict, and the jurors' expressions of anger and feelings of exhaustion reflected that an emotional, political battle had been fought. Michael Hastings told Richardson that she had been right to follow her conscience. He lost a battle with the majority of jurors who were "upper class and expected you to obey your boss no matter what."

Eara James confirmed that this was the political dynamic:

Another thing against her, she took it to the students. She had her superiors; she should have gone to them.

Tying the dean's hands would open the door for others to do the same. He would lose respect. I was involved in a similar situation with the Masons. The Grand Matron had a fight with the Grand Patron. She took it in the wrong direction. Like me at work. I have a supervisor who has to take his orders from people. I can tell him he's wrong, but I can't tell the people below him. The law may protect you on paper, but it just doesn't work.

Margaret MacDonald agreed:

The first two questions [in the special interrogatories] were not terribly difficult. Right away we agreed. The third was the one that nipped it in the bud. We came to the conclusion that he was her boss. . . .

Was the dean telling the truth? In certain aspects, no; you had proved he wasn't. You proved beyond a shadow of doubt that he was avoiding issues, maybe even lying. But even then, he was dean; he had the upper hand.

After a judgment is entered, the losing side has thirty days to file a notice of appeal. Our decision not to appeal the Richardson verdict was physical, emotional, and political rather than legal. We felt that legal errors in the instructions and special questions to the jury provided ample grounds for appeal. On the other hand, the *Pickering* defense—presented only obliquely to the jury—would undoubtedly have provided big appellate ammunition to BU. Richardson after all had been a member of Nesmith's "administrative team." *He* defined her function: as administration spokesperson and flak-catcher. Many a federal court decision had already held that even affirmative action officers in management positions could be fired for rebelling from the company line. Surely, BU could argue, had the tables been turned—had Nesmith been the affirmative action enthusiast and Richardson the foot-dragger—he would have had a right to get rid of her. This was, of course, the fundamental perplexity that beset Richardson's case from the start.

The case had been undertaken because those still at the School of Theology, and others loyal to it, did not want to acquiesce without struggle in yet another termination of another valuable ally. The Richardson litigation became symbolic, not because her supporters claimed it was, but because Dean Nesmith had made it so, explicitly, most every time he talked or wrote about the decision. Much was at stake, but it was at stake at STH, not in the courthouse.

So when, on the twenty-ninth day after the verdict, the final decision had to be made, it appeared that the energy and élan were no longer there. The students had begun to scatter; new ones had only heard of Nancy Richardson as a name on an impassioned leaflet. Professor Bob Treese was near retirement, with Paul Deats not far behind him. Jim Fraser, whose contract was not renewed, had already moved to the University of Massachusetts. Lynn Rhodes was off to join Stephen Reid at the Pacific School of Religion in Berkeley. Elizabeth Bettenhausen and Linda Clark, both still on the STH faculty, faced an uphill and uncertain battle for tenure.

And Richardson, who had been persuaded to pursue this difficult, exhausting, and expensive case, to endure the mudslinging and insults, because her issue had become symbolic to those remaining at STH, had surely done her share. She had little stomach for repeating the experience. And she had much to do that faced forward, not back. The new Women's Theological Center in Boston, which she headed, seemed a more constructive project and demanded her energy.

Even a successful appeal, moreover, would mean only a retrial. And what sense would that make, two or three years down the road? The troops were feeling too scattered, depleted, discouraged, to derive much sustenance from the prospect of a prolonged appeal based on what seemed to be a bunch of legal technicalities, with the ultimate reward, perhaps, a chance to go through it all again. The jury had heard the testimony and found for Nesmith; did the details of legal instructions or the wording on verdict forms really make a difference?

Of course, forgoing an appeal may in its way have been wise. Our claims had been novel ones; BU's objections to their viability, generally rejected by the liberal Judge Garrity, could well have persuaded a higher court. An appeal could have backfired by generating a decision severely narrowing the scope of the state civil rights act or the common law, or announcing, as Mr. Parrott had so often urged, that affirmative action was not public policy.

"It was a hard decision," Eara James said of the deliberations. "People changed their minds overnight. By the second night it was 9–3 against her. But the next morning two guys changed their minds, so it was 7–5. We had to go at it again. Then with the press of the holiday two more gave up. I wouldn't want to go through it again. It takes its toll on you."

A jury trial is not a safe business for anybody, particularly intellectuals, academics, idealists, political minorities. But playing out the School of Theology's sometimes rarefied disputes over the philosophy of affirmative action in the Suffolk County Superior Court may not have been quite so lunatic as it sometimes seemed in retrospect. We went into the case with eyes open, comprehending that it was political, and that politics would largely decide the outcome. We felt that the investment was worth it, not only because we might win, not only because Richard Nesmith should not simply get away with what he did to Richardson, and STH, without answering for it, not only because there were people at the school who were carrying on that debate, and for whom Richardson's termination had resonance. Despite its difficulty, affirmative action is, as Judge Garrity knew, a concept and an issue and a debate that must be carried to people on juries and in courtrooms and in the mass media. It's a political question.

CHAPTER 20

THE SECOND RECONSTRUCTION

THE U.S. Supreme Court's multiple opinions in the *Bakke* case represented a holding action, a political compromise, a Solomonic decision. Its *Weber* and *Fullilove* cases, though likewise narrowly and cautiously written, approved and encouraged affirmative action. Lower courts continued to order race-conscious remedies and settlements. And federal agencies, in their cumbersome way, continued to monitor the affirmative action plans of government contractors and fund beneficiaries, and to perform compliance reviews.

It was not until June 12, 1984, that the Supreme Court delivered its first serious blow to race-conscious affirmative action. *Firefighters Local No. 1784 v. Stotts* was a case about seniority in employment, about the clash, during a period of economic downturn and layoffs, between vested seniority rights of white workers and claims to remedial justice on the part of their more recently hired minority counterparts. In the *Stotts* case those minority firefighters had been hired because of a consent decree, a settlement entered to end a race discrimination Title VII lawsuit.

But the consent decree had not anticipated, or if it anticipated, had not dealt with, layoffs, and so when the time came, the minority beneficiaries of the settlement would, under the standard collective bargaining seniority system, be the first to go. This layoff dilemma was replicated in hundreds of employment settings nationwide where affirmative action had produced its first tentative improvements. In *Stotts*, the federal trial court, to preserve the purpose and effect of the settlement, entered an order requiring affirmative action in the layoff process. The Supreme Court reversed this order.

The Court majority, per Justice White, said that Title VII, because of the special protection it extends to "bona fide seniority systems," did not authorize the affirmative action layoff order. But there was broader language in the *Stotts* opinion, language about the limitations that Title VII imposes on judges' remedial power, language that inspired great hopes in the new occupants of the Reagan White House and Justice Department, and equally great fears in the proponents of affirmative action.

"[M]ere membership in the disadvantaged class," wrote Justice White (who, it will be recalled, had sided with the Brennan group in *Bakke*),

> is insufficient to warrant a seniority award; each individual must prove that the discriminatory practice had an impact on him. . . . Here, there was no finding that any of the blacks protected from layoff had been a victim of discrimination and no award of competitive seniority to any of them. . . . It therefore seems to us that . . . the Court of Appeals [which had affirmed the trial court's order] imposed on the parties as an adjunct of settlement something that could not have been ordered had the case gone to trial and the plaintiffs proved that a pattern or practice of discrimination existed.

> Our ruling . . . that a court can award competitive seniority only when the beneficiary of the award has actually been a victim of illegal discrimination is consistent with the policy behind §706(g) of Title VII, which affects the remedies available in Title VII litigation. That policy, which is to provide make-whole relief only to those who have been actual victims of illegal discrimination, was repeatedly expressed by the sponsors of the Act during the congressional debates. Opponents of the legislation that became Title VII charged that if the bill were enacted, employers could be ordered to hire and promote persons in order to achieve a racially-balanced work force even though those persons had not been victims of illegal discrimination. Responding to these charges, Senator Humphrey explained the limits on a court's remedial powers as follows:
>> "No court order can require hiring, reinstatement, admission to membership, or payment of back pay for anyone who was not fired, refused employment or advancement or admission to a union by an act of discrimination forbidden by this title. . . ."
> An interpretive memorandum of the bill entered into the Congressional Record by Senators Clark and Case likewise made clear that a court was not authorized to give preferential

treatment to non-victims. "No court order can require hiring, reinstatement, admission to membership, or payment of back pay for anyone who was not discriminated against in violation of [Title VII]."

These statements of Senators Humphrey, Clark, and Case, made during the legislative battle over Title VII, had in the past been relied upon in judicial opinions dissenting from the approval of affirmative action remedies. To use this language in the *Stotts* majority opinion was startling. For affirmative action, often in the form of specific hiring or promotion goals, had been ordered as an across-the-board remedy for classwide discrimination so frequently that it hardly raised a legal eyebrow anymore. In such class action suits, individualized proof that thousands of single plaintiffs were the victims of thousands of single acts of discrimination had not been required as a prerequisite to classwide relief, nor, obviously, could it realistically be. Indeed, in *United Steelworkers v. Weber*, just four years earlier, the Court had relied on other portions of the voluminous legislative history of Title VII to emphasize its consistency with voluntary job preferences for those historically victimized by racism. The comments by Senator Humphrey, and the Clark-Case memorandum, explained the *Weber* Court, "were not addressed to temporary, voluntary, affirmative action measures undertaken to eliminate manifest racial imbalance in traditionally segregated job categories."

The Reagan Justice Department seized eagerly upon the broad language in *Stotts* that "make-whole relief" is available "only to those who have been actual victims of illegal discrimination." The Justice Department now began arguing in courts, in negotiating sessions, and in the public arena that the *Stotts* opinion heralded a major change in civil rights law. Henceforth, said the administration, any race-conscious affirmative action preference was unlawful, unless justified as a specific remedy for a specific individual victimized by a specific discriminatory act—at which point, of course, it is no longer an affirmative action preference at all.

The Civil Rights Division of the Justice Department, headed by William Bradford Reynolds, began a two-pronged attack on the many affirmative action settlements that it had, under previous administrations, laboriously negotiated. Letters from Justice went out to fifty-one state and local governments (including Boston) instructing them to modify their affirmative action hiring plans in response to *Stotts*. Most municipalities either ignored or explicitly defied these instructions. The Department encouraged legal attacks by white employees on all aspects of such plans, and intervened in support of these plaintiffs where it could.

The U.S. Equal Employment Opportunity Commission now began a review of its former reliance on statistics in investigating discrimination charges. The built-in headwinds–business necessity analysis, spawned by the Supreme Court's 1972 opinion in *Griggs v. Duke Power Company*, was attacked by Reagan Civil Rights Commission staff director Linda Chavez because it put pressure on employers "to eliminate valid tests in favor of quota selection." In August of 1985, plans were announced to repeal all of the numerically-keyed affirmative action requirements for contractors doing business with the federal government. The applicability of those requirements had already been narrowed several years before when the administration increased the threshold amount of the federal contract that would trigger a contractor's affirmative action obligations.

Did *Stotts* really mean all that Mr. Reynolds and company said it did? Or was it just a narrow decision with some unfortunately ambiguous language, a decision limited to seniority and layoffs and the remedial power of Title VII courts? The Lawyers Committee for Civil Rights Under Law, the NAACP Legal Defense and Education Fund, other longtime legal advocates of affirmative action, and many of the local governments whose plans were now under attack, argued that *Stotts* was so limited, and the federal courts generally seemed to agree. Certainly if the Supreme Court had intended to overrule *United Steelworkers v. Weber*, which four years before had upheld a racial quota in admissions to a craft worker training program, it would have said so.

But there were further ominous signs. In January of 1985 three Supreme Court justices dissented from a denial of certiorari (a refusal to review) in one of the many cases that challenged affirmative action remedies post-*Stotts*. The case involved serious statistical disparities between white and minority candidates in a civil service correction-officers exam, and the State of New York's decision to raise the scores of the minority applicants by establishing two separate grading curves. The state's action, although voluntary, was motivated in part by the fact that two previous exams had been challenged as discriminatory, and in part by its belief that minorities would perform equally well in the job. The voluntary plan had been upheld by the federal court of appeals, relying on *Weber*.

The three Supreme Court justices who wanted to review this case wrote that they doubted that *Weber*, a Title VII decision, should apply to government employers whose hiring practices are challenged under the Equal Protection Clause of the Fourteenth Amendment. "This Court has never taken the position that, consistent with the restraints of the Fourteenth Amendment, a State agency may establish preferential classifications on the basis of race in the absence of rulings by an appropriate body that constitutional or statutory violations have occurred."

The justices who expressed this view included the eminently predictable William Rehnquist, but also then Chief Justice Burger, who had written the decision upholding a quota in *Fullilove v. Klutznick*, and Byron White, who had approved race-conscious affirmative action in *Bakke*, *Weber*, and *Fullilove*. If, as the dissent of these three suggested, the tide was turning, then whatever anguished debates were still occurring, at Boston University or elsewhere, over what affirmative action truly meant, and how best to implement its remedies, would become largely theoretical.

Several months later, the Supreme Court did accept the first of what would be a trilogy of affirmative action cases to be decided in 1986. The facts of this case were so weak that the granting of certiorari generated widespread fear in the civil rights community that the Court had picked the case, of the many it had to choose from, precisely in order to demonstrate the infirmities of affirmative action plans that are voluntarily negotiated by government employers. For in *Wygant v. Jackson Board of Education* there was virtually nothing in the factual record to show a history of racial discrimination in the hiring of teachers that might justify preferences for minorities under the standards the Court had earlier set forth in *Bakke* and *Fullilove*. Although there had been a history of complaints about racial discrimination in the Jackson, Michigan, school system, and there had been significant statistical disparities before the affirmative action program began, the earlier complaints had been settled, and what facts existed to show a history of discrimination had not been entered in the court record in the *Wygant* case. Instead, the federal judge who heard this "reverse discrimination" suit by a number of white teachers, challenging a section of their collective bargaining agreement that injected race as a factor in layoff decisions, dismissed the claims without a trial, on a very sparse record, and the federal appeals court affirmed.

What the Supreme Court had before it, then, was a relatively clearcut racial preference, voluntarily agreed to, apparently without adequate historical justification. Under the collective bargaining contract, layoffs were to be made in order of seniority, except that the existing percentage of minority teachers was not to be reduced. Since minority teachers generally had less seniority, indeed were largely beneficiaries of the school system's recent affirmative action efforts in hiring, some of them would be retained while white teachers with greater seniority would be laid off.

The school system's affirmative action goals, moreover, were keyed not to the percentage of qualified minority teachers in the area's labor pool, but to the percentage of minority students. This was not an unknown technique in school desegregation remedies where teachers as well as students had been segregated, and there was certainly sociological support for the importance of same-race role models for children. But given the Supreme Court's rejection of similar justifications for racial preferences in *Bakke* several years before, the way the Jackson Board of Education and its teachers union had arrived at their statistical goals was an additional source of concern for those defending the lower court decisions in *Wygant*, or at least hoping to limit the damage that a Supreme Court reversal might to do affirmative action generally.

A final ominous note in *Wygant* was that this was a layoff case. Under Title VII, seniority systems, and layoffs based on seniority, had special protection; that was the narrow reason for the Court's holding in *Stotts*. Under the Fourteenth Amendment, applicable to state and local governments like the city of Jackson, seniority and layoffs did not have any such special status, but the fact of the matter was that the Supreme Court seemed to be particularly sensitive to the harms suffered and resentments harbored by whites who were laid off from jobs they already had. Somehow race preferences in hiring did not seem to create the same level of political turmoil, or the same judicial solicitude. That the Supreme Court had taken a layoff case to make what would probably be a major statement about affirmative action, in a situation where the U.S. Justice Department for the first time was arguing strenuously against any sort of race-consciousness at all, gave ample reason for concern.

No sooner were the briefs filed in *Wygant* than the Supreme Court took two additional affirmative action cases for review. *Firefighters v. Cleveland* and *Sheet Metal Workers v. EEOC* both had much stronger factual records than *Wygant*, which gave some cause for hope that the Justice Department's arguments for total color blindness would not prevail. On the other hand, with *Wygant* as the lead case, the more pessimistic among affirmative action advocates could reasonably fear that the Court intended to do its worst damage first; the facts in *Wygant*, and thus the justifications for race-conscious remedies, were weak. Then the Court could apply its new rules in terse opinions to the more sympathetic facts of the *Cleveland* and *Sheet Metal Workers* cases.

That the Court certainly intended to make a major statement was evident now from its acceptance of three cases whose facts and procedural postures spanned the various situations in which the affirmative action issue arises. *Wygant* involved a voluntary (not court-ordered) layoff plan, agreed to by a local government and thus raising questions not merely under a statute (Title VII) but under the Fourteenth Amendment to the U.S. Constitution. *Local 93, International Association of Firefighters v. Cleveland* involved a consent decree, a voluntary settlement but approved by a court and with the force of a court order, in a Title VII race discrimination lawsuit originally brought by the Vanguards, an organization of black and Hispanic firefighters. The predominantly white union, relying primarily upon *Stotts*, was now claiming the consent decree's numerical goals for promotion of minority firefighters violated Title VII.

The third case, *Local 28 of the Sheet Metal Workers' International Association v. Equal Employment Opportunity Commission*, involved court-ordered goals for admission to an apprenticeship program that the union had intransigently attempted to maintain as a white prerogative in the face of increasing anger and impatience from the federal court. The union in this case challenged the affirmative action remedy on both statutory (Title VII) and constitutional grounds. An irony in the case was that it had been brought by the EEOC, an agency of a federal government that now so adamantly opposed affirmative action in any form.

Wygant was decided on May 19, 1986. The justices split a number of different ways; there were five separate opinions. By a vote of five to four, the Court struck down the Jackson layoff plan. But more importantly, the Court announced its continuing approval, in proper circumstances, of race-conscious affirmative action remedies. Such remedies are justified under the Constitution, wrote Justice Powell, where there is "convincing evidence of prior discrimination." In *Wygant* the Court found no such evidence; moreover, the layoff plan was not "narrowly tailored" to achieve the remedial purpose:

> We have recognized . . . that in order to remedy the effects of prior discrimination, it may be necessary to take race into account. As part of this Nation's dedication to eradicating racial discrimination, innocent persons may be called upon to bear some of the burden of the remedy. "When effectuating a limited and properly tailored remedy to cure the effect of prior discrimination, such a 'sharing of the burden' by innocent parties is not impermissible."

> Significantly, none of the cases [in which such remedies were approved] involved layoffs. Here, by contrast, the means chosen to achieve the Board's asserted purposes is that of laying off nonminority teachers with greater seniority in order to retain minority teachers with less seniority. We have previously expressed concern over the burden that a preferential layoffs

scheme imposes on innocent parties. See *Firefighters v. Stotts.*
. . . In cases involving valid *hiring* goals, the burden to be
borne by innocent individuals is diffused to a considerable extent among society generally. Though hiring goals may burden
some innocent individuals, they simply do not impose the
same kind of injury that layoffs impose. Denial of a future employment opportunity is not as intrusive as loss of an existing
job.

Many of our cases involve union seniority plans with employees who are typically heavily dependent on wages for their
day-to-day living. Even a temporary layoff may have adverse
financial as well as psychological effects. A worker may invest
many productive years in one job and one city with the expectation of earning the stability and security of seniority. "At
that point, the rights and expectations surrounding seniority
make up what is probably the most valuable capital asset that
the worker 'owns,' worth even more than the current equity in
his home." . . . Layoffs disrupt these settled expectations in a
way that general hiring goals do not.

While hiring goals impose a diffuse burden, often foreclosing
only one of several opportunities, layoffs impose the entire
burden of achieving racial equality on particular individuals,
often resulting in serious disruption of their lives. That burden
is too intrusive. We therefore hold that, as a means of accomplishing purposes that otherwise may be legitimate, the Board's
layoff plan is not sufficiently narrowly tailored. Other, less intrusive means of accomplishing similar purposes—such as the
adoption of hiring goals—are available. For these reasons, the
Board's selection of layoffs as the means to accomplish even a
valid purpose cannot satisfy the demands of the Equal Protection Clause.

Justice Powell's argument here, although politically canny, ignores
the problem that led to affirmative action in layoffs to begin with. Where
the job market is shrinking, not expanding, hiring goals don't do a great
deal of good. A few years earlier, this Powell opinion in *Wygant* would
have been viewed as a defeat for affirmative action in principle and for
minority job gains in the real world. It is a measure of the political distance
traveled backward since the heyday of enthusiasm for affirmative action,
even since the Supreme Court's decision in *Weber*, that *Wygant* was greeted
with relief and jubilation in the civil rights community.

After *Wygant*, the other two 1986 affirmative action decisions, handed down on July 2, were anticlimactic. Justice Brennan was the author of both decisions, and their language was considerably more generous to the long-sought goal of racial equality than Powell's in *Wygant* had been. In the *Sheet Metal Workers* case Brennan took some pleasure in reminding readers of the Justice Department's change of position on affirmative action, and on the legislative history of Title VII since the days of *Weber*. Reagan appointee Sandra Day O'Connor provided a crucial vote upholding the affirmative action remedies in both cases.

Despite the apparent clarity of the signals sent by the *Wygant–Firefighters–Sheet Metal* trilogy in 1986, the media unleashed a near-sensationalist fanfare when in March of the following year the Supreme Court for the first time approved an affirmative action plan that benefited women. The Santa Clara, California, Transportation Agency had never had a woman in any of its 238 skilled craft worker jobs until Diane Joyce was promoted to the position of road dispatcher in 1980. Seven applicants had been deemed qualified for this job, having accumulated the necessary skill and experience, and scored above seventy points on an interview. Two men scored seventy-five; Diane Joyce, seventy-three. One of these men, Paul Johnson, sued.

What was fascinating about the reportage of this decision, in which Justice Brennan's majority opinion reaffirmed the ruling in *Weber* that voluntary affirmative action plans did not necessarily violate Title VII, was that the press almost uniformly trumpeted it as an approval of hiring a "less qualified woman" over a "more qualified" man. Despite a long discussion that I had about the case with a Boston TV reporter in which we fully agreed on the absurdity of this description, her station that night nevertheless (and I suspect over her objection) led off with the wire services' "less qualified" characterization. And *The New York Times* lead article the next day piously reported that the Supreme Court had ruled that "employers may sometimes favor women and minorities over better-qualified men and whites."

Not a word in the Supreme Court decision supported this loaded characterization of the case. (It was, however, the central theme in Justice Scalia's vehement dissent.) Justice Brennan, in the majority opinion, went out of his way to emphasize that Joyce and Johnson were equally qualified, that in fact her marginally lower score on an oral interview conducted by men may have been attributable to the expressed view of one such man that she was a "rebel-rousing, skirt-wearing person." The meaningless two-point difference in score in a subjective interview process controlled by males actually served to highlight the very point that most of the media so assiduously missed: the irony, indeed latent bigotry, that often resides in conclusory descriptions of competency or qualifications.

The *Johnson* case involved no quotas and only the softest of numerical goals. A Supreme Court decision a month earlier, carrying the mellifluous name of *United States v. Paradise*, received less notice but went further, upholding a temporary fifty-percent promotion requirement that had been set by a federal court to remedy a particularly stubborn bias against black employees of the Alabama Department of Public Safety. Despite the imposition of a less rigorous affirmative action remedy in 1972 (after a finding of racism so pervasive that not one black person had been hired at any level in the department for thirty-seven years), Alabama still had no black state troopers at or above the rank of corporal in 1981 when the *Paradise* court ordered its quota.

The U.S. Department of Justice, which had originally intervened in the *Paradise* case on the plaintiff's side, had by now switched loyalties and argued to the Supreme Court that the fifty-percent affirmative action remedy was an impermissible attempt to impose a particular racial balance on the upper ranks of the department. The Supreme Court majority rejected this contention: the fifty-percent order was necessary because of the department's continuing refusal to operate a "promotion process without adverse impact on blacks and to eradicate the effects of its past delay and discrimination." Justice Brennan's majority opinion, and a concurrence by Justice John Paul Stevens, both cited the Court's long line of school desegregation cases in stressing the broad, flexible power of courts to fashion race-conscious remedies for violations of constitutional rights.

These victories were heartening, if tenuous. In *Paradise*, four justices—Rehnquist; White; and the two Reagan appointees, Scalia and O'Connor—dissented.

The civil rights movement of the 1950s and 1960s, culminating in the Civil Rights Act of 1964, has sometimes been likened to the formal establishment of emancipation after the Civil War, while the remedial efforts by courts and others to make that formal equality a political and social reality have been compared to Reconstruction. Like the first Reconstruction, affirmative action both in theory and practice has encountered steep resistance. It has been argued that affirmative action is too radical, too sweeping, too threatening to established practices of selecting students or employees, especially at the higher echelons of money and power. An alternative argument, however, might be that affirmative action, as practiced in the 1970s, did not go nearly far enough in uprooting the assumptions that perpetuate the racial—and sexual—sins of the past. Instead, affirmative action proponents too often settled for numerical balance as a superficial goal while generally refusing to scratch beneath that surface at the implicit racial and cultural biases that inform all our notions of merit. In the process, old civil rights coalitions were sundered and the stereotype of the unqualified woman or minority, the unworthy beneficiary of affirmative action, replaced that of the obsequious servant or minstrel singer.

"At some point during those long months of waiting for the decision in *Bakke*," wrote Professor Derrick Bell, Jr, in 1979,

> I dreamed that a new professional aptitude test had been devised. The new test measured with amazing accuracy not performance in the first year of law or medical school, but the student's potential for providing quality legal representation or medical care after admission to practice.
>
> When announced, the new "Potential for Effective Practice" test (PEP) was hailed by the legal and medical professions. But then sample test results revealed that blacks and other minorities scored an average of two hundred points above whites. Careful studies were made, but they simply confirmed these initial findings. Evidently, experts surmised, the varied array of survival skills that had enabled minority students to reach professional school were also the characteristics that were essential to success in practice. Indeed, the gap between scores of minorities and whites on the PEP test was the exact reverse of that evidenced in the traditional, standardized tests. And if the PEP test replaced present admissions standards, it was estimated that few, if any, whites could gain admission to professional schools.
>
> As the dream ended, national conferences were being called to study the test, and congressional committees were voting to investigate the test's authors. Neo-conservative social scientists were finding merit in racially heterogeneous environments, while condemning meritocratic policies as hopelessly elitist. Legal scholars researched the Constitution's history and found that it was indeed "color conscious," while rejected white applicants, contending that the PEP test did not reflect mainstream American culture, planned to challenge the test's validity in the courts.

The Supreme Court's affirmative action decisions in 1986 and 1987 did not cite Professor Bell's writings or discuss the subtle issues that he raises. Perhaps it is not a court's job to delve into such mysteries or to speculate upon the most just means for eradicating discrimination from society. The 1986 and 1987 cases were important because they left the door open, or at least ajar, for remedial consideration of race or sex in employment decisions. Whether anything more creative, or novel, or radical is done with the affirmative action concept depends on the existence, persistence, and survival of people like Nancy Richardson at places like Boston University.

EPILOGUE

THE year after her termination from Boston University, Nancy Richardson went to work as a part-time consultant on women's issues at the Episcopal Divinity School in Cambridge, Massachusetts. She also, as the dean had suggested she do during their famous meeting in May of 1981, completed her thesis, and became a doctor of philosophy.

Plans for a Women's Theological Center in Boston were brewing as early as 1982. As envisioned by Richardson and others, the center would offer one year of graduate study, the credits to be accepted at degree-conferring seminaries and graduate schools. The course of study would focus on religious issues of concern to women, and on women's religious experiences, particularly women of Latin American, African, and other non-European backgrounds. New styles of worship and liturgy, including dance, song, chanting, and poetry, were much a part of the center's life.

Richardson began co-directing the center at its inception and was still at it in 1987 as this volume went to press. Another one of her projects was *God's Fierce Whimsy*, published in 1985, a book about "Christian Feminism and Theological Education," co-authored by seven feminist theologians including Carter Heyward, professor at the Episcopal Divinity School, and Beverly Harrison of Union Theological Seminary in New York. This book addressed itself to women "players . . . in the grandiose games of misogynist academic gynmastics."

God's Fierce Whimsy had many deeply felt things to say about religion, sex, racism, justice, male theological hegemony, and "excellence." Among them:

> The large majority of white male theologians have been educated to regard only their own experience as normative in the

making of Christian doctrine. And the content of the "great" theological systems confirms this methodological assumption. To do theology, so we are told by these men, is to assess the nature and character of universals, to sweep with broad strokes the particularities of personal and specific events, to bypass the nitty-gritty pains and problems, whims and fantasies, of the common folk . . .

Feminist theology represents a fundamental challenge to this tradition. "[K]nowledge of our intellectual/spiritual power as rooted in our feelings and passions is new among us white women from the traditions of Northern Europe."

The significance of this theological movement among Christian women of our generation cannot be underestimated. It is to this day the spark of much provocative and excellent Christian theological work being done in this country. There is, among women scholars and ministers, growing clarity that the methodological assumptions of feminist theology are transforming the epistemological underpinnings of theology itself. And there is growing excitement that the fruit of feminist theology is less bitter, more sensual, and more spiritually edifying than non-feminist (masculinist) theological approaches. . . .

In a feminist course on Augustine, for example, no one's questions or opinions about Augustine's social location or his views on women or sexuality would be dismissed as irrelevant. They would be taken seriously as questions yielding insights. It *is* possible to teach Augustine, Thomist philosophy, Reformation history, canon law, the history and theology of the black church, and certainly the Bible, on the basis of feminist method. . . .

"The fundamental goal of theological education must be the doing of justice," the authors concluded. This means:

1. Education is never neutral. It is either for justice, which requires the liberation of all people from structures of oppression, or against it.

2. The scholar who is indifferent to justice in his or her scholarly work is not an excellent scholar.

Beverly Harrison produced another book in the years after her rejection by Boston University. *Our Right to Choose: Toward a New Ethic of*

Abortion is a comprehensive, intellectually formidable scholarly work tracing attitudes toward abortion through theological history, and probing the moral dilemmas raised but by no means resolved by the existence of fetal life within the body of a woman. It was not long after this work was published that Harrison received a feeler from BU School of Theology about a vacancy in an endowed chair in social ethics, a vacancy created by the recent retirement of Professor Paul Deats. Deats had been given the Muelder chair after Harrison's appointment was turned down in 1978. Now it was available again. This time, Harrison did not even nibble.

Judge Paul Garrity resigned from the bench in 1984 after achieving photojournalistic fame by posing dramatically in front of Boston Harbor, clad in judicial robes, in connection with an article about a pollution case he was handling. He joined a small private law firm and was much seen about town, usually in his bow tie. Charles Parrott continued his successful trial practice, as did his assistant in the Richardson case, Alan Rose.

Boston University and John Silber remained, and remain, in the news long after the brouhaha over the 1981 termination of an outspoken administrator at the School of Theology ended. Silber was a member of President Reagan's task force on Central America in 1985, testified frequently in Congress, ardently supported the Solomon Amendment, which made certification of draft status a prerequisite for college students' federal financial aid, and even imposed the same certification requirement on all students receiving aid from Boston University. Three STH seminarians, conscientious objectors to any cooperation with Selective Service, brought an ACLU-sponsored lawsuit to challenge Silber's and the government's policy. They won a temporary victory, which enabled them to retain their financial aid through graduation, but the U.S. Court of Appeals ultimately upheld the linkage of financial aid with certification of compliance with the draft.

In another lawsuit, tried in federal district court in the summer of 1987, a jury found Silber and BU guilty of sex discrimination in refusing to tenure an English professor, Julia Brown, despite her outstanding qualifications. The BU president, according to one witness, had referred to the English Department as a "damned matriarchy." It had seven tenured women and twenty tenured male professors at the time.

In August 1986 BU received a federal grant to train refugees from the Soviet-dominated regime in Afghanistan as journalists. It was reported that the dean of BU's College of Communications and much of the journalism faculty felt that the training should take place at BU, that a Pakistan-based program would be viewed more as a propaganda effort than a journalistic one, but that Silber and the U.S. Information Agency preferred Pakistan, where many of the refugees are living. "The proposal from the university was submitted by the provost because Dean [Bernard] Redmont [of the Communications College] refused to endorse a Pakistan-based training program," according to *The New York Times*.

Last month Dean Redmont resigned his administrative post. According to people close to the situation, who asked not to be identified, the resignation was a result of administrative friction with the university's president, John R. Silber, in the Pakistan debate.

Also in 1986, another free speech battle developed at Boston University. Four undergraduates were threatened with various sanctions—one was notified of eviction from his dormitory—because they persisted in hanging anti-apartheid, pro-divestment posters and banners from their dormitory windows. BU claimed it had a blanket rule against such displays, driven by aesthetic concerns as well as a desire not to be a censor. News of this rule, however, came as a surprise to much of the BU community, since numerous signs and banners in fact adorned dormitory windows throughout the sprawling campus. The Civil Liberties Union of Massachusetts represented the four activists in a lawsuit, *Yosef Abramowitz v. Boston University*. After a one day trial in December 1986 Superior Court Judge Haskell Freedman ruled that the university had impermissibly punished the students because of what they had to say. The administration had approved or tolerated banners advertising student government elections, athletic events, and blood drives—as well as images of athletes and rock musicians, beer advertisements, Batman insignia, traffic signs, and replicas of flamingos and palm trees. "The testimony in this action," wrote the judge,

> does not reveal a single instance in which the defendant asked a student to remove a sign, poster or banner from a dormitory window before the plaintiffs began posting signs and banners in their dormitory windows urging the university to divest its stock in companies doing business in South Africa. Far more plausible than the defendant's "see no evil" explanation is the likelihood that the defendant tolerated these signs, posters and banners because they were neither controversial nor critical of the defendant's policies.

Relying upon the Massachusetts baby civil rights act, the same law that had been invoked by Nancy Richardson when she was fired by

Richard Nesmith because of her unacceptable pedogogical and ideological proclivities, Judge Freedman ruled in the BU banner case that the university had illegally sought to retaliate against the students "because of their display of signs, posters and banners communicating views on a controversial subject" with which the university disagreed. "[N]owhere in our society," declared the judge, "is the protection of the free flow of ideas more important than in the university community, the quintessential 'marketplace of ideas.' "

BIBLIOGRAPHICAL NOTES

CHAPTER 1

Beverly Wildung Harrison, Nancy Richardson, Nelle Slater, Lynn Rhodes, Robert Treese, and Richard Nesmith (in pretrial deposition testimony) supplied the information for Chapter 1. I also used documents that were produced during pretrial discovery, a number of which became exhibits that were entered into evidence at trial. Beverly Harrison's article, "The New Consciousness of Women: A Socio-Political Resource," was published in the Winter 1975 issue of *Cross Currents*. John Silber's article, "Above the Rabble," was published in the September 1, 1976, *New York Times*. His comment about "rejecting excellence in the interest of women and minorities" is quoted by Nora Ephron in "Academic Gore" *(Esquire,* September 1977).

CHAPTER 2

In the late 1970s John Silber's administrative style at Boston University inspired much journalistic attention. I have relied primarily upon Nora Ephron's "Academic Gore" *(Esquire,* September 1977), Stephen Arons's "The Teachers and the Tyrant" *(Saturday Review,* March 15, 1980), Howard Zinn's "A Showcase of Repression" *(The Progressive,* June 1980), "The First Hurrah" *(Newsweek,* January 4, 1971), "Rich Man, Poor Man" *(Newsweek,* March 27, 1978), "Silber Tightens Grasp on BU Media" *(The Real Paper,* November 19, 1977), "The Silberization of WBUR" *(The Real Paper,* August 29, 1977), and *New York Times* articles in April and May 1976, regarding the faculty's vote of no-confidence in Silber. Interviews with Professors Paul Deats and Howard Zinn were also valuable.

Information on the battle over the *bu exposure*, and the subsequent litigation, came from Civil Liberties Union of Massachusetts legal files, as well as my own experiences as an attorney for the plaintiffs during the later stages of the lawsuit that *exposure* staffers brought against Silber and the university to recover the funds that had been withheld. (That suit, filed in 1978, ended with a $7,500 settlement in 1984.)

Internal documents that I have quoted, relating to the School of Theology's early disputes with President Silber, were given to me by various faculty members. The description of Martin Luther King, Jr. as a "spellbinding" preacher during his graduate student days at BU comes from J. Anthony Lucas's *Common Ground* (Knopf, 1985). Other material on King's BU years, including the fact that he chose it for graduate school above Yale, is found in David Garrow's *Bearing the Cross: Martin Luther King, Jr. and the Southern Christian Leadership Conference* (William Morrow, 1987).

CHAPTER 3

Dean Nesmith's 1980 letter to the Methodist minister in Virginia was produced by BU as part of pre-trial discovery in the *Richardson* case. J. Stanley Pottinger's remarks are quoted from his essay, "The Drive Toward Equality," in *Reverse Discrimination* (Barry R. Gross, ed., Prometheus Books, 1977). "The nature of the violation determines the scope of the remedy," is from the Supreme Court's 1971 decision, *Swann v. Charlotte-Mecklenburg Board of Education*, 402 U.S. 1, 16 (1971) in the official United States Supreme Court Reports. Brown v. Board of Education is reported at 347 U.S. 483 (1954) and 349 U.S. 294 (1955).

The comparison of older male and female candidates for an academic post is recounted by F. K. Barasch, "HEW, the University, and Women," in *Reverse Discrimination*. Professor Randall Kennedy's article, "Persuasion and Distrust: A Comment on the Affirmative Action Debate," was published in 99 *Harvard Law Review* 1327 (1986). Mary Daly's book was *Beyond God the Father* (Beacon Press, 1973). Nesmith's memo on a "woman's woman" was produced during pre-trial discovery in *Richardson v. Trustees of Boston University*.

CHAPTER 4

The material in this chapter comes almost entirely from trial and pre-trial documents in *Richardson v. BU*, from discussions with Nancy Richardson, Paul Deats, Robert Treese, Odette Lockwood-Stewart, and other STH staff, faculty, and former students, from memoranda and other documents given to me by BU staff and faculty, and from trial and deposition transcripts.

CHAPTER 5

The test questions on the Rhode Island police exam were reported on October 14, 1985, in the *Boston Globe*. Howard A. Glickstein is the former Civil Rights Commission director, whose letter is quoted in Todorovich and Glickstein, "Discrimination in Higher Education: A Debate on Faculty Employment," in *Reverse Discrimination*. Professor Thomas Sowell's comment is also from *Reverse Discrimination;* his essay is "Affirmative Action Reconsidered." The front-page *New York Times* article whose headline I quote was "City to Use Racial Quota to Pick at Least 1,000 Police Sergeants," by Joyce Purnick, November 18, 1985.

Griggs v. Duke Power Company is reported at 401 U.S. 424 (1971) in the official U.S. Reports. The federal court that noted the unfairness of permitting subjective evaluations by white supervisors was the United States Court of Appeals for the Fifth Circuit in *Rowe v. General Motors Corporation*, 457 F. 2d 348, 359 (1972). ("F.2d" is a series of volumes published by West Publishing Company containing decisions of the United States Courts of Appeals.)

CHAPTER 6

This material comes from pre-trial and trial documents and testimony, and discussions with Paul Deats, Robert Treese, Lynn Rhodes, James Fraser, Nancy Richardson, John Cartwright, and a number of BUSTH students. Peter Berger's *A Rumor of Angels* was published by Doubleday Anchor in 1970.

CHAPTER 7

The lower court and Supreme Court opinions, the voluminous briefs, and the equally voluminous law review literature on the *Bakke* case, form the basis for much of this chapter. *Bakke* is reported at 438 U.S. 265 (1978). The California Supreme Court decision in *Bakke* is found at 18 Cal. 3d 34 (1976) (volume 18 of the third installment of the official California Supreme Court Reporter).

Joel Dreyfuss and Charles Lawrence III's *The Bakke Case* (Harcourt Brace Jovanovich, 1979), was also a source, on the history of the litigation as well as on standardized testing. Dreyfuss and Lawrence quote a 1972 study by Ralph Friedan and others which concluded that "the criteria for selecting medical applicants correlate poorly with the student's performance in medical school and not at all with their performance as physicians."

David M. White's articles, "Culturally Biased Testing and Predictive Invalidity: Putting Them on the Record," in 14 *Harvard Civil Rights–Civil Liberties Law Review (CRCL)* 89 (1979), and "The Definition of Legal Competence: Will the Circle Be Unbroken?" 18 *Santa Clara Law Review* 641 (1978), were sources for much of the information regarding the SAT, MCAT, LSAT, and other standardized tests. White cites a number of studies for the negative correlation that has been found between MCAT scores and clinical ratings of physicians: Helper and Kriska, "Predictors of Clinical Performance," 49 *Journal of Medical Education* 338 (1974); Howell and Vincent, "The Medical College Admission Test as Related to Achievement Tests in Medicine and to Supervisory Evaluations of Clinical Performance," 42 *Journal of Medical Education* 1037 (1967); Richards, Taylor and Price, "The Prediction of Medical Intern Performance," 46 *Journal of Applied Psychology* 142 (1962). The quotations discussing test questions about grocery shopping and Indian tribes, and black and white test performance gaps are all from White's *CRCL* article.

The material on BUSTH's hiring efforts and anti-racism recommendations comes from pre-trial documents in *Richardson v. BU*, as well as interviews with Paul Deats, Willard Rose, and others.

CHAPTER 8

Professor Derrick Bell's comments on *Bakke* were published in "Introduction: Awakening After *Bakke*," 14 *Harvard Civil Rights–Civil Liberties Law Review* 1 (1979). Professor Kent Greenawalt was responsible for the perception that law schools might choose to admit "those who would make better lawyers in preference to those who would make better law students." ("Judicial Scrutiny of 'Benign' Racial Preference in Law School Admissions," 75 *Columbia Law Review* 559 (1975)). The *New York Times* article on Johns Hopkins was "Top Medical School Dropping Standardized Admission Test," May 13, 1985.

CHAPTERS 9 AND 10

Sources for these chapters were trial and deposition testimony, litigation documents, and discussions with the participants, including former seminarians Marjorie Mollar and Jon Hattaway.

CHAPTER 11

The *Weber* and *Fullilove* decisions are found in the official United States Supreme Court Reports at 443 U.S. 193 (1979) and 448 U.S. 448 (1980), respectively.

CHAPTERS 12 THROUGH 19

Litigation documents, trial transcript, and interviews with jurors by me and Nancy Richardson, are the sources for these chapters.

CHAPTER 20

The Reagan Administration's campaign to eliminate affirmative action, particularly in the period after the *Stotts* decision, was reported regularly in the press and documented in briefs filed during this period and memoranda emanating from the Justice Department. Derrick Bell's dream about the PEP test is recorded in "Introduction: Awakening After *Bakke*," 14 *Harvard Civil Rights–Civil Liberties Law Review* 1 (1979). The affirmative action case that three justices wanted to accept for review in January 1985 was *Bushey v. New York State Civil Service Commission*, reported at 105 S.Ct. 803 (1985), the West Publishing Company's series reporting Supreme Court decisions.

Firefighters Local Union No. 1784 v. Stotts is reported at 467 U.S. 561 (1984). *Wygant* is at 106 S.Ct. 1842 (1986); *Firefighters v. Cleveland*, 106 S.Ct. 3063 (1986); and *Sheet Metal Workers v. EEOC*, 106 S.Ct. 3019 (1986). *United States v. Paradise* is found at 107 S.Ct. 1053 (1987), and *Johnson v. Transportation Agency, Santa Clara County*, at 107 S.Ct. 1442 (1987). The *New York*

Times reported the *Johnson* decision with a three-column front-page headline on March 26, 1987.

EPILOGUE

God's Fierce Whimsy, by the Mud Flower Collective, was published by Pilgrim Press in 1985. Information in the Epilogue also comes from interviews with Nancy Richardson and Beverly Wildung Harrison, and my own experiences in subsequent lawsuits against Boston University. BU's involvement with the USIA in training Afghan journalists, and Dean Redmont's resignation over the issue, were reported in The *New York Times* ("U.S. Will Help Train Afghan Journalists," August 18, 1986).

INDEX